MACROECONOMIC POLICY

During the postwar era there was a broad consensus about the aims and potential of macroeconomic policy. The Keynesian approach was predicated on the belief that it was both possible and desirable to control the levels of aggregate demand and unemployment. The stagflation of the 1970s indicated that macroeconomic policy ought not to be so ambitious, and gave credibility to a macroeconomic school that advocated a more limited role of government: the Monetarists.

Macroeconomic Policy examines the central tenets of both Keynesian and Monetarist schools. (It is aimed at those who have had one course in macroeconomics and presents its arguments in a clear and non-technical way.) It begins by examining the aims of macroeconomic policy: low unemployment, low inflation, high levels of output and high rates of growth. In practice these goals interact and policies which promote one are often detrimental to another.

As well as examining how the different schools manage the trade-off between goals, the book also considers their distinctive attitude to markets, how they manage concepts of the short and long run and their different reactions to uncertainty.

MACROECONOMIC POLICY

Alan Marin

London and New York

First published 1992
by Routledge
11 New Fetter Lane, London EC4P 4EE

Transferred to Digital Printing 2004

Simultaneously published in the USA and Canada
by Routledge
a division of Routledge, Chapman and Hall, Inc.
29 West 35th Street, New York, NY 10001

Typeset in 10/12pt Garamond by
Ponting–Green Publishing Services, Sunninghill

British Library Cataloguing in Publication Data
A catalogue record for this book is available
from the British Library

ISBN   0–415–08379–6
0–415–08380–X pbk

Library of Congress Cataloging-in-Publication Data
Marin, Alan, 1941–
Macroeconomic policy / Alan Marin.
p.   cm.
Includes bibliographical references and index.
ISBN 0–415–08379–6
1. Macroeconomics.   2. Economic policy   I. Title.
HB172.5.M363   1992
339.5–dc20   91–47133
CIP

To Della and Harry

CONTENTS

LIST OF FIGURES AND TABLES

FIGURES

TABLES

PREFACE

This book has its origins in discussions with my friend and colleague, Kurt Klappholz. Both of us had been teaching courses on economic policy to students who were not going on to take the series of courses suitable for those intending to become economics specialists. We found a serious lack of a macro textbook suitable for such students. Their reading lists comprised articles from a variety of sources, such as the UK 'bank reviews', but nothing that could accompany the lectures in providing them with a coherent framework through which they could relate the various arguments they came across in the articles.

Our other teaching and tutorial experience also convinced us that many students who were intending to take further specialist courses did not see the relevance and inter-relationships of the topics in macroeconomic analysis that they had studied. Most of these students would complete their economics education at the undergraduate level and have policy issues as their primary interest, rather than economic analysis as an end in itself.

The other spur to writing this book was that as we talked together about statements on economic policy issues that had been made to the press, etc. by people who apparently had learned some economics (and even by some professional economists), too many seemed to us to contain confusions or rely on inconsistent implicit assumptions. We would have liked to be confident that those who studied economics would be able to analyse intelligently the validity of comments on macroeconomic policy, and to see what assumptions were inherent in the various views.

This book is aimed at students who have already taken an introductory course in economics. Some will be non-specialists who then study policy and take no more economics principles courses. Others will be studying a more standard intermediate macroeconomic theory course, but will also require a book that concentrates on the policy relevance of the theory and on how the pieces of analysis fit together in views about the way that the economy works and about the options open to policy-makers and their advisers.

Many of the notes in this book refer to ideas that some of the readers, but not all, will have come across in other courses. Because the IS-LM analysis is now taught in some introductory courses but not in others, and similarly for the AS-AD analysis, the text of the book does not require a formal knowledge of these diagrams, but the notes mentions them in ways that should make it easy for students familiar with them to draw the diagrams for themselves. The references to articles and books are of two kinds: first, to original sources, especially where students are likely to see the ideas referred to elsewhere by the names of the originators; second, to articles and books which provide a fuller treatment at an analytical level which should be accessible to most readers of this book. The latter are usually indicated by 'see ...'.

Originally Kurt Klappholz was going to co-author this book. Although, in the end, after taking early retirement he decided not to, I have left all the first person statements in the plural rather than the singular – they are not intended to denote delusions of grandeur on my part.

Especially in writing a textbook, which has no pretensions to originality, but draws heavily on the ideas of others, debts are incurred. In the case of the subject matter of this book, mine go back to all those from whom I have learned economics ever since I was a student myself. They include my colleagues at the LSE from whom I have learned much, both during informal discussions and in seminars. I am also grateful to the students whose questions and ideas have ensured that I have not become too complacent about the bases of my own understanding.

I mentioned above that the impetus for this book originally came from Kurt Klappholz. During the ensuing period, I have often been unsure whether this was a reason for gratitude to him or the reverse. However I am definitely grateful to him for our many discussions over the years on all sorts of topics. His concern for intellectual honesty, and his constant questioning, have been a continuing stimulus.

Since this book was first mooted, I have dealt with a series of helpful editors at George, Allen & Unwin and its successors through to Routledge. I also received useful comments from the readers to whom the publishers sent the manuscript. Not all of their suggestions were accepted, but many were, and I am grateful for the trouble they took.

The first and subsequent drafts of the manuscript were typed with exceptional accuracy by Sue Kirkbride. More recently, Louise Johnson has provided capable secretarial assistance.

I have left till last the mention of my greatest gratitude – to my wife Jennifer. As far as this book is concerned my gratitude is for her unfailing encouragement and support even when the process of writing and re-drafting seemed to drag on interminably.

Alan Marin, April 1992

1

WHAT NEEDS EXPLAINING?

THE CHANGE

Those of us who learned our Economics before 1970 would have been incredulous if told that there would be unemployment rates in double digits in many developed countries, and that it would be widely claimed that nothing could be done about the problem. To be more precise, economists who learnt their subject between, let us say, 1950 and 1970, and those who taught them, would have shared this view with only a few exceptions. In addition, governments and political commentators both at the academic and the journalistic ends of the scale, would have shared the assumption that governments which presided over such unemployment would not last beyond the next general election. Furthermore, it was felt that such electoral punishment would be justified – governments had the ability to avoid widespread unemployment if only they managed the economies suitably. A few economists had not gone along with the consensus, but they were a small minority and their views were generally ignored. Their appeal to academic economists was beginning to widen slightly, but had not yet spread at all into the wider world. Until the late 1960s, even amongst academic economists, these dissenters (often the followers of Milton Friedman) were known primarily for other aspects where they disagreed with the mainstream consensus, and their views about the possibility or desirability of controlling unemployment were generally downplayed.

Our aim in this book is to try to clarify the issues involved in the arguments over whether governments can and should control the level of employment and output by the use of macroeconomic policies. In the process of discussing disagreements over whether governments could have prevented the rise in unemployment in the past two decades, we shall also deal with views as to why unemployment has risen, and whether government macroeconomic policies have themselves contributed to the rise. At the end of the book, in Chapter 7, we also examine some other reasons suggested for the rise in unemployment that have not been dealt with in the preceding chapters.

In the early years of the 1980s, British Prime Minister Margaret Thatcher

1

was sometimes referred to by her opponents, with a degree of derision, by the name 'Tina' – these also being the initial letters of her oft-repeated statement that 'there is no alternative'. One way of summarising the question that this book tries to examine is whether it is correct to claim that there is no alternative to the types of policies, and their results, that have been adopted in most, though not all, countries in the past decade.

THE APPROACH OF THIS BOOK

Those who have already studied some economics will have come across some of the issues which are debated in the disagreements over macroeconomic policies. However, all too often, because they have been introduced in passing while teaching the techniques of macroeconomic analysis, the knowledge of even these policy issues is not coherent. Unfortunately, there is insufficient understanding of the interrelationship between the issues, and of whether agreeing with one side of the debate on one issue entails taking a particular position on one of the others.

We hope to provide a framework which will enable our readers to see where the issues fit in, both those that they have already studied and those which are probably less familiar. One way that we shall try to do this is to provide, especially in the earlier chapters, a 'quasi-historical' approach. We call it 'quasi-historical' because we are not concerned with chronological questions which are legitimately important to a truly historical account. For example, for our purposes it will not be relevant when exactly a particular idea was first proposed or, necessarily, by whom. In particular, if after its initial appearance the idea lay dormant and was not taken up and discussed by others, we shall only consider it at the point where it did become the focus of argument. Nevertheless, because current debates often contain bits taken from discussions that occurred earlier, and, most importantly, these 'bits' remain disconnected if no account is taken of the context in which they were debated, a coherent framework does require some view of how the subject of macroeconomic policy management has developed. Furthermore, under-standing the relevance of many of the points which crop up in debates over the role of government in controlling economic activity, involves a realisation of the extent to which they were put forward as a rebuttal of arguments made by those who took a different view.

The reference to opposing viewpoints in the previous paragraph leads to another aspect of our approach which is controversial amongst economists. At various points in the book we shall refer to views of 'Monetarists' and 'Keynesians'. Some economists dislike the splitting of views into opposing camps, feeling that this seems to reduce economics to little more than a football match between two sides. In addition, they think that there is too much heterogeneity of opinion to classify the arguments into just two opposing groups. We do recognise that there are many disagreements within what we shall categorise as 'Monetarist' or 'Keynesian' views, and we intend to try to avoid the temptation of exaggerating the internal consistency within groups, or the breadth of the disagreements between them, just because it might add a little extra spurious dramatic colour to what might otherwise be considered dry analysis – anyway, we consider the subject-matter interesting enough not to need extra excitement. However, we do feel that there is enough of a thread running through the debates over macroeconomic policy so that there is a sense in which there is a continuous Monetarist view and a continuous Keynesian one. This is despite the fact that as we treat the issues in our 'quasi-historical' approach, we shall recognise the way the arguments have changed over time. We shall draw attention to these changes, and to the differences between economists whom we shall describe as being, in some sense, within the same camp.

Despite these caveats, we do think that there is enough continuity and similarity of outlook within each of the two groups that we shall characterise as Monetarist and Keynesian, to make such a distinction illuminating rather than the reverse. Just what these continuities and consistencies of outlook consist of, will, we hope, become clear in the succeeding chapters.

Although, very often, the differences seem to lead to policy prescriptions that come out fairly consistently on one side or another of the political divide in many countries, our primary interest is in the *economic* analyses behind these prescriptions. We do not intend to try to judge whether any, some, or all of the economists involved came to their policy recommendations because they were convinced by the economic arguments, or whether their judgement over the relative validity of the economic argument was coloured by their political inclinations.[1]

One final point needs to be made in this section. Because we think it clarifies the policy debates to put them into what we have described as a 'quasi-historical' context, there may be a danger of giving the impression that the Monetarists are simply reacting to the Keynesian arguments, and have had no coherent outlook of their own. This is not the case. The various strands in the Monetarist analyses do represent a coherent and consistent approach. However, because of the predominance of Keynesian macroeconomics over the past half-century viewed as a whole (for example, in the vast majority of introductory and intermediate textbooks), for much of the time Monetarist arguments have emerged into wider debates as objections to what they have seen as the prevailing 'orthodoxy'. Some Monetarist writing has even seemed to enjoy taking the position of underdog and iconoclast.

OVERVIEW OF SOME OF THE ISSUES

A wide range of issues will be covered in the discussions of macroeconomic policy. Some will recur rather more frequently than others, in various contexts. At this point it might be helpful to indicate briefly a few of these

3

themes, as a set of signposts for some of the more detailed treatments in the contexts of the particular policy debates. Readers will find it worthwhile to return to this section after they have studied the subsequent chapters.

Aims

In any discussion over macroeconomic policies, some disagreements may simply reflect disagreements over what should be the aims of public policies. Sometimes it may be that some people think that there is one aim which is paramount and that others are completely unimportant. More often, perhaps, there may be disagreements over the relative weights to be given to the aims when there is a trade-off, because the fuller achievement of one aim entails a lesser achievement of another.

The aims of macroeconomic policy are commonly considered to be: (i) low unemployment, (ii) low inflation, (iii) high levels of output and (iv) high rates of growth of output. These are often considered to be 'obviously' desirable, though, as we shall see, not invariably so. A satisfactory exchange rate or the avoidance of a balance of payments deficit are sometimes also considered as aims, but these are probably more correctly seen as constraints in the achievement of the other aims.

As we shall see later in this book, varying importance has been ascribed to these aims. For example, in the early years of Keynesian pre-eminence, particular stress was laid on low unemployment as the overriding aim of macroeconomic policy. Conversely, it has been suggested, some Monetarists worry primarily about controlling inflation and downplay concern with unemployment by analysing it as always voluntary.

Although we shall be dealing with macroeconomic policies, it is necessary to remember that not only may there be conflicts between the macroeconomic aims to which the policies are directed, but that these policies may interact with what are usually considered microeconomic issues. For example, the desirability of a rise in tax rates for purposes of reducing aggregate consumption when there is inflation may interact with consideration of the incentive and income distribution aspects of the level of taxation.

Relevance of markets

In the previous section we referred to our view that despite changes within what we shall call Monetarist and Keynesian views, there are important continuities. We start with a fundamental division between the two sets of views that seems to have persisted over time. Even when the focus of argument has shifted, and where the disagreements do not seem to centre on this fundamental issue, those on either side still seem to differ in their views on this very basic issue in their other statements.

The issue: the neo-classical paradigm of microeconomics is of a perfectly competitive market which moves smoothly and reasonably quickly from one equilibrium to another. Even within microeconomics there is an analysis of monopoly and other 'imperfections', but outside the specialist field of industrial economics, or in the pages of journals at the frontiers of research, the focus is usually on the perfectly competitive market. Those who take Monetarist positions in macroeconomics, tend to assume that the economy as a whole can be described as fitting this neo-classical paradigm with only trivial exceptions. In contrast, Keynesians assume that there is at least one important market that does not act according to the perfectly competitive paradigm. The obvious candidate for such a market would seem to be the labour market (although in recent years Keynesians have extended their analysis to product markets as well). It seems to us, that it is because the labour market is the obvious candidate for such an imperfection, if one believes that there is such a widespread imperfection anywhere, that many of the arguments over the years have focused on the labour market. For example, even when the discussions are over the causes of inflation, which is defined in terms of product price changes, the disagreements always focus on wage setting.

Short and long term

There is another common division between analyses of macroeconomic problems which is somewhat related to the previous one. This one also often divides Keynesian and Monetarist views, though not invariably.

Both Monetarist and Keynesian analyses of the economy are most often equilibrium ones. Yet the notion of equilibrium is not identical. In the Monetarist approach, as in standard neo-classical microeconomics, prices and wages are flexible. They move in response to supply and demand, and (as indicated above), ensure that following any changes a new equilibrium is smoothly and reasonably quickly reached. In this equilibrium prices are such that supply equals demand. In many Keynesian models, however, there is a sort of equilibrium, but this is not attained via price and wage flexibility. There can in a sense be excess supply even in equilibrium.[2] For example 'Keynesian unemployment' equilibrium implies an excess supply of labour.

Some economists have therefore adopted the position that although Keynesian analysis is relevant for the short term, over the long term the Classical or Monetarist analysis is pertinent – since even if prices and/or wages are sluggish in the short term, eventually they will be flexible and alter in response to prolonged excess demand or supply.

For policy proposals, the question still remains which set of assumptions is more relevant. Keynes himself coined the phrase 'In the long-run we are all dead' as a riposte to those whose policies were based an anlyses of long-run equilibria. Conversely some Monetarists assume that the long-run equilibrium will be reached soon enough for it to be relevant even for all policy discussions (this is especially, though not exclusively, true of the 'New

Monetarists' to be discussed in Chapter 5). Others sometimes argue that even if the long-run equilibrium is not 'just round the corner', a stress on short-run outcomes ignores the long-term implications and that these must also be taken into account. On this argument, mistakes would be made from ignoring any undesirable longer-term effects that would cumulate from a succession of policies myopically aimed at their short-term benefits.

Knowledge, ignorance and risk

It is relatively easy to draw diagrams on blackboards or in books, or to write down equations, which show the relationship between some variables; e.g. a consumption function showing how consumption would vary as income changed. In practice, however, there is always a lack of certainty, which itself may affect policy prescriptions.

The uncertainty covers various aspects. In the consumption function example just given, it may concern just how reliable are the numerical estimates of the marginal propensity to consume, and therefore, for example, the magnitude of the multiplier linking changes in fiscal policy to changes in income. The same applies to all the other relationships involved in predicting the quantitative effect of any policy. Often there will be a range of estimates from different studies, in addition to the variability inherent in each single statistically-based estimate. Even when there is substantial consensus over the size of any eventual impact, there may be uncertainties over the time taken to reach close to the final impact.

Frequently there is uncertainty about the current situation. Data on such variables as aggregate output or the balance of payments are often substantially revised as information is collected and collated. The initial estimates may therefore be misleading, yet some policy stance is necessary – keeping fiscal/monetary policies constant is itself a policy response.[3]

Some of the disagreements between economists are related to the problem of over how to react given the lack of certainty. Examples will occur throughout this book. It has often been considered that Keynesians were typically more confident about what was reliably knowable than Monetarists. This will, however, turn out to be another case where some of the splits within the groups are also significant (especially in Chapter 5).

If the views expressed in this section are correct, then clearly the disagreements between Keynesians and Monetarists are not restricted to disagreements over the role of the money supply or of monetary policy. Even if disagreements over the flexibility of labour markets are not as central as was suggested earlier in this section (pp. 4–5), the next four chapters will confirm that Keynesians and Monetarists often divide over non-monetary issues. Nevertheless, because it is by now such a well-established usage, we shall continue to use the term 'Monetarist' to describe those who oppose the Keynesian viewpoint.

PREREQUISITES AND TECHNIQUES

This book is intended for those who have taken an introductory course in macroeconomics. It is likely to be useful also for some of those who have taken further courses in the subject, as experience suggests that they may still sometimes be confused about the interrelationships between the issues to be covered. Although we shall assume that readers are familiar with the basic terms and concepts such as national income, the multiplier, what is usually meant by the money supply, and so on, some introductory material will be repeated where it is relevant to the policy issues, yet where the particular items are often treated as incidental and isolated examples when basic analytical techniques are taught.

One aspect of the Keynesian model which is sometimes covered in introductory texts and sometimes not is the IS–LM model. We shall therefore not assume a prior knowledge of the IS–LM approach, but will at times refer to it in notes where this may be illuminating for those who have understood the approach. Those readers who are familiar with IS–LM analysis should find it straightforward to draw the diagrams for themselves to illustrate the points in such notes.[4]

In any study of economic issues, the perennial question is what level of technical analysis to use. Our primary method will be to use verbal analysis, occasionally supplemented by diagrams. In addition, occasionally it is useful to summarise an argument by expressing it via equations, but no calculus or other mathematical techniques of that level, let alone above, will be required. Our aim is not to teach further economic analysis for its own sake, nor to follow up topics which are not strictly relevant to our main theme, even if they are often treated in more depth in standard second-level (or 'inter-mediate' level) textbooks on macroeconomic analysis Our aim is not to provide a foundation for further economic theory. Instead it is to provide a basis for understanding policy issues which are commonly discussed, but where the arguments depend, often implicitly, upon reasoning and assumptions, the relevance of which may not be realised and whose contentiousness may not be appreciated.

2

THE KEYNESIAN VIEW OF UNEMPLOYMENT

INTRODUCTION

This chapter reviews the Keynesian answer to the following problem: on the one hand, scarcity and rational behaviour should ensure that 'full employment' prevails – scarcity means that people's wants are not fully satiated and therefore they would like to consume more goods, therefore anybody who would be prepared to work to help produce those goods should be able to find employment; on the other hand, how can we account for 'the "obvious" large-scale divergences ... (from full employment) ... that we think we see, especially in prolonged depressions?'.[1] The reason for the quotation marks round the adjective 'obvious' will become apparent in the course of this book.

In the second section (pp. 9–14) we review the Keynesian answer. In line with our comments in the previous chapter, we consider the Keynesian interpretation of Keynes' answer, rather than what were necessarily Keynes' own views. Keynes' *General Theory* is a complex and, arguably, not always self-consistent book. For our purposes what matters is not what Keynes 'really meant', but the model of the economy that was accepted by Keynesians at different times. In the third section (pp. 14–23) we deal with the implications of the Keynesian model for government policies concerning unemployment, and how it led to the belief that unemployment was curable and to the commitment by governments to cure it. Partly reflecting the period when Keynesian ideas were first adopted, their primary focus was initially on unemployment as the overriding macroeconomic problem, and the exposition here reflects this. In later chapters we shall consider the possible conflicts between 'curing' unemployment and other policy aims.

To a greater extent than in succeeding chapters, the material in this chapter should already have been encountered by students who have read an introductory textbook on macroeconomics. Our treatment is therefore to be taken as a review, which emphasises the points which are salient for our subsequent discussion of policies towards macroeconomic policy.

THE KEYNESIAN MODEL OF THE DETERMINATION OF OUTPUT AND EMPLOYMENT

It is difficult to pick on any one point as the basic one that distinguishes the Keynesian model from alternatives. Like the alternatives, it is an interlocking whole in which the various components reinforce one another. One possible starting-point that seems to be taken for granted in the Keynesian way of looking at the world, is the notion that aggregate real demand for goods and services is determined by the components of desired expenditure – consumption, investment, government expenditure, and exports net of imports. If, for now, we concentrate on a closed economy so that we can ignore trade, then in standard symbols we have equation (2.1):

$$Y = C + I + G \qquad (2.1)$$

The Keynesian approach relies on the notion that, if consistently defined, the Y on the left-hand side of equation (2.1) can refer both to expenditure and to income and output. In the early years following the publication in 1936 of *The General Theory* there was some confused discussion of the relationship between the equivalence of income, output and expenditure viewed as an identity following from consistent national income definitions, and the requirement that they be equal in equilibrium. The latter obviously carried the implication that they could be unequal out of equilibrium. However, this was soon cleared up and a useful way of seeing why the three different ways of looking at national income have to be equal for there to be an equilibrium, is to say that since the realised values of income, output and expenditure must be equal when we look back at any particular period, if the planned or desired expenditure, output or income were not equal, then these plans must have been inconsistent. If they were mutually inconsistent they could not all be realised, and, if we assume that when people find that their plans have not been realised they change what they intend to do, it is only when the plans are consistent that there can be an equilibrium.

There was a similar initial confusion that was soon cleared up over the equivalent statement that savings must equal investment in equilibrium.[2] Putting the proposition in terms of equation (2.2)

$$I + G = S + T \qquad (2.2)$$

is formally exactly the same as equation (2.1), given the way income can be spent. Equation (2.2) can be derived from the former whether as an equilibrium condition or as an implication of the national income accounting identity.[3] Nevertheless, Keynesian treatments still often drew attention to the savings/investment relationship because it typified two other aspects of this approach.

First. Decisions about saving and consumption are themselves seen as dependent upon the level of income. This relationship plays a crucial role in solving for the equilibrium level of income, and in working out how much income will change if there is a change in some exogenous variable – including government expenditure. For working out the comparative statics of an economy which corresponds to the model, a key parameter is the marginal propensity to consume or its mirror image, the marginal propensity to save. This, together with the marginal tax rate, determines the multiplier for a closed economy.[4] Politically, the choice of the word 'multiplier' was important, especially when combined with the prediction that the multiplier would be greater than one for reasonable values of the marginal propensity to consume and the tax rate.[5] It seemed to carry the implication that a relatively acceptable increase in government expenditure would have a powerful effect on the level of income and output, and therefore on employment.[6] Furthermore, the demonstration that there was a multiplier of unity even for increases in government expenditure financed by tax increases, rather than by government borrowing, could be used to reassure those who were worried about the size of the national debt, and persuade them that it was worthwhile undertaking a fiscal expansion even in a form which would not increase the government budget deficit.

Second. The expression of the equilibrium condition in terms of saving and investment made it easier for Keynesians to draw attention to what was seen by them as a vital difference between a modern economy and the 'Robinson Crusoe' exposition often used to illustrate economic principles.[7] In the Robinson Crusoe economy the equality of saving and investment is unproblematic. Saving must equal investment because the only way that saving can occur is by putting aside goods which could be consumed now, in order to enhance consumption in future years.[8] In contrast, in a modern economy, the existence of financial institutions and assets separates the act of saving from that of investment. Much more investment is undertaken by different people than those who save. For example, firms may undertake investment in any one year either by borrowing from financial institutions or by liquidating their own financial assets which have been built up over a period of years. Conversely, households can save by acquiring financial assets, such as bank deposits or building society accounts, as well as such assets as stocks and shares.[9] Because investment and saving decisions are made by different people, in the Keynesian view there may be no mechanism which can ensure that the amount of intended investment is sufficient to provide a demand for enough output to create full employment. There is thus the possibility, to say the least, that we could end up with an equilibrium level of income and output which involves unemployment.

Whichever way it is approached, the Keynesian conclusion is that the economy may end up in a position in which the total desired expenditure is below the expenditure which would provide full employment. Keynesians assume that in these circumstances it is the level of income which will adjust, in such a way that the level of savings at the actual level of income then equals investment.

Even if firms were to try to produce more during a slump, the extra income thus generated would not in and of itself produce enough extra demand to absorb the goods which have been produced. This is a result of assuming that the marginal propensity to consume is less than one. Thus once in an unemployment equilibrium, there will be no tendency to leave it. Keynes expressed this as being his denial of what he called Say's Law – the proposition that 'supply creates its own demand'. In particular, the mere existence of excess capacity and spare labour will not automatically lead to an increase in output and employment, in the Keynesian view. Only an increase in one of the components of desired expenditure will lead to an increase in output. In terms of equation (2.1), an increase in government expenditure, investment, or the exogenous component of consumption is required. An increase in investment could occur either because of an exogenous shift in investment (for example, due to more optimistic expectations about the future irrespective of the current *level* of income) or because a fall in the interest rate has been engineered, with investment inversely dependent on the level of interest rates.

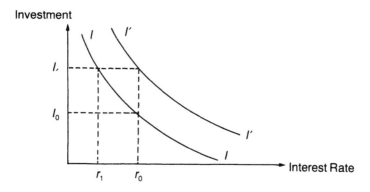

Figure 2.1 Increase in investment

In terms of Fig. 2.1 investment could increase from I_0 to I_1 either because of a shift in the whole investment function from I to I', or because of a fall in interest rates from r_0 to r_1. Should investment be completely insensitive to changes in interest rates, then only the former exogenous shift in investment is possible. Consumption can change either because of a shift in the consumption function, or because of a change in taxation – the latter will change the relationship between income and disposable income, and therefore between consumption and income, even if the relationship between consumption and disposable income is unaltered. As normally noted in introductory textbooks, a change in consumption due to a change in income is a movement along a given consumption function, not a shift in the function, and therefore any such movements are to be treated as reflections of changes in the equilibrium level of income occurring for other reasons, not as initiators of such a change in income. In the standard Keynesian model, changes in government expenditure are considered to be solely a result of government decisions.[10]

Keynes' stress on the importance of incorporating the likelihood of less than full-employment output and income into the way one thinks about the economy was crucial for his refutation of the 'Treasury View' which he fought in the late 1920s/early 1930s. This was the view (still sometimes implicit in statements nowadays) that any increase in government expenditure must always be fully offset by the fall in private investment that it would 'crowd out'. In terms of the left-hand side of equation (2.2), any increase in G must be fully offset by a fall in I, to maintain the equality of the left- and right-hand sides. Keynes' theory implied that this 'Treasury View' was incorrect: the equality between the two sides of equation (2.2) could be maintained by a rise in S on the right-hand side.

Parenthetically, we might note that the expression 'crowding out' is sometimes used in different ways. It always refers to an induced change in the opposite direction of one of the other components of expenditure resulting from a change in government spending. However, some writers use the unqualified term 'crowding out' for *complete* crowding out, i.e. when the induced change *fully* offsets the initial change in government expenditure, and therefore income is unaltered. Others (probably the vast majority of economists) use 'crowding out' for *any* induced change, even if only partially offsetting, and qualify the term by the adjectives 'full' or 'complete' when they want to indicate that the offsetting completely nullifies the change in government expenditure. Obviously confusion can result from mixing the two usages. All too often one comes across commentators claiming that some policy action, e.g. fiscal policy, would be useless because of crowding out whereas the formal prediction is only of partial, not full, crowding out. We shall try to always add 'full' or 'complete' where relevant, and use 'crowding out' for even partial offsetting.

This may be a suitable point in the discussion to note another, modern, terminological development which can lead to serious confusion. In the last few years, initially in the US, some commentators, followed by some economists, have started to use the word 'saving' as a shorthand for another relatively new term in this context: 'national saving'. By 'national saving' they mean the sum of saving as usually defined, i.e. private sector saving, plus the government budget surplus, which they call 'public sector saving'. This is equivalent to private sector saving minus the budget deficit. In the notation above:

$$\text{'National saving'} = S + T - G = S - (G - T) = I$$

It is possible that this usage of 'saving' may initially have had a political purpose – whether or not it was ever consciously misleading is not for us to say – it enabled those opposed to the US budget deficit to say that it had caused a reduction in saving among its other effects. There have even been writers who referred to 'saving', in the context of an open economy, where what they meant was $(S - I) - (G - T)$. This must always, by definition, be equal to the Trade Deficit of the Balance of Payments. They could thus claim that the Trade Deficit was 'caused' by the drop in saving which was itself due to the budget deficit. The claim that the US balance of payments problem could be attributed to the government budget deficit might be correct. The claim that this was *proved* by the National Income Accounting identities was false. Of course, changes in taxation or government expenditure may themselves affect investment and saving as more usually defined. To avoid the confusion resulting from switching between the conventional and the altered definitions, we shall continue to stick to the conventional and accepted meaning of 'saving' throughout this book.

Returning now to substantive issues, we have concentrated in this section on the possibility that the level of desired expenditure would be less than that which would give full employment. Formally, the Keynesian approach is symmetrical and there could also be the possibility that the demand for goods will be greater than could be supplied even if all the labour force were fully employed. This gives rise to Keynes' own theory of inflation, the notion of an 'inflationary gap' – the excess of desired expenditure over full employment output. However, although this would predict *when* inflation might occur, it does not tell us *how much* inflation will be, and it is this which is required for a theory of inflation. We shall return to this point in Chapter 4. Because the Keynesian theory appeared during the Great Depression and because Keynesians were typically much more concerned about unemployment in the early years, the Keynesian theory of the inflationary gap tended to be given far less attention.

If we turn our attention away from inflation, which concerns the speed with which prices are changing, and instead look at the price *level* during periods of unemployment, we encounter a vital split within the Keynesian approach. In the formal model within *The General Theory*, although money wages are treated as rigid while there is unemployment, the price level is treated as flexible. The price level is determined by the interception of an aggregate demand and aggregate supply curve.[11] However, for perhaps 30–40 years, most Keynesian discussions of the determination of output and employment paid no attention to changes in the price level and how they might feed back on to the level of output. Even empirical models of the economy tended to be structured so that real expenditure determined output, and then employment and output determined inflation. But the causation was in one direction only. This divorce between the formal model including aggregate demand and most of the models attempting to explain or predict the economy, was not just a case of the Keynesians failing to grasp the Master's insights. In a fascinating unpublished thesis, Dr Jennifer Roberts has shown that in the 1930s Keynes himself was completely split in his attitude towards this problem. Sometimes, as in some of *The General Theory*, Keynes viewed prices as flexible and as having to rise to induce firms to produce more output – given the assumption of a rising marginal cost curve at the microeconomic level. Because money wages are viewed as fixed, this is the same as the statement that *real* wages have to fall for an expansion of employment and output. Much of the rest of the time, Keynes himself took the view that with widespread excess capacity firms would be happy to supply more output without raising their prices. This, of course, therefore implies that real wages can remain constant while employment expands.

We shall try to be clear about when we are assuming that prices are constant, and when we are treating them as variable. For the rest of this chapter and most of the next one, since we shall be considering the policies proposed by Keynesians to counter unemployment, as put forward and widely accepted in the early post-World War Two period, we shall stick to the fixed price version.

MONETARY AND FISCAL POLICIES TO INCREASE OUTPUT

As stated in the previous section, if the economy is in an equilibrium with less than full employment, the suggested solution was to increase aggregate expenditure by increasing either government expenditure or investment. The former would constitute an expansionary fiscal policy, the latter could be achieved via monetary policy. An expansionary fiscal policy could also consist of a cut in taxes or an increase in transfer payments in order to increase consumption at each level of income, but for simplicity we shall restrict attention to increases in government expenditure.

In general, there will be a one-to-one relationship between increases in the money supply and decreases in the rate of interest, for a given set of consumption and investment functions, and a given demand for money function.[12] The modern academic usage is to define monetary policy in terms of the quantity of money. For example, a constant monetary policy would consist of having a constant supply of money, while an expansionary monetary policy would be an increase in the supply of money. At various times, however, monetary policy has been thought of as the attempt by the Central Bank to fix a particular level of interest rates, so that an expansionary monetary policy, for example, would be the reduction of interest rates by the Central Bank. We shall adhere to the modern academic usage, but it is worth taking a few paragraphs to indicate why there was an alternative terminology, as this has at times affected the terms in which policy debates have been carried on; and monetary policy is still often defined implicitly in terms of interest rate changes and manipulation in much media commentary. There are several reasons:

(1) In the Keynesian explanation of how an increase in the money supply could lead to an increase in income, the so-called 'transmission mechanism' (that is the route by which an increase in the money supply was transmitted into an increase in expenditure) was that the increase in money supply led to a reduction in interest rates; the reduction in interest rates then induced more investment, and the increase in investment then led to an increase in income and further expenditure. Since it is the fall in interest rates which leads to the increase in investment and expenditure, under conditions of uncertainty when the Central Bank cannot be quite sure whether there are random fluctuations (or even longer-run alterations) in some of the relevant functions, it seems to make sense for the Bank to concentrate on the nearer link in the causal chain, that is on interest rates, rather than on the more distant money supply as the tool for affecting income.[13]

(2) In many (most?) countries the Central Bank does not directly control the supply of money, not even the monetary base.[14] Even when the official aim of the Central Bank is said to be to achieve a particular level of the 'money supply', this is something of a misnomer in such countries, and might better be called a 'quantity of money' target, rather than a 'money supply' target. The reason is that in these countries the Central Bank has an explicit or implicit commitment to lend reserves to the Commercial Banking system, if the banks feel that their reserves are running too low. Under these circumstances consider what would happen if the Central Bank tries to reduce the money stock by open market operations. It would sell bonds to the public, and as the members of the public wrote out their cheques to the Central Bank this should reduce the Commercial Banks' reserves with the Central Bank. In the standard description of open market operations, this ought to lead to the banks having to reduce customers' deposits and replenish their reserves (for example, by calling in loans), thus reducing the money supply.[15]

However, if the Commercial Banking system can instead always replenish its reserves simply by borrowing from the Central Bank, there will be no need to reduce deposits. Therefore the money supply will not fall. Instead what open market operations are doing is to enforce the level of interest rates desired by the Central Bank. If the interest rate desired by the Central Bank is higher than that currently being charged by the Commercial Banks, by conducting open market operations it can force the Commercial Banks to borrow from it at the rate it sets. If they are paying a higher rate on their borrowings from the Central Bank than they are earning from their loans to customers, the banks will be losing money on these loans. Therefore they will be forced to raise the interest rate that they charge for their loans, thereby achieving the aim of the Central Bank to raise interest rates. The explanation when the Central Bank wishes to reduce interest rates is essentially similar, except that the reduction in the rates charged by the Commercial Banks will be induced by their competition for customers at a time when they can obtain funds more cheaply.

Given the inability of the Central Bank to directly control the money supply in such a system, if the aim of its monetary policy is to achieve a particular stock of money rather than a particular interest rate, what it is doing is trying to pick an interest rate that will lead to the desired stock of money being demanded. In this case, the interest rate is an intermediate tool. This is illustrated in Figs 2.2 and 2.3. In both diagrams the downward sloping curve M_d shows the amount of money balances that people wish to hold at each rate of interest.[16]

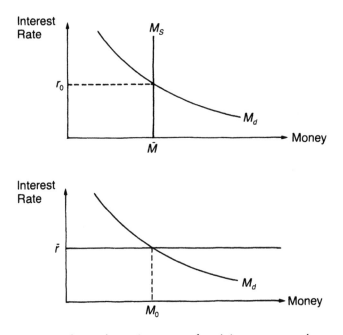

Figures 2.2 and 2.3 Alternative means of attaining money stock target

In Fig. 2.2 the vertical line at $\bar{M}$ indicates the money supply in a case where the Central Bank could control the money supply, and has a target for it equal to $\bar{M}$. Equilibrium in the money market would imply that the interest rate would settle down at r_0. Alternatively the Central Bank can control the interest rate at $\bar{r}$, as shown in Fig. 2.3, and the demand for money would then settle down at M_0. If $\bar{r}$ is chosen to be equal to r_0, then M_0 will be equal to $\bar{M}$. Therefore, the Central Bank may frame its policy in terms of a desired quantity of money and achieve it by the enforcement of a suitable interest rate.[17] Thus even when monetary policy is framed in terms of a money stock target, its implementation may be via interest rates, and therefore people in general may still think of monetary policy as being interest rate policy.[18]

(3) Some Central Banks have wished to control the level of interest rates for reasons other than those mentioned under (1). We shall deal with the aim of protecting the exchange rate in Chapter 6. Central Banks may also wish to keep interest rates low at times, in particular the interest rate on long-term assets, in order to encourage investment – not because of investment's role in generating sufficient expenditure to achieve full employment, but because of its role as an engine for long-run growth in the economy. They have also at times seen the maintenance of steady (and low) interest rates as desirable in themselves, because of the implication of interest rate changes for bond price changes. This aim has gone under different names at different times and in different countries: for example the desire for 'orderly markets' or the need to protect 'widows and orphans'.[19] Although economists have sometimes scoffed at these arguments, they may also be a reflection of the fact that the Central Banks have more than one legitimate function. In addition to running monetary policy for its macroeconomic effects, they also have the responsibility of selling government debt in order to fund budget deficits. In general, if people have confidence that the price of bond is not going to vary by very much, then it will be possible to sell them those bonds with only a very small drop in price – they will feel that they are getting a particularly good deal and be prepared to buy. On the other hand, if it is known that bond prices are extremely variable, it may require a much larger drop in their price in order to persuade people that *now* is the time to buy them, rather than postponing the purchase because prices might drop further. Thus if bond prices have a history of being steady, and therefore people expect them to continue to be steady, government deficits can be funded on more advantageous terms, thereby minimising the future continuing burden on taxpayers of meeting the interest payments on the debt. For successful fulfilment of this role, therefore, the Central Bank would wish to keep interest rates steady at a low level.

These other aims of low and/or stable interest rates may not only explain some of the view of monetary policy as interest-rate policy, but also may involve clashes and trade-offs with the use of monetary policy for maintaining full employment.

Despite recognising that monetary policy can mean control of interest rates, we shall follow the current majority of economists and continue to treat Central Banks as if they controlled the money supply. By an 'expansionary monetary policy' we shall mean an increase in the money supply and, similarly, steady (or contractionary) policies will refer to a constant level of the money stock (or a drop in it).

We can now return to the question of whether an expansionary monetary or fiscal policy will always help to raise output and employment, starting from an unemployment equilibrium in a Keynesian model.

The answer is clear. In general, either an increase in government expenditure or an expansionary monetary policy, leading to an increase in investment via lower interest rates, will lead to an increase in output. Nevertheless, for many years, and to some extent even now, there is the view that Keynesians believe that only fiscal policy can affect income and output, while Monetarists believe that only monetary policy can have such an effect. It turns out that in certain special cases only fiscal policy works, and in another special case only monetary policy works. Monetarists have accused Keynesians of unrealistically believing in the special case which would validate fiscal but not monetary policy, while Keynesians have said the opposite about Monetarists. Part of the confusion is probably a result of polemics, especially in writings intended to have a more popular appeal. Partly it is also, as we shall show later, the result of something of a tendency of each group to fall back on different special cases when trying to give a simplified exposition of their views.

Only fiscal policy will work, and monetary policy will not have any effect, if one of the links between changes in the money supply and changes in investment is broken.[20] The link that accounts of Keynesian theory tend to concentrate on is that between the increase in the money supply and the fall in interest rates. One can conceive of a situation where, as interest rates become very low, the demand for money curve in Figs 2.2 and 2.3 becomes horizontal.[21] This situation is described as a 'liquidity trap'. Its occurrence could be explained in various ways, such as that the extra return from holding bonds as compared to money does not compensate for the risk of future capital loss on the bonds should their price fall (which is equivalent to the interest rate rising in the future). The important implication of the liquidity trap is that once the rate of interest has fallen to the level at which the liquidity trap occurs, an increase in the money supply will not reduce the interest rate any further. Therefore, if the level of investment which would occur at this minimum rate of interest is still not great enough to provide expenditure equal to full employment output, then monetary policy will not be able to increase investment and thereby restore full employment by this route. However, in a liquidity trap an increase in government expenditure will still increase output. In fact, as long as we remain in the liquidity trap, an increase in government expenditure will have the full effect on income predicted by the multiplier – because interest rates do not rise at all there is no crowding out of private investment to offset any of the effects of the increase in government expenditure.

As just mentioned, the accounts of Keynesian theory concentrate on the liquidity trap as the extreme Keynesian special case. Those who accuse Keynesians of believing that only fiscal policy can work, and that monetary policy cannot, then point out the extreme unlikelihood of a liquidity trap, and the lack of evidence that it has ever occurred. They can even point to Keynes' own statements implying that it is primarily a theoretical possibility rather than a realistic description of what happens even during a depression.[22] It seems to us, however, that most of those Keynesians who claimed that monetary policy cannot raise income did not have the liquidity trap in mind. Instead they usually based their view on the other link between monetary policy and investment. If investment is completely insensitive to the rate of interest, then monetary policy will have no effect even if it does lead to a fall in the interest rate. Empirically, many of the Keynesian studies of investment behaviour, including those incorporated into some of the early statistical forecasting models, did not find that investment depended on interest rates at all. This would seem to be the real basis of those Keynesians who downplayed monetary policy. Our impression is that it was only in the mid to late 1960s that many of the Keynesian-style forecasting models and empirical studies began to find quantitatively significant responses of investment to changes in interest rates. By now, virtually all economists accept that investment *is* sensitive to interest rates.

Nevertheless it remains true that the general theoretical framework accepted by Keynesians from the beginning indicated that provided that the economy was not in a liquidity trap and provided that there was some sensitivity of investment to interest rates, monetary policy would affect output and employment.[23] This is now accepted as the empirically relevant case.

The converse case, in which monetary policy can affect income while fiscal policy is powerless to do so, will also not occur in the general Keynesian model. However, there was a period, particularly in the late 1950s and 1960s, when this view was ascribed to Monetarists. It can occur in a special case, which is also usually thought of as being a component of the pre-Keynesian 'Classical' theory.[24] This component is the 'Quantity Theory of Money'. The Quantity Theory can be put in various ways which are equivalent for our purpose. The traditional way is to say that the velocity of circulation of money is constant. Perhaps more revealingly for our purpose, it can be stated as the assertion that the demand for money is independent of the rate of interest.[25]

The implication of the Quantity Theory can be seen from the first formulation by considering equation (2.3),

$$MV = PY \qquad (2.3)$$

where M stands for the stock of money, V stands for the velocity of circulation, P stands for an index of the price level and, as before, Y stands for income.[26] The right-hand side of equation (2.3) is, therefore, the *value* of national income, or nominal income. If velocity, V, is simply defined as equal to the value of national income divided by the money stock (that is $V \equiv PY/M$) then equation (2.3) is simply true by definition and tells us nothing about the world. The Quantity Theory is the assertion that V is in fact exogenous and constant over short periods – it may change slowly over time but any changes in velocity are not themselves a result of other changes in macroeconomic variables which alter as a result of government macroeconomic policies. If V is a constant, then equation (2.3) tells us that there is a one-to-one relationship between changes in the stock of money and changes in the value of national income. If, in addition, as in the present context of our discussion of monetary and fiscal policy, we keep the price level, P, fixed, then the only way that Y can change is if M changes. The implication is that any other change, such as a change in government expenditure, will not affect the level of real income. Hence fiscal policy must be powerless, while monetary policy will affect real output.[27]

Although the implication of equation (2.3) is that fiscal policy cannot affect national income, it does not indicate the sort of mechanism by which an increase in government expenditure will fail to affect income. This is indicated more by the second way of putting the Quantity Theory, which can be written as in equation (2.4)

$$M_d \;=\; kPY \qquad\qquad (2.4)$$

where M_d indicates the demand for money, k is a constant, and, as before, PY is the value of national income. This version represents the idea that the demand for money is purely for transactions purposes, and that this transactions demand is independent of the rate of interest. (If the demand did depend on the rate of interest, then k would not be a constant.) Furthermore, since in equilibrium the demand for money must equal the supply of money, the M_d on the left-hand side can simply be replaced by M to give equation (2.5)

$$M \;=\; kPY \qquad\qquad (2.5)$$

In a formal sense equations (2.3) and (2.5) are completely equivalent once we add the assumptions that V in equation (2.3) and k in equation (2.5) are both constant: k is then simply the reciprocal of V, and vice versa.[28] However, by considering equation (2.4) as a demand for money which is not dependent at all on interest rates, one has the idea that there is one, and only one, level of national income which would lead to a demand for money balances which is equal to the exogenously given supply of money. This suggests that if there is an increase in one of the components of desired expenditure, such as government expenditure, what will happen is that there will be an excess demand for funds which will drive up the interest rate in the financial markets. The process will only stop when enough investment has been crowded out by the rise in interest rates so as to leave total expenditure back at its old level.

We have indicated the dynamic process of change between the old and the new equilibria in a purposefully vague manner. The formal analysis only compares the equilibria themselves, and does not specify the processes of change. The end result of the process is, however, clear from the formal model. An increase in government expenditure will lead to a drop in private investment of exactly the same quantitative amount, leaving total expenditure and output unchanged. In terms of equation (2.1) the increase in G will be matched by a fall in I, and there is full crowding out. Hence fiscal policy cannot have any effect in the special case where the demand for money is completely insensitive to interest rates.[29]

If we were only interested in the predictions of the Keynesian model, and not in the policy issues that are still current, we could leave the matter of the efficacy of monetary and fiscal policy at this point, with the conclusions that in general either policy will work. In the special cases where one of the two policies cannot affect output and employment, the other policy will still have an effect – in fact a more powerful effect than in the general case. However, this is a convenient point to jump forward in time and deal with a policy relevant issue that still causes much confusion. We mentioned above that there was a tendency for Monetarists to say that Keynesians believed only in fiscal policy and for Keynesians to accuse Monetarists of believing only in monetary policy. This 'debate' was particularly noticeable during the 1960s.

We have already indicated that there were some Keynesians who felt, as a matter of the way they saw the evidence, that the case where only fiscal policy could affect output was empirically relevant. On the other side of the divide, the issue was mixed up with the meaning given to the phrase 'Quantity Theory of Money'. The confusion over the meaning and implications of this theory is still found in some books and articles today. The source, perhaps, is a famous article by the economist identified as the outstanding Monetarist of the 1950s and 1960s, namely Milton Friedman. In his 1956 article 'The Quantity Theory of Money – A Restatement', Friedman amongst other things provided an analysis of the demand for money where the demand for money depended on several variables, including interest rates, and therefore the numerical value of k in equation (2.4) or of V in equation (2.3) was not constant. He claimed that the Quantity Theory only required that the measured velocity of circulation should be a stable *function* of other variables, not a constant number. This of course would be perfectly compatible with the general Keynesian case, and would not in itself give any other predictions about policy. At most, it might lead to a different focus on particular aspects of the processes. However, in work which was published shortly after-wards,[30] Friedman claimed that when investigated statistically, in fact the demand for money was not sensitive to interest rates, even though in theory it might have been so. As already shown, this empirical finding carried the implication that 'only money matters'. The confusion arises because this strong statement, with which Monetarism was popularly identified for a long time afterwards, does depend on velocity being a constant number, and not merely on it being possible to write it as a stable *function* of other variables. Because of the conjunction of Friedman's attempted rehabilitation of the title 'Quantity Theory' and his statement that only monetary policy will have an effect on income, many people assumed (without thinking the matter through adequately) that this policy prediction that only monetary policy can have an effect was compatible with the notion that it suffices for the demand for money to be a stable function, and is not limited to the case where velocity is a constant number. As we have shown, this is simply wrong.

By the end of the 1960s, other economists who in many ways were sympathetic to other aspects of the Monetarist approach to managing the economy, had investigated the demand for money empirically. They, like Keynesians, found that the demand for money *did* depend upon the rate of interest, and that Friedman's earlier findings did not stand up to more sophisticated but more correct statistical analysis. Thus, by about 1970, both Monetarists and Keynesians were agreed that one could use either monetary or fiscal policy to affect the level of economic activity.[31] Partly because of the long lag between what appears in the academic journals and discussions, and the messages relayed and understood by 'practical men of affairs' and politicians, the belief that Monetarists had shown that all that mattered was to get the money supply correct (and that fiscal policy was irrelevant to the level of output) persisted for much longer and has been influential right up to the present.[32,33]

We have stressed that in their serious work, except perhaps for some years in the 1960s, most Keynesians and most Monetarists agreed that it is neither true that 'only money matters' nor is it true that 'money does not matter', but 'money matters' and so does fiscal policy. Nevertheless, the identification of each group with a special case has persisted, and, in our view, this may not be due just to ignorance and inertia on the part of non-economists. At times, one is tempted to simplify, and it may be the case that different economists have a tendency to fall back on the particular simplification of one of the special cases whenever they give in to the temptation.

One advantage of the special cases is that they make predictions very easy, without having to calculate and keep in mind a large number of parameters. Economists may at times want to give an off-the-cuff prediction of the results of some macroeconomic policy change. For example, one may be sitting as an 'expert' in a television or radio studio on the night that a budget has been announced. One may even be sitting in a bar with some acquaintances, and not wish to appear too ignorant. Under these circumstances, it requires no more than the memorisation of a reasonable number for the multiplier to predict the effect on income of a particular budget change, *if* one is prepared to take the extreme 'Keynesian special case' simplification. For example, in the special case, if the multiplier is equal to 2 and the increase in government expenditure is equal to £3 billion it does not require very much mathematical ability to state that income will rise by £6 billion. Conversely, *if* one is prepared to use the constant velocity simplification, the implication is that the result of an increase in the money supply would be an equal percentage increase in nominal national income. Again, it requires no great mathematical sophistication to say that a 5% increase in the money supply will lead to a 5% increase in income. To make predictions, if one insists on sticking to the more general cases that the same economists use in their serious work, would require knowing many more parameters and in general not be susceptible to 'back of envelope' calculation. Until portable computers become small enough and cheap enough for most of us to carry them around with us the whole time, the temptation to simplify will still persist. What we are suggesting is that economists who in other ways think of themselves as Keynesians will tend to fall back on the over-simplified case in which the multiplier alone gives a prediction (that is also the case in which fiscal policy only would work). Conversely, economists who in other ways might identify with the Monetarist position, will tend to fall back on the over-simplification involving a constant velocity of circulation (that is, the case in which only monetary policy can work).[34]

One final reason for the persistence of the identification of Keynesians with the special case in which only fiscal policy can work, is the need to introduce new ideas in economics to beginners in the most simple context. As a result, students are typically introduced to the Keynesian model in the form of the 45-degree diagram (sometimes also called the 'Keynesian cross' diagram) and the equivalent savings/investment diagram in which investment is treated as exogenous. Similarly they are taught to calculate the change in income that would result from a change in government expenditure or investment, by using the multiplier without any modification for the feedback on to investment from induced changes in interest rates. This is, again, only strictly valid in the unrealistic special cases where either we are in a liquidity trap or investment does not depend at all on interest rates.

RELATIONSHIP OF MONETARY TO FISCAL POLICY

From the analysis of the previous section, together with what are now accepted as the empirically relevant relationships connecting interest rates to investment and to the demand for money, it follows that either monetary or fiscal policy, or both, can be used to alter the level of expenditure. The choice of the combination of monetary and fiscal policy could be determined by other aims, since different combinations imply different rates of interest. If continued over longer periods they also imply different levels of the stocks of money and of National Debt (i.e. government bonds). The more expansionary the fiscal policy stance, and the less expansionary the monetary policy stance, the higher will be the rate of interest. Conversely an increase in the money supply, together with a contractionary fiscal policy, could reduce interest rates without altering expenditure. (For those familiar with an IS–LM analysis, the argument is illustrated in Fig. 2.4.)

If the government has other aims which depend on interest rates, this will help to determine the combination of monetary and fiscal policy. To use one of the examples mentioned earlier in this chapter, a lower interest rate implies higher private investment and this may be desired for its longer-term effects on capital accumulation and growth. This would imply a preference for increasing income via an expansionary monetary policy rather than a fiscal one. On the other hand, there may be a feeling that lower tax rates are also good for growth, and (if there are limits as to how far government expenditure

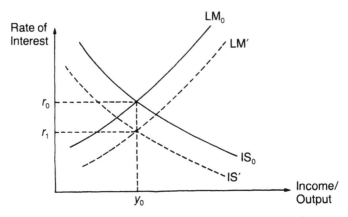

Figure 2.4 IS–LM representation of reducing the interest rate (from r_0 to r_1) while leaving output unchanged by expansionary monetary policy (LM_0 to LM') and contractionary fiscal policy (IS_0 to IS')

can be squeezed) governments might wish to have an expansionary fiscal policy in the form of reduced taxes. Similarly, some forms of government expenditure may be desired for themselves, e.g. education may be an aim in itself, or help towards other aims besides increasing aggregate expenditure, e.g. education may increase technological progress and growth. Thus the 'best' combination of monetary and fiscal policies will depend on considering a range of both micro- and macroeconomic aims, constraints and trade-offs.[35]

The relationship between the use of monetary and fiscal policies may also be affected by institutional arrangements which vary between countries. In some countries (e.g. the UK, France) monetary and fiscal policies are both effectively under the control of the government. In others (e.g. US, Germany) monetary policy is the responsibility of a largely independent Central Bank. Even in the former group, co-ordination can be a problem. In the latter group some seem to avoid major problems (Germany) while others seem to go through periods of tension (US), with apparently contradictory monetary and fiscal policies leading to undesired results.[36]

Although it takes us well past the early Keynesian stress on unemployment as the primary focus of macroeconomics, we might mention here that at the time of writing (late 1990) the issue has been given prominence in the EEC in the discussion about the possible role and constitution of any future joint EEC Central Bank. Those in favour point particularly to the success of the German Central Bank (the Bundesbank). This success is the low level of inflation in (West) Germany in the 1970s and 1980s – the record on growth and unemployment is less outstanding. This success is attributed to the existence of an independent Central Bank with a constitutional commitment to restrain inflation. It thus involves ideas to be discussed in Chapter 4, but the two main arguments commonly advanced can be outlined here: (i) by

24

enabling monetary policy to be determined by the long-term effects on inflation, lower inflation is achieved over the long term; (ii) an independent Central Bank can resist pressures from governments seeking re-election for an unwise expansion in the money supply to reduce interest rates.

The second argument obviously takes us into more explicitly political considerations, though not completely outside the realms of economics (see the next chapter). The first argument on its own does not imply the need for independence of monetary policy. As already noted in this section, both monetary and fiscal policy have various impacts on other aims of government policy which need to be considered in settling the balance between them, and, for that matter, between employment and the other aims. Were it not for the other (political) argument, there seems no reason why artificially separating monetary from fiscal policy should improve the balance chosen.

CONCLUSIONS

In this chapter we have reviewed the Keynesian approach to the determination of output and employment, with its implication that an equilibrium can exist with output at less than the level corresponding to the full employment of the labour force. We have also shown that in this approach it is always possible to increase output up to its full employment level by a judicious use of fiscal policy, monetary policy or both. Only in extreme cases did the theory imply that *only* fiscal policy would increase employment or that it could not increase it at all. Except in the former extreme case monetary policy could also be used. Except in the latter extreme case even fiscal policy alone would work. In all cases, the government could increase the level of employment when the economy started in an equilibrium with unemployment.

Once this argument was widely accepted, since the government *could* reduce unemployment due to a lack of sufficient aggregate expenditure on goods and services, it seemed obvious that it should undertake the responsibility to act in such a way. Hence the pressure on governments to undertake the commitment to the maintenance of full employment, and the widespread view that any failure to keep the economy at full employment was the fault of the government. It would be a sign of either incompetence or irresponsibility. Either way, the conventional political wisdom became that governments must use macroeconomic policy to keep employment high, and that any failure to do so would deservedly result in loss of office in a democracy.

3

DEFICIENCIES IN THE KEYNESIAN EXPLANATION AND POLICY PROPOSALS

INTRODUCTION

The Keynesian model and policy prescription reviewed in the previous chapter quickly gained widespread acceptance, both amongst economists and in terms of political commitments. In the United States the New Deal was quickly viewed as a kind of proto-Keynesianism; although even as late as the 1960s some Republicans remained publicly opposed to 'deficit spending'. The return of a Democratic President, Kennedy, in 1960 inaugurated a period in which some of the leading Keynesian economists in the United States played a prominent role in economic policy-making. Until 1980, it is probably correct to say that Keynesian policies were followed even under Republican Presidents.[1] In most other developed countries, there was a much quicker acceptance of Keynesian policies by political parties spanning the political spectrum. For example, in the United Kingdom a bipartisan commitment to the government's responsibility for the achievement of full employment was based on a report which was completed even before the end of the Second World War.

Despite this policy acceptance, and the acceptance of the Keynesian approach by most economists, there continued to be discussions amongst economists over what were seen as some of the weaknesses in the Keynesian approach. Some economists saw these points as merely minor blemishes in the Keynesian explanation of unemployment and the economy, others saw them as fundamental flaws. The latter, a dissenting minority during the heyday of Keynesianism, have become much more influential since the later 1960s. The points in this chapter are, therefore, still the focus of much disagreement – affecting not only the theoretical explanations, but also the policy prescriptions. In the next section we consider the arguments over Keynes' assumption that the money wage is to be treated as simply given at any period in time. As was stated in Chapter 1, to this day, in our view, many differences of views about economic policies can be reduced to differences of views regarding the operation of the labour market. One way of rephrasing the above arguments is by asking whether all unemployment is 'voluntary'.

This aspect is dealt with in the section entitled 'Is unemployment always voluntary?'.

The problems of the exogeneity of money wages and the voluntariness, or otherwise, of unemployment lead on to consideration of the relationship between unemployment and *real* wages. This is dealt with on pages 35–40 and considers the question of whether real wages have to be cut in order to increase employment, and whether a cut in money wages would actually lead to a fall in real wages, or merely to an equivalent proportional cut in prices.

'Equilibrium or disequilibrium unemployment', later in this chapter, relates the exogeneity of the money wage to the whole stress on unemployment *equilibrium*.

The ideas covered on pages 27–42 are all interrelated, but unfortunately people can only read words in an order, not simultaneously. For the purposes of exposition we have put these ideas in what we think is the best sequence, but the reader may find it rewarding to think back on (or reread) the earlier sections after having read the later ones, in order to get more feel for the interdependencies.

The final section (pp. 42–50) looks at the relationship between debates over a model which formally deals with *equilibrium* unemployment, to the continuing disagreements over whether governments should try to stabilise economic *fluctuations*.

THE EXOGENEITY OF MONEY WAGES

In the standard Keynesian models of the economy, it is assumed that as long as there is unemployment money wages are fixed.[2] Because, in the Keynesian view of the world, when there is widespread unemployment there is an excess supply of labour, normal market theory would imply that we would expect there to be downward pressure on wages; just as when there is excess supply in any other market we expect the price of the relevant product to fall. The assumption that money wages remain constant during periods of unemployment is therefore often expressed as the view that 'money wages are rigid downward'.

Although in much of the discussion over the policy implications of the assumption of exogenous money wages, it is the *downward* rigidity of money wages which is important, Keynes also assumed in *The General Theory* that as long as employment remains below the full-employment level, then wages will not actually rise[3] even if there is a change in the price level. This implied that although money wages are constant, real wages are not. In particular, if money wages remain constant when there is a rise in the price level, then real wages fall. This seems to carry the implication that in the wage-setting process workers (and possibly employers) are concerned about the money wage but not about the real wage. This implication profoundly disturbs some economists. One of the fundamental results of microeconomic

27

analysis is that behaviour, and therefore resource allocation, should depend not on *nominal* values but upon *relative* prices. In the context of the labour market and workers' behaviour in supplying labour, the nominal value is the money wage and the relative price of labour is the money wage relative to the price level: i.e. the real wage. Therefore an assumption that workers do not react to changes in real wages contradicts what economists usually think of as 'rational' behaviour. Behaviour which responds to nominal, and not to real, values is also often described as 'money illusion'. People are allowing themselves to be fooled into inappropriate behaviour (i.e. actions which do not maximise their utility) because they are looking at a wage or price simply as a number of £s rather than the command over resources that those £s represent.

The strong negative emotive connotations of words like 'irrationality' and 'illusion' is not just a matter of chance. As already stated, the assumptions of much (most) of microeconomic analysis and its predictions would be vitiated if such behaviour were found to be widespread. Hence the unease at Keynes' assumption that money wages may be rigid even when the Retail Price Index changes.[4] The subsequent discussions have mainly dealt with the case where a rise in the price level means that real wages fall if workers do not seek a rise in the money wage.

The two issues, of whether money wages will fall when the supply of labour exceeds its demand and whether they will fail to rise when prices rise, are conceptually separate. One could argue that one is realistic without necessarily accepting the other. In recent years, in fact, some Keynesians have offered explanations of the labour market that deal only with one of the two assumptions. Keynes himself gave an account of the way he saw labour market behaviour which he thought justified both aspects of the rigid money wage assumption. Since, as mentioned in the previous chapter, *The General Theory* did allow for prices which were flexible, and which rose when output expanded even at times of unemployment (so that real wages fall when output expands), Keynes was concerned with both aspects of wage rigidity. Because for a long time after the late 1930s most Keynesians ignored the possibility of price rises during periods of unemployment, they tended to simply worry about defending the assumption that money wages do not fall even when there is excess supply of labour. However, recently there have been attempts by Keynesians to justify an assumption of rigid money wages even while prices rise.

We shall not attempt to give an exhaustive account of all of the different possible explanations which have been proffered by Keynesian economists in order to justify the assumption of rigid wages, but shall mention a few to give the flavour of the sorts of arguments advanced. Amongst the earliest is the view that workers are concerned about *relative* wages because these are supposed to indicate their relative worth. By worth, in this context, we do not mean their marginal productivity, but in a sense the esteem in which they are held. For any particular worker or group of workers to take a wage cut, when they cannot be absolutely certain that all other workers are taking a cut in wages, might also imply a drop in their relative social standing. One could rephrase the argument by saying that, in the view of those who find it plausible, a person's relative wage indicates their 'value' – where the word has the meaning given to it in Oscar Wilde's famous epigram 'A cynic is a man who knows the price of everything and the value of nothing'. Because a rise in the price level which reduces the real value of all money wages does not alter the relative wage, workers would be prepared to accept a cut in the real wage brought about in this way, even while they would reject being the first to start a process of cuts in real wages brought about by a reduction in their money wage during a period of unemployment. Hence this sort of explanation deals with both forms of wage rigidity.

Some more modern Keynesian versions of a somewhat similar approach stress such things as the importance of social norms which inhibit unemployed workers from offering to take the jobs of the currently employed, at least during periods of non-catastrophic unemployment, or fears of offending against feelings of 'fairness'.[5] The latter can also be linked to theories of the labour market which predict that not only will workers resist wage cuts but that employers may not wish to cut wages even if they could hire currently unemployed workers at a lower wage than they are paying their existing employees. In the fairness version of these theories (a type of what are often called 'efficiency wage' theories) if wage cuts on existing employees are pushed through by using the threat of hiring the currently unemployed, the resentment engendered amongst employees will lead to them putting in the minimum effort that they can get away with. The lack of willing commitment by the workers will lead not only to a drop in the actual amount of work done, but may also lead to a slapdash approach to quality. Thus it is in the employers' own interest not to cut wages.[6] Other versions of 'efficiency wage' theories stress other reasons that employers may have for not wishing to cut wages. These include: the incentive to avoid incurring the cost of training newly hired workers, which can be helped by keeping a wage which is above the 'going' wage rate for the job and thus discouraging existing workers from quitting; the extra incentive for workers to avoid being sacked for shirking if the wage they are currently earning is above that which they could hope to earn if they were forced to try to find another job; and that there is a danger that paying lower wages will discourage the potentially more productive workers from joining the firm.

The justifications for assuming rigid wages, in the sample which has just been given, have in common that they do not rely on the 'imperfection' of trade unions. Another strand in the Keynesian tradition, though not stressed by Keynes himself, focuses on the role of trade unions. The importance of trade unions would then be not so much that their motivation for resisting wage cuts is greater than that of their members, but that unlike unorganised workers they might have the power to prevent wage cuts. Essentially, the threat of a strike if some existing workers were to be replaced by the unemployed at a lower wage rate, might be enough to prevent a cut in wages. However, at least in countries where the proportion of the labour force which belongs to trade unions is well under 100%, unions alone are not enough to justify an assumption that all money wages are rigid downwards. Even if unionised firms did not cut money wages, non-unionised firms could do so and as a result they would produce their goods at lower prices than unionised firms, and thus the latter would be driven out of business. Even if some whole industries were unionised, if non-unionised industries were in a position to reduce their relative prices then demand would switch to them. The emphasis on trade union power as at least a partial explanation of downward wage rigidity seems to us to vary between countries and between times according to the relative size and apparent strength of trade unions.

As indicated earlier, those economists who oppose the Keynesian approach have often found these Keynesian explanations of wage rigidity unconvincing. Partly this is a feeling that whatever the obstacles, in the end 'market forces' must prevail. It is sometimes stated as a disbelief that it is possible for mutually advantageous trades to be possible and yet not be undertaken.[7] If there is an unemployed worker who would be better off working even at a lower wage than currently paid by a particular employer, and the employer could cut costs and therefore increase profit by employing this worker at a lower wage, then it is treated as axiomatic that a mutually advantageous agreement will be reached and implemented. The more recent Keynesian explanations of wage rigidities which were referred to in the previous paragraph can be seen as an attempt to answer this attack on the earlier Keynesian explanations. What they have in common is the implication that in fact a wage-cutting deal between employers and the currently unemployed would not be mutually advantageous. At least one of the two potential contractors would not wish to implement such a deal. In the approach which appeals to 'social norms' it is the unemployed who do not wish to offer to replace current workers at lower wages. Social pressures outweigh their self-interest as it is more narrowly defined in traditional economic approaches to utility maximisation. In the efficiency wage versions it is not in the employer's self-interest, even defined narrowly as profit maximisation, to replace some of the existing labour force by new workers hired from the ranks of the unemployed at a lower wage. In either approach, because the threat of hiring other workers if the current labour force do not agree to a wage cut is not credible, the existing workers will not agree to such a cut.

In general, Monetarists do not find these descriptions of the labour market to be realistic. Their view of the world is that if unemployment persists for any length of time, then wages will fall unless the apparently unemployed prefer to remain in that situation. Whichever of the explanations they accept, most Keynesians do feel that there can be long periods of unemployment

without appreciable falls in money wages, even though many of the unemployed would be prepared to take a job at a real wage somewhat lower than
the going rate – if only they were offered a job.

IS UNEMPLOYMENT ALWAYS VOLUNTARY?

The question of whether there are times when much of the unemployment
can be considered involuntary is one which has divided economists ever since
Keynes first introduced his notion of involuntary unemployment. Although
Keynes provided a neutral definition of his use of the term 'involuntary
unemployment', the passion of much of the disagreements over whether the
phenomenon can exist slips between formal definitions and ordinary usage
and implications. In ordinary usage 'involuntary' carries the connotation that
there is no option. Because there is no alternative there is no choice to be
made. To quote one dictionary, involuntary means 'without the exercise of
will'. Thus those who deny that there can be involuntary unemployment
typically mean to say that the unemployed could find some other job, if only
they were prepared to make the sacrifices necessary. They see unemployment
as being voluntary because it is a result of the choice to remain unemployed
rather than to take a job which is considered even less desirable than
unemployment.

Monetarists typically claim that even if it is not possible for the unemployed
to find the sort of job, using the sort of skills, and paying the level of wages
that they would like, there are always some possibilities for employment. It
may be understandable that an unemployed worker who has spent years
acquiring experience in some skilled occupation may not want to take a job at
minimal wages washing up dishes, or go around offering to polish people's
shoes, but since the choice is there their continued unemployment should
instead be described as 'voluntary'. This view is obviously related to the
Keynesian/Monetarist disagreement of the previous section over the rigidity
of wages. The view that in the ultimate analysis all unemployment is
voluntary says that there are always some sectors where it is possible to find
work if one is prepared to cut one's wage demand enough.[8]

Those Keynesians who are prepared to argue about the voluntariness of
unemployment within this particular context make various replies. One is to
assert that within a modern industrialised economy such sectors, where the
possibility of finding a low wage job still exists, are of trivial importance.
During periods of mass unemployment, they could not absorb all of the
unemployed, even if all the unemployed were prepared to work in such
sectors. In addition, within a Keynesian framework, some argue that even if
some of the currently unemployed do reduce their wage demands enough to
find work as dish-washers etc., they will merely displace the existing people in
those low wage/low skill occupations. Thus the composition of the unemployed might alter, but there would not be a decrease in the total number

of unemployed workers unless there were an increase in demand. Thus we are back with the Keynesian view that during periods of unemployment, output is dependent upon aggregate demand. In the absence of an expansion in total expenditure, aggregate output will not increase and therefore total unemployment will not fall.[9] More generally, when not discussed simply as a defence against the attack mentioned in the previous paragraph, the Keynesian argument for treating most unemployment (during recessions) as involuntary, has various strands. One strand goes back to Keynes' formal, technical, definition in *The General Theory*. Others try to use a notion of involuntary unemployment that picks up more of the everyday notion of voluntariness.

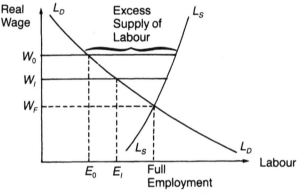

Figure 3.1 Unemployment with rigid money wages

Keynes' definition was that unemployment is involuntary if a rise in the price level relative to the money wage would increase the volume of employment. In other words, a fall in the *real* wage would persuade firms to employ more workers, and (what is essential in this notion of involuntary unemployment) there would be a supply of workers available to fill the extra jobs even at this lower real wage. The definition is illustrated in Fig. 3.1, where the downward-sloping curve L_D is the demand for labour – so that a lower real wage leads to a higher quantity of labour being demanded – while L_S shows the ordinary supply curve for labour as a function of the real wage. Some Keynesians would consider the supply curve to be virtually vertical, at least for prime-age workers, if we consider labour measured in terms of the number of workers rather than in terms of man-hours worked, as they do not think that people's decisions about whether to work at all are very sensitive to the real wage.[10] Nothing much in the argument hinges on whether or not the supply curve is vertical. If initially we have a real wage of w_0 then the amount of labour demanded, and therefore employment, is given by E_0. At this real wage more workers would be prepared to work than are in fact employed. If the price level were to be higher, with the money wage unchanged, then the real wage would be lower. In Fig. 3.1 consider a lower real wage of w_1 where if W denotes the money wage and P denotes the price level we have

$$\text{and} \quad \begin{aligned} W_0/P_0 &= w_0 \\ W_0/P_1 &= w_1 \end{aligned}$$

with P_1 higher than P_0. Employment at w_1 would be E_1. The unemployment at E_0 was involuntary because the extra demand for labour can be filled from the unemployed even at this lower real wage. The same would be true for any increase in employment up to the full employment level.

What gives this definition of involuntary unemployment whatever force and appeal it has is, we think, due to embedding it within a model of the economy that treats the money wage as downwardly rigid. In the example, the fall in the real wage occurred even while the money wage is fixed at W_0, because of the rise in the price level from P_0 to P_1. A rise in prices is not within the power of workers to achieve, especially during a slump when they are not raising money wages. As long as the money wage is simply treated as exogenous, workers cannot achieve the necessary cut in their real wage. Since they are 'off' their supply curve, Keynes could feel justified in describing such unemployment as 'involuntary'.[11] What workers would *like* to do is expressed precisely by the supply curve of labour.

Keynes' definition of involuntary unemployment and his explanation of changes in involuntary unemployment fit within his model of the economy in which changes in the volume of employment are inversely linked to changes to the real wage. In Fig 3.1, workers are off their supply curves as long as real wages are above w_F, but firms are on their demand curves for labour and unemployment varies with changes in the real wage as firms move up or down their demand curves. As already indicated, many Keynesian discussions for a long time (and to some extent even now) treated the price level as well as the money wage as inflexible during periods when expenditure is not high enough to ensure output equal to its full employment level. Therefore some of the other strands within the later Keynesian arguments that unemployment may be involuntary are not directly linked to Keynes' own definition. They are compatible with analyses that allow unemployment to change in response to changes in expenditure without concomitant changes in the real wage.

One such approach is to claim that during a depression the unemployed may be described as being involuntarily unemployed if not only were they previously employed at a real wage at which they cannot now find jobs, but in addition they could reasonably expect that normal types of jobs will be available once again on terms that they would be prepared to accept. Their jobs have been lost not because of some fundamental change in the structure of the economy (whether in the *pattern* of demand or of efficient production), but simply because of a lack of *aggregate* demand. When 'normal times' return, they will once again be able to obtain ordinary jobs. If workers hold such views, and if they are justified in holding them, then their reluctance to seek out very low paid, menial, jobs does not mean that their unemployment is voluntary. Thus this version of the Keynesian argument is meant to counter the Monetarist view discussed earlier and illustrated by our example of dish-washing. Keynesians often point to the anecdotal evidence of newspaper reports concerning the queues of applicants for ordinary jobs if some firm announces that it is hiring workers during a recession. The acceptability of this Keynesian view depends, at least in part, on the correctness of its assertion that an increase in expenditure would lead to 'ordinary' jobs becoming available at 'acceptable' wages.[12]

The Keynesian argument just discussed can be viewed as an amplification of Keynes' own definition. However, it is not limited to a case where the 'acceptable' real wages which will accompany higher employment, are necessarily lower than the real wages while unemployment was higher. Both approaches, as with the arguments of those who insist that unemployment is to be considered always as voluntary, do depend on a more general view of what is considered to be an adequate model of macroeconomics. Given that much (in our own casual judgement, most) of the subsequent discussion has not been limited to Keynes' original definition of involuntary unemployment, one might well ask why there has been so much intense debate over whether the term 'involuntary' should ever be applied to unemployment. Keynes could be seen as having merely given the technical definition within his particular model of the economy, and it is commonly argued that definitions are merely shorthand to save having to rewrite a long phrase each time one wishes to refer to the concept. Why, then, should economists working with models which differ either to a greater or lesser extent from that in *The General Theory* continue to argue over whether unemployment should be called voluntary or involuntary? One might speculate that a large part of the answer to this question is that even though we can define words in some neutral way, they still retain their emotive connotations. Keynes' choice of the word 'involuntary' was not, in this view, purely coincidental. For example, he could have chosen some other phrase such as 'excess supply' or 'high real wage' unemployment. However, calling it involuntary carried the message that it was undesirable, and that something should be done about it if possible. As we have discussed, he was successful in gaining acceptance of a commitment not to accept widespread unemployment. In his model, and for that matter in later Keynesian discussions, unemployment is undesirable in the sense that it would be welfare improving to reduce it. Precisely because workers are off their supply curve of labour, an increase in employment, even at a somewhat lower real wage, will benefit the unemployed without harming employers.[13] Although this would have still been an implication of the model whatever name was given to the type of unemployment, calling it involuntary would leave the desired impression even with those readers who had forgotten the precise definition, or even with those who had never read the book but merely vaguely heard about its ideas from some second-hand report.

Those who feel that all unemployment is voluntary would usually argue that there is no *problem* of unemployment. Since workers are on their supply curve and unconstrained in any meaningful sense, there is no need for any policy to try to alter the level of employment. The level of employment is the result of demand and supply decisions by firms and workers, and can be assumed to have the usual optimality properties of market equilibria. Government action to affect labour markets is no more justified than in any other market – at most (on this sort of Monetarist view) it should be limited to removing imperfections, such as the imperfections due to trade union power.

Many economists would disagree, but our opinion is that it is not at all uncommon in economics for persuasive terms to be used *and* to have an effect on people's general perceptions. One could think of such phrases as 'perfect' competition, or 'free' trade. In both cases one can give, and is normally given, a purely technical definition. Yet the fact that one type of competition is called perfect is likely to leave the impression that there is something desirable about such a form of competition, even to those who have never thought through a formal welfare economic analysis of the assumptions and value judgements under which it is desirable. Somehow competition which is 'perfect' must be better than 'imperfect'.[14] Similarly, the designation of the absence of tariffs as 'free' trade carries the implication that it is better than the alternative: what is 'unfree' must be inferior to freedom.[15] Our conjecture is that the continued arguments over the appropriateness of calling unemployment 'involuntary' are due to similar persuasive connotations for policy of the choice of adjective.[16]

Whether or not we are justified in our speculations as to why the arguments over the suitable description of the unemployed have continued, we are convinced that the issue remains one of the crucial ones distinguishing those who we have described as Keynesian from those we have described as Monetarists. In particular, those who feel that unemployment is primarily voluntary seem also to be those who feel that governments should not, or cannot, use macroeconomic policy to affect the level of employment and output. On the other hand, those who feel that unemployment can often be described as involuntary also always seem to feel that the problem could be solved by government, macroeconomic, action.

REAL WAGES AND UNEMPLOYMENT

In one important respect, Keynes did not depart from the views of his predecessors in his treatment of employment in *The General Theory*: changes in the level of employment were inversely related to changes in real wages. As illustrated in Fig. 3.1, changes in employment occurred as firms moved up and down their demand for labour curves. For Keynes, at least as long as there was involuntary unemployment as he defined it, the change in real wages occurred via changes in prices while money wages remained constant. Nevertheless, the proposition that a decline in unemployment would typically require a fall in real wages was not one that would be opposed by those economists with whom Keynes thought himself in disagreement. Where they differed, typically, was in their views over whether it was necessary for governments to intervene in order to achieve the necessary fall in real wages. Keynes' insistence that money wages were typically downwardly rigid, and his stress that there could be unemployment equilibrium (as we shall discuss in the next section), meant that he was not prepared to advocate waiting for money wages to fall in order to eliminate involuntary unemployment. At the policy level, this is an example of Keynes' predilection for concentrating on what he saw as the immediate problem at hand, rather than rely on what a long-run equilibrium would be: 'in the long-run we are all dead'.

According to Keynes' analysis, an expansionary monetary or fiscal policy would raise employment. However, in conjunction with his analysis of the labour market, as in Fig. 3.1, this can only occur if the expansionary monetary or fiscal policies lead to a rise in the price level.[17] From the very beginning, some of Keynes' opponents, such as Lionel Robbins, objected to his proposals (particularly in the more politically orientated pamphlets that Keynes wrote in the early 1930s) because they felt that he was avoiding the issue. In Robbins' view, if the cure for unemployment involved a fall in real wages, it was the professional duty of economists to state this honestly and explicitly. It would then be a political choice as to whether there was a preference for achieving the cut in real wages by policies which raised the price level, or by allowing money wages to fall. He felt that Keynes' approach was misleading: the advocacy of expansionary policies, let alone Keynes' acceptance of either devaluation or tariffs, was politically appealing precisely because most people did not realise that it was a disguised way of achieving real wage cuts. (Similar arguments still occur, particularly in discussions about using exchange rate depreciation to increase output and employment.)

Part of the problem was that Keynes was, in fact, not always consistent over the issue (as we mentioned in the previous chapter). Although his formal model did imply a fall in real wages, his less formal statements did, at times, proceed on the assumption that it would be possible to achieve a fall in unemployment without any cut in real wages. However, even within the analysis of *The General Theory*, the structure of the argument allowed a defence of the reliance upon expansionary policies to reduce unemployment. The first stage is the argument, already discussed, that in fact money wages are inflexible downwards. In the real world confronting the policy-maker, therefore, it would be extremely unwise to rely upon a fall in money wages induced by the continuing excess supply of labour to solve the problem of unemployment. Furthermore, even as a matter of theory, it might be that a cut in money wages would fail to lead to an increase in employment. There could be situations in which a cut in money wages would simply lead to an equal proportionate fall in the price level – thus leaving real wages unaltered. The circumstances under which this would occur are those which we referred to in the last chapter as the 'special Keynesian case'.

To see why the two special Keynesian cases, of (1) investment completely insensitive to interest rates or (2) a liquidity trap, would lead to equivalent falls in nominal wages and prices, it is necessary to think about the way that employment and output are determined within a Keynesian framework. Clearly, in this or any other approach, employment will only increase if output is increased. When we think back to the national income accounting identity, and the resulting equilibrium relationships, as in equation (2.1), output will only increase if there is an increase in consumption, investment, or government expenditure. Therefore if a cut in money wages is to lead to a higher equilibrium level of employment, and therefore output, it must lead to an increase in one of these components of expenditure. However, consumption is assumed to be related to income, and therefore consumption will only increase if income (which is equal to output) has been increased.[18] Since there is no reason to expect a cut in money wages to lead to an increase in government expenditure, then in a closed economy the only possible way that cutting money wages can lead to an increase in output is if it leads to an increase in investment.

The mechanism by which this could occur is as follows. A cut in money wages will cut firms' costs of production, and therefore lead to a downward shift in their supply curves. Thus prices will fall. However, a fall in prices with a constant money supply means that the *real* supply of money has increased. The excess supply of money will lead to a fall in interest rates and it is the fall in interest rates which will lead to an increase in investment. It is because investment has increased, and therefore total desired expenditure has increased, that the real demand for goods increases and limits the fall in prices. Therefore prices will not fall as much as money wages have fallen, and so real wages have declined – even though the fall in real wages is less than the fall in money wages. Hence in the standard case, if money wages were to fall then there would be an increase in output and employment. However, in the special Keynesian cases, as discussed in the last chapter, the link between increases in the real money supply and increases in investment is snapped. In the first of the Keynesian cases the fall in interest rate does not lead to an increase in investment, in the second the increase in the real money supply does not lead to a fall in interest rate.

We can summarise the preceding argument in either of two equivalent ways. *First*, a cut in money wages will not lead to an increase in employment in the special Keynesian cases, because the demand for goods does not increase and therefore we end up with the same level of output as before. *Second*, in the special Keynesian cases an attempt to cut real wages by reducing the nominal wages level will fail because prices will fall by the same proportion leaving real wages unchanged. Hence Keynes' argument was that not only should one not expect it to be easy, if at all possible, for an excess supply of labour to lead to a sufficient cut in money wages, but it was not even theoretically definite that a cut in money wages would solve unemployment.[19]

It should also be noted, that in the 'normal' case where a cut in money wages would help employment, so would an increase in the nominal money supply. Thus anything that can be achieved via a cut in money wages can also be achieved via an expansionary monetary policy. This reinforces Keynes' stress on the folly of relying on wage cutting as the cure for unemployment. In his view it would probably never occur on its own, even if it did it might not achieve the desired goal, and even if it could achieve the desired goal a more certain way of achieving the exact same result would be to run an expansionary monetary policy.

There are other reasons that led Keynes to oppose trying to return to full employment by a policy of cutting money wages accompanied by (even if to a lesser degree) falling prices. These arguments cannot be adequately dealt with in a formally static model, but nevertheless were stressed both by Keynes and by some of his contemporaries.[20] Part of the argument is that the *process* of falling prices will discourage postponable spending – it will pay to wait before buying durable goods in order to take advantage of their subsequent lower prices. Another argument is that, given that many debts are fixed in nominal terms, lower prices increase the real value of debt, and thus imply a redistribution of wealth away from debtors towards creditors. It is plausible to suggest that people who are in debt are likely to have a larger propensity to spend than creditors and other owners of assets.[21]

As already mentioned, Keynes himself did not always rely on his formal model of the labour market in which increases in output could only occur if there was a decline in real wages. As also mentioned in the last chapter, for a long time most subsequent Keynesian discussions of economic events and policies also ignored this aspect of the analysis in *The General Theory*. One reason why Keynesians tended to ignore the inverse link between real wages and employment was that it was felt that the evidence suggested that there was no such link. In the past fifty years there have been many studies trying to establish whether or not real wages are counter-cyclical: that is, whether when the economy is in a slump real wages are high and when there is a boom real wages are low. Our impression is there is still no overwhelming consensus. For a while, in the late 1930s and afterwards, the majority view was that statistical studies showed that there was no link at all between real wages and employment and this is still probably accepted by the majority of economists. Nevertheless, some more recent studies have claimed to find an inverse correlation, others still maintain the lack of a relationship. At the very least, the data on fluctuations in real wages and employment do not show enough variability and clear-cut patterns for the findings to be independent of the particular time period, place and statistical techniques used in different studies.[22]

The result is that different economists can feel free to have different beliefs over the relationship between changes in real wages and changes in unemployment, or the same economist can even make different assumptions in different pieces of analysis, or may genuinely feel that there are times when unemployment is associated with too high a level of real wages and times when it is not.[23] Because of the lack of conclusive direct evidence on the relationship between real wages and employment, the view one takes on the issue may also be affected by the way one views related issues. In particular, if one accepts that money wages are downwardly rigid during periods of high unemployment, then (as we have seen in the preceding two sections) it is only possible for cuts in real wages to reduce the unemployment if prices rise. Conversely, if prices do not rise during slumps, then real wages will remain rigid. Hence views on the relationship between real wages and employment are closely linked to views on whether prices, and not only money wages, are inflexible. Those Keynesian treatments which implied that real wages do not have to fall for an improvement in employment and output, often did so because they assumed – either implicity or explicitly – that firms will increase their production without requiring a rise in prices during periods of depression. Most of the time, if any justification at all was offered, it was simply along the lines that during a slump firms have large amounts of excess capacity and will therefore be prepared to increase their volume of sales if only they could sell the output, even without requiring a higher price. Sometimes slightly more attention was given to the pricing behaviour of firms than was implied by the view. Keynesian empirical models very often employed the 'mark-up pricing' approach. In this approach firms charge a price which includes some constant margin over what their costs of production would be at normal levels of output.

More recently, there have been other Keynesian attempts to provide a firmer theoretically acceptable microeconomic foundation for the proposition that prices may be inflexible – or at least only move sluggishly – in the face of shifts in the demand facing the firm. Some are somewhat similar to some of the theories explaining wage rigidity that we mentioned earlier, stressing such notions as customer/supplier relationships over a long period and the resulting need for mutual confidence that neither side will attempt to take unfair advantage of the other, and will provide predictability.[24] Others use the idea of 'menu costs', in which firms incur costs if they change their prices frequently: for example, because of the need to print new catalogues and distribute new price lists.[25] Most of these Keynesian justifications for price rigidity, the newer ones as well as the mark-up pricing approach, assume that there is widespread imperfection in product markets.[26] In this sense, they go easily together with the Keynesian view that labour markets do not work according to a simple market paradigm, with its flexible responses to situations of excess supply or excess demand.

Categorisation of the current beliefs of economists on the issues discussed in this section is not straightforward. Although non-Keynesians typically treat prices as flexible, and therefore goods markets as clearing,[27] Keynesians tend to differ amongst themselves. Some treatments assume that prices will vary with output even if wage costs remain unchanged.[28] Other Keynesian discussions, sometimes even by the same people, treat prices as constant as long as wages remain unchanged, i.e. as long as output remains below the level corresponding to full employment.[29] Similarly, many (but not all) Keynesian empirical models of the economy continue to use some version of mark-up pricing.

Similar divisions continue with respect to whether real wages have to fall in order to reduce unemployment. As we have seen, this is an implication of views on price flexibility. Thus, typically, non-Keynesians assume that it is necessary for real wages to fall if employment is to be increased.[30] Some Keynesians also continue to follow Keynes in also making this assumption.[31] Other Keynesians assume, sometimes implicitly by not bothering to give an explicit model of the labour market at all but just assuming price rigidity as well as money wage rigidity, that it is often possible to increase employment without having to reduce real wages.[32,33] Furthermore, some Keynesian discussions of particular episodes of high unemployment posited that there could be some periods when unemployment was due to real wages being too high, while at other times unemployment could be due to a lack of aggregate expenditure, even though real wages were not above the level that would be consistent with full employment.

Even for those who feel that it is typically necessary to reduce real wages in order to reduce unemployment, there is still the additional question of the best way to achieve such a cut in real wages. As we have seen, those Keynesians who do accept the need to cut real wages feel that it is more sensible to attempt to do this by policies which will lead to a rise in prices, while money wages remain unchanged.

Finally in this section, although it takes us beyond the debates discussed in this chapter and touches on the material more fully dealt with in the next, we might also note that there is no Keynesian consensus over whether unemployment during periods of ongoing inflation would on its own lead to money wages rising less fast than prices are rising, thereby cutting real wages.

On the other hand, during periods in which there is some ongoing inflation, it is not unknown for government ministers or spokespeople to appeal for 'restraint' in wage negotiations and give two reasons in the same speech.[34] *First* because lower wages would lead to increased employment. *Second* because lower wages will reduce inflation. They do not seem to realise that the two reasons are not necessarily consistent. The first requires that prices should rise while wages stop rising (or rise more slowly), in order to reduce real wages. The second reason implies that a slowdown in money wage increases will be matched by a slowdown in inflation – by which is meant price inflation.

EQUILIBRIUM OR DISEQUILIBRIUM UNEMPLOYMENT

The standard Keynesian analysis is of an equilibrium level of unemployment.[35] There are at least two questions that have bothered some Keynesians: *First* does the possibility of equilibrium unemployment depend on the assumption of rigid money wages? Given the vulnerability of this assumption to attacks on its lack of firm, theoretically acceptable, microeconomic foundations (as detailed on pp. 28–31), it might be preferable if this assumption could be dropped and yet the standard results retained. *Second*, particularly if the equilibrium predictions do depend on the less than fully satisfactory assumption of money wages being completely inflexible downwards, might it not be better (and more realistic?) to view unemployment as a disequilibrium phenomenon?

The answer to the first question is straightforward. If, by an equilibrium, we mean a situation in which all variables are constant, including wages, and if by flexible money wages we mean that wages will fall if there is an excess supply of labour (i.e. employment less than full employment), then by definition unemployment equilibrium requires rigid wages. If wages are flexible, and there is unemployment, wages will be falling and this situation is not an equilibrium one.

The answer to the second question is not as simple. As explained in the previous section, even if wages are flexible downwards this does not imply that they should be relied on to solve unemployment. It is tautologically correct that there cannot be equilibrium unemployment with flexible wages, but there might be continuing disequilibrium unemployment. As also already explained, in the special extreme Keynesian cases, flexible wages will simply lead to a continuing downward spiral of money wages and prices. Even without the special Keynesian cases, the arguments mentioned above concerning what might happen during the *process* of falling wages and prices mean that if money wages were flexible, and if they were to start to fall, the process might be an unstable one. That is, that during the disequilibrium process, forces may be set up that will actually lead to overshooting of the equilibrium – in our case, money wages (and real wages) will fall below the levels that would have restored full employment were it not for the deflationary effects of the disequilibrium process itself. Finally, even if money wages are flexible downwards, they may be sluggish enough that it would take an inordinately long time to return to full-employment equilibrium, relying just on this flexibility itself.[36] Thus downward flexibility is irrelevant for policy purposes, on Keynesian priorities of stressing immediate rather than longer-run problems and possibilities.

For all of these reasons, some Keynesians have preferred to think of their approach as not being limited to a model which predicts that there will be an unemployment *equilibrium*, but instead consistent with an analysis of unemployment as a continuing disequilibrium.[37] For these Keynesians, what is essential in the Keynesian message, is the prescription that at times of unemployment one should not, or even cannot (where the problem is one of instability), rely on endogenous market forces to solve the problem. Instead, expansionary macroeconomic policies are required.

Although there is such a Keynesian view, held by some eminent Keynesians, it remains true that most Keynesians have followed Keynes himself in limiting their formal analysis to one of equilibrium unemployment. There have been various suggestions as to why Keynes, and his followers, have limited themselves to equilibrium analyses. Historically, it is perhaps relevant that in the United Kingdom, unlike many other countries, the second half of the 1920s was a period of high unemployment. It was not limited to the Great Depression starting in 1929. Thus Keynes, writing a book published in 1936, was living in a country which had experienced more than a decade of high unemployment. Under these circumstances, it may have seemed sensible to concentrate on high unemployment viewed as an equilibrium.

One might also note, and it is not a trivial point, that it is much more difficult to do a rigorous disequilibrium analysis than an equilibrium one. Even now, most formal analysis, microeconomic as well as macroeconomic, is an equilibrium analysis for this reason.

It is also possible that, whether consciously or subconsciously, the political appeal of the Keynesian proposed recourse to expansionary macroeconomic policies, was better served by a prediction of equilibrium unemployment. If unemployment had been discussed as a disequilibrium phenomenon, the proposed policies would have been more open to the riposte that 'Well, since unemployment is only a disequilibrium situation, we might as well rely on the market to solve the problem, rather than interfering by printing money or running a budget deficit' (both of which were, and are, opposed by some people for other reasons). Merely claiming that it might take longer to return to full employment if there were a non-interventionist stance, might be a less compelling argument than that high unemployment was an equilibrium. The latter carried the connotation that it would last indefinitely if nothing were done.

BUSINESS CYCLES AND STABILISATION

Although Keynes himself had concentrated on the problem of equilibrium unemployment and policies to restore full employment, Keynesians soon began to turn their attention to the problem of dealing with *fluctuations* in output and employment. Looking over the experience of industrialised countries, many economists thought that history showed a pattern of fairly regular cycles in output. Although there were those who denied that there was a regular 'business cycle', most economists felt that business cycles were more than a statistical artefact – even if they were not perfectly regular.

A wide variety of explanations have been offered for business cycles, going back well before Keynes. Some of the earliest Keynesian theories were built around the notion that investment is determined by *changes* in the level of income, as well as possibly by interest rates.[38] In combination with other lags in the operation of expenditure, or with some bounds which eventually limited any expansion or contraction of income, these theories could explain business cycles. Other Keynesians stressed the volatility of the expectations of future profits on which investment depended. These swings in the 'animal spirits' of entrepreneurs could then be used as part of an explanation for fluctuations in output.[39] For our purposes, it is unnecessary to give further examples from this extensive literature, or to go further into the details of the suggested mechanisms. What is important is that if a business cycle exists, then government policies towards unemployment must be seen as having as their aim stabilising the level of employment close to that corresponding to full employment. Furthermore, if the counterpart to the high unemployment slumps are booms with inflationary pressures, part of the aim of the conduct of government macroeconomic policies might be to restrain the booms in order to dampen down inflation.[40]

The aim of stabilisation of economic fluctuations is thus seen by some economists as keeping employment as high as possible, subject to not allowing expansion to lead to unacceptable 'over-heating'. Others, however, see stabilisation as an extra aim in its own right. Fluctuations in output (or in the rate of growth of output) are considered undesirable and should be minimised. The undesirability of fluctuations is often simply taken for granted and the reasons not explicitly spelled out. It may be that the uncertainty and risk that go with variations in income and output are disliked, as people are assumed to be risk averse. It may be that wide fluctuations in output discourage investment and hence reduce longer-term economic growth.

Whichever view is accepted as to why stabilisation is desired, the Keynesian approach to income determination and macroeconomic policies seemed to imply how governments should combat business cycles. Given the view of how monetary and fiscal policies could affect desired expenditure, the obvious prescription was to have expansionary policies during the depression phase of the cycle and contractionary policies during the boom phase.

However, in the late 1940s, Milton Friedman published an eventually influential attack on the attempt to stabilise economic activities by use of macroeconomic policies.[41] Although his attack had some effect on thinking at the time, it was soon largely overshadowed by the other Keynesian/Monetarist debate in terms of the desirability of monetary *versus* fiscal policy, with Friedman himself identified as the leader of the Monetarist school. His argument against stabilisation, which could be expressed as saying that neither monetary nor fiscal policy should be actively used to try to control unemployment, became really influential amongst non-economists as well as economists after the monetary *versus* fiscal debate died down – at least in the academic literature, that is, in the late 1960s.

The essence of the view that governments should not try to stabilise economic activity was that such attempts were likely to exacerbate fluctuations rather than reduce them. One strand of the argument hinges on the point that governments cannot always get the timing of the effects of their policies exactly right. There may well be lags in the process. The result of such lags can be illustrated most simply as in Fig. 3.2.[42]

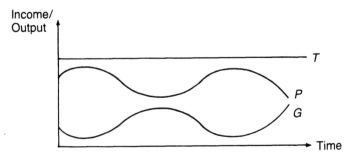

Figure 3.2 Sucessful government stabilisation policy

In this diagram of a hypothetical economy, the vertical axis measures output and the horizontal axis time. For simplicity we show an economy which has no trend growth and just regular cycles. The curve P represents the level of income that would exist as a result of private actions in the absence of any government stabilisation policy. A situation where there would be a perfectly regular business cycle, for some reason or other, is depicted. The curve G shows the effects of government macroeconomic policy: for example, government spending amplified by the relevant multiplier. T shows the total level of income, i.e. the sum of the result of private and government-influenced activities, so that $T = P + G$. Figure 3.2 shows what the government would like the result to be – its spending fluctuates so as to just offset privately influenced fluctuations and the result is a perfectly steady level of income.

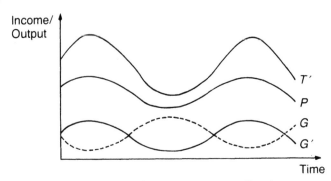

Figure 3.3 Destabilising government policy: lags

In Fig. 3.3 curve P is exactly the same as in the preceding diagram. Dotted line G is also exactly the same as in the preceding diagram. However, line G' shows the worst possible result of lagged effects. It has the same magnitude as G but is lagged in its effects so that the results of government policies affect the economy with a lag – the worst possible case, shown here, is when the lag is exactly half of the length of the cycle. The resulting level of total income, T', fluctuates much more than if the government had never tried to stabilise income at all (in the particular case chosen here the fluctuations are twice as wide). Even if the lags in the effects of government policies affecting the economy are not as long as those chosen here to illustrate the worst possible case, it is clearly possible for lagged effects to exacerbate cyclical swings.

To put the logic of the argument loosely into words, the position is as follows. The government sees that there is a slump and takes expansionary action. However, by the time that the expansionary action begins to have strong effects on expenditure, the economy is already, on its own, coming out of the recession. As it is moving into an expansionary phase along comes the extra effect of the government activity and pushes the economy into a position of higher excess aggregate demand than would have occurred otherwise. When the government sees that there is too much of a boom, the government takes some contractionary monetary and/or fiscal policies in order to try to return the economy to a more reasonable level of expenditure. However, if there are again long lags, it may be that the boom has begun to slacken on its own just when the contractionary effects of the government policy hit expenditure. The result is then to push the economy into a recession that might not have otherwise occurred, or into a deeper recession than would otherwise have occurred.

A similar result (though less discussed) could also occur if governments were ignorant about the *size* of the responses to monetary/fiscal policies. An attempt at an expansionary policy to avert a slump could take the economy not just back to full–employment output, but way past it if there were a stronger response than expected (e.g. if the size of the multiplier had been seriously underestimated). This case is illustrated in Fig. 3.4 where again P is the same as in the preceding two diagrams and dotted line G is also the same. Line G'' shows what could happen if the government underestimates the effects of its policies – the width of the swings in total income, T'', are greater than those in P, i.e. greater than would have occurred with G constant. In other words, because of ignorance about the magnitude of its impacts, the government has converted 'mild' recessions into 'major' booms and 'minor' booms into 'severe' slumps.

The conclusion of this line of argument is that well-intentioned government attempts to stabilise the level of income and employment may very well turn out to be perverse, and to make fluctuations worse. In the face of such uncertainty, given an aversion to risk, governments should avoid activist macroeconomic policies.

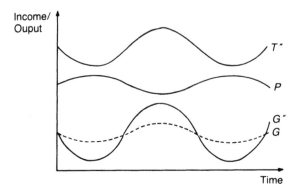

Figure 3.4 Destabilising government policy: overreaction

Debates on the merits or demerits of attempting to stabilise the economy took several routes. Most concentrated on lags, rather than the magnitude of multipliers and similar determinants of the size of responses, probably because it was felt that reasonably reliable estimates were available. One set of discussions tried to analyse what the possible sources of lags were, how important they were, and if it was felt that stabilisation policy was never-theless desirable, how the lags might be shortened by suitable institutional or policy changes. There was a categorisation of the types of lags.[43]

Chronologically the first lag would be the 'recognition lag'. This is the time taken for the government to realise that there was a problem. Given that there are difficulties in collecting accurate and up-to-date data, that initial estimates are often substantially revised, and that it is often not obvious whether a particular observation is a 'one-off' aberration or reflects the emergence of a new situation, the recognition lag may be substantial.

There are then lags before action can be taken. These lags, as well as the others mentioned, may well differ between countries. For example, in the United States, where budget changes have to be negotiated between a President and a Congress, which can have a majority of a different political party, there may well be long delays in enacting changes in fiscal policy, whereas monetary policy can be altered more quickly by the Federal Reserve Board. Other countries, where the government and the parliamentary majority are typically of the same political party, may not face this particular problem. There may, however, be a tradition that budgets are only presented annually, and any extra budget in between may be taken as a politically unacceptable admission of error. There may also be certain asymmetries, especially, when fiscal policy would involve raising taxes.[44]

There may then be further lags between the taking of action by the government and the time that individuals are affected. For example, once a change in profits tax has been given legislative approval, firms may pay tax in arrears so that it only affects the tax bills in a subsequent year. There is then a final lag between the time that the individuals are affected and the time that they change their spending behaviour. For example, a change in interest rates may only affect investment spending with a long delay, because of the gap between changes in orders for investment goods and the actual delivery of these goods and payment for them.

Empirical work suggested that average lags for some sorts of policies in some countries could well be measured in years rather than months.

One response to such findings was to say that no stabilisation policy should be attempted. In particular, if one looked just at post-World War Two business cycles, they typically seem to be of 4–5-year duration. Thus lags stretching over a year could well be destabilising. It was suggested that attempts to 'fine-tune' the economy, i.e. to try to correct even small divergences from desired levels of output, would not only fail but actually make things worse.

Keynesian responses tended rather to look at ways that the lags could be shortened. Legislative changes could be introduced, and in some countries *were* introduced, in order to shorten the legislative lags and to speed up the implementation of policy once the changes had been decided upon. An alternative, and possibly complementary, response was to try to avoid the problem by improving the ability to forecast future levels of activity. The recognition lag could be by-passed if it were possible to know in advance where the economy was likely to be in, let us say, a year's time. Appropriate action could be taken now, even if the relevant policy would not have its effects for a year. It was partly for this reason that the building of ever more elaborate econometrically-based forecasting models came to be seen as a typical Keynesian economists' activity.[45] Improvements in the ability to estimate the size of the likely responses to alternative policies would also reduce the chance of the second reason for destabilisation mentioned above. This relationship between the ability to forecast economic events, and the improvement of stabilisation policies, may also explain why when, in the 1980s, some governments decided to abjure stabilisation policies they also made derogatory remarks about econometric forecasting models – even those run by their own government departments.[46]

Another strand of the Keynesian reply was to claim that they were not worried about 'fine-tuning', but that there could still be *major* swings in the level of expenditure that were worth trying to even-out somewhat, and where at least a dampening of the fluctuations could be successfully achieved.

The last Keynesian reply suggests, perhaps, that it is also possible to see the Monetarist-Keynesian debate over stabilisation policy as reflecting not just a concern with the possibility of lags, but a much more fundamental disagreement over the nature of the economy. In a sense, the disagreement is whether the economy could be described as stable. In most economic theory, 'stability' means that if, as a result of some past disturbance, a variable is not at its equilibrium then it will converge to an equilibrium. The policy disagreements between Keynesians and Monetarists, based on disagreements over whether employment and output are stable, are concerned with stability in two related but somewhat broader aspects. The Monetarist view assumes, often implicitly, that if the government does not unwisely intervene, following some disturbance, employment and output will (i) not diverge too far from equilibrium and (ii) *quickly* return to equilibrium. For example, left to itself, the economy will experience neither very deep nor very prolonged slumps. Conversely, Keynesians based their recommendations, often implicitly, on the view that in the absence of government intervention, the economy could experience periods of very high unemployment that also last for a long time.[47]

Since we do not generally see very rapid changes in very short periods in output and employment, these two aspects of stability are interrelated. To give an exaggerated example, if we were to have unemployment today at 20% of the labour force, it is unlikely that next week unemployment would fall to 5%.

This fundamental disagreement that some have seen between Monetarists and Keynesians, has clear implications both for the desirability and the practicality of government macroeconomic stabilisation policy. If one believed that deep recessions are unlikely, and that any recession will soon cure itself, then there is no urgent need for government expansionary policy. In addition, if the economy is likely soon to move out of the mild and temporary recession, then any government-attempted expansionary policy is likely to prove destabilising. If there are any lags at all, it is likely that by the time the government monetary/fiscal expansion has its effects the economy will already be back close to the full-employment level, and therefore the expansionary policies will have the undesirable effects of creating an unnecessary period of inflationary pressure. From the Keynesian viewpoint, however, the opposite is true. Because they believe that there can be periods of severe unemployment, it is desirable to take action to reduce such unemployment. Furthermore because, in the absence of government policy, there would not be a quick return to full employment, there is little danger that expansionary policies during a slump will prove to be destabilising. If the slump is likely to be protracted, then even if there are some lags in the effects of monetary/fiscal policies, the economy will still have room for expansion (in other words there will still be excess capacity and unemployment) by the time the policies take effect.

Although we have described as fundamental these differences over whether a modern economy is self-correcting as far as aggregate employment and output are concerned, they rest on beliefs about the stability of the economy rather than testable hypotheses. Our explanation of each side's beliefs purposely uses such vague terms as 'temporary' as contrasted to 'protracted' or 'mild' as contrasted to 'severe' recessions. The two sets of beliefs are more often implicit than explicit foundations for the views on stabilisation policy, and are not formulated in a way that would allow for any sort of decisive testing between them.

The policy debate over whether stabilisation should be attempted is often summarised as whether a government should be allowed *discretion* to actively attempt to control aggregate economic activity or should be bound by *rules* which it has to follow passively. The sort of rules proposed would be to always have a balanced budget and a steady growth in the money supply, irrespective of the level of economic activity.

Keynesians objected, both by empirical analyses and theoretical arguments, that following such simple rules would lead to worse results than would sensible attempts at stabilisation.[48] Furthermore, they claimed that simple rules were impossible to follow. For example, as income varied government receipts/expenditures would automatically vary and so balancing the budget would require an active response to the state of the economy; and could well be destabilising as it would require cutting government expenditure when transfer payments were high because of a slump.[49]

Another argument is sometimes raised against allowing governments discretion to alter monetary/fiscal policies. This is more obviously political: it is the fear the governments may try to manipulate the economy so that booms occur in the run-up to elections. They would hope that the resulting bad effects of an over-expansion of demand would not appear until after the election had been won. At that point a much severer squeeze than would otherwise have been necessary would be required, but (with luck) the induced slump would have worked its effects before the next election and a new boom could be engineered. Although the worries about 'electoral business-cycles' have sometimes been used as an argument against discretion by the same economists who also argue that ignorance and lags make attempted stabil-isation dangerous, the two arguments are inconsistent. To time the boom to occur in the months before an election requires a good knowledge of the lags, and therefore genuinely attempted stabilisation would not exacerbate the cycle.[50]

The reaction against stabilisation policy probably reached its peak among policy-makers in the early 1980s. To some degree, since then there has been a return to espousal of discretion.[51] However, to an extent there has also been a switch to worrying more about inflation and less about unemployment as the prime focus of monetary/fiscal policy, further complicated by more attention to the balance of payments/exchange rate effects of policies. These will be analysed in subsequent chapters.

CONCLUSIONS

Although the issues dealt with in the different sections of this chapter at first sight seem disparate, as was stated in the introduction there are in fact interrelationships between them. In terms of the policy implications, the Keynesian positions tend to support the desirability and practicality of government macroeconomic intervention. The views we have labelled

Monetarist tend to deny either the necessity or the desirable outcome of such an activist approach to macroeconomic policy. In terms of the economic theory involved, many (but not all) are linked to the theme we have mentioned several times: are there important sections of a modern economy which are not adequately captured by the type of neo-classical microeconomic model of competitive markets in which prices move smoothly so as to ensure equilibrium?

4

DEMAND MANAGEMENT AND INFLATION

INTRODUCTION

Almost as soon as government commitments to maintain 'full employment' were suggested, the fear was expressed that such commitments would have inflationary consequences. However, the early Keynesian approach did not have a theory of what determined inflation. At most it predicted that there would be inflation if desired expenditure exceeded the level of output corresponding to full employment, but it did not predict or explain *how much* inflation there would be. After some review of definitions, we discuss how this gap was filled in by the famous 'Phillips Curve' and its explanations, and the resulting implications for policy.

However, within a decade the theory was subject to fundamental criticism and shortly afterwards it became apparent the empirical basis of the Phillips Curve was unreliable. The criticisms and the way they were used to undercut much of the Keynesian approach to controlling unemployment are dealt with in the sections on pages 63–72.

It is possible to accept some of the implications of the developments associated with the concept of the 'natural rate', and yet retain much of the Keynesian approach to policy. The section on pages 72–8 discusses the arguments used, and their implications, and the section on pages 78–81 discusses the view that inflation depends solely on the growth of the money supply.

DEFINITIONS

Inflation

Before moving on to the explanations of inflation and the associated policy prescriptions, it might be worthwhile reviewing the standard definition of inflation as there is a surprising amount of confusion over what is meant. Some disagreements which are apparently over other issues may merely reflect differing implicit definitions. Inflation is usually defined by phrases equivalent to 'a process of rising prices', or 'a continuing rise in prices', and it is usually measured by the percentage change in one of the indices of the cost of living.[1] The definition has various aspects which are important in economists' approaches.

First it distinguishes inflation as an ongoing process of rising prices from discrete jumps in the price *level*. Much of elementary macroeconomic theory discusses the price level and changes in the level as a result of some exogenous change (e.g. in the level of the money supply).[2] This is not the same as a discussion of inflation.

The sort of confusion that can arise from muddling the distinction between a once-and-for-all rise in the price level and a continuing process of rising prices can be illustrated by a scene that has recurred fairly often, e.g. in the UK Parliament. The Chancellor of the Exchequer stands up and during his speech announces that to combat inflation the interest rate or taxation will be raised, e.g. the duty on tobacco or petrol. The Opposition speakers point out that if taxes (or interest rates) are increased prices (or the cost-of-living including housing costs) will rise. Thus instead of combating inflation, the Chancellor will be increasing it. What may be behind this recurrent argument is a different view of what is meant by inflation. The Chancellor's action will admittedly raise prices, but he hopes that this will be a once-and-for-all rise and that the fall in aggregate expenditure due to rise in taxation (or interest rates) will actually cut into the process of rising prices. What the Opposition spokesmen are saying is that they view any rise in prices, even if it may be a once-and-for-all rise, as part of inflation. Therefore, since the rise in taxation will increase prices, on their implicit definition it will increase inflation. The definition that has been proposed here, as being in accord with economists' usage, would rule out the second argument.[3]

Second: the other aspect of the definition that has been proposed here, as a convenient one that catches the majority opinion about what we mean by inflation, is to distinguish between prices in general and one particular price. The distinction that we wish to make is between a change in all prices and a change in the relative price of one particular product. On this definition it would be misleading to say that consumption of a particular good, e.g. meat, has fallen because of inflation. On the basis of elementary price theory we would expect that the consumption of meat would not be affected if, for example, all wages rose last year by 30% and all prices rose by 30%, including that of meat. What would be expected to affect the consumption of meat would be a faster rise in the price of meat than in the prices of other products and of wages. From this point of view you might expect that the consumption of meat would alter in the same way if the price of meat goes up by 40% at a time when other wages and prices are going up by 30%, as it would if the price of meat went up by 10% and there was no inflation at all in general wages or prices.[4]

Another definitional point might be raised here. One far too often comes across the statement, purporting to be a definition, that 'inflation is a process of too much money chasing too few goods'. This purported definition is, in fact, an implicit explanation of inflation, not a definition, and it will be discussed under the causes of inflation and not as part of the definition.

Demand-pull and cost-push

Much of the early attempts to explain inflation often divided the theories into two groups: *first* demand-pull, *second* cost-push. There are various meanings given to this distinction and these meanings have changed over time to an extent that the terms are often unclear and therefore we shall try to restrict our use to those cases where there should be no confusion. At one time the distinction was between those who believed that inflation was caused by shifts in aggregate demand as compared to those who thought that inflation was caused by shifts in aggregate supply. This distinction relates to the simplest of price theory models. If in Fig. 4.1 we consider a single market initially in equilibriumat a price P_0 then the price can rise to P_1 for one of two reasons: either because the demand curve shifted from $d_0 d_0$ to $d'd'$ while the supply curve remains at $s_0 s_0$ or because the supply curve shifted from $s_0 s_0$ to $s's'$ while the demand curve remains unchanged. Either of these would lead to a rise in price in the case of a single product and the demand-pull/cost-push distinction was simply applying this model to the economy as a whole.

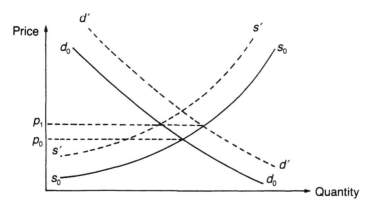

Figure 4.1 Change in equilibrium price level following shift in demand or supply

Our impression is that distinguishing demand-pull from cost-push on this basis is now much less popular. The reason is that the distinction just described will only be useful in the case of a once-and-for-all price rise rather than in the case of a continuing process of inflation. It perhaps made sense 30–40 years ago, when the rule was assumed to be stable prices and the question asked was what started off a particular episode of inflation. Once inflation has been going on for decades, the question of what originally started it so many years ago is not a very relevant one, as compared to discussing the conditions that allow inflation to continue. The demand-pull/cost-push distinction of demand curve shift versus supply curve shift is less useful for this. Once inflation has got under way, a shift in the demand curve may itself lead to a rise in the supply curve as workers want higher wages and feel that firms can afford to pay them. Similarly, an increase in the supply curve could lead to a rise in the demand curve for products because workers have more money income.

In the 1960s a different distinction between demand-pull and cost-push became more widespread. This later distinction also tried to apply the simplest of price theory models to the economy as a whole. However, it concentrated on a rather different aspect of the neo-classical paradigm. This latter aspect of the market model is the explanation given for rising prices. In this model we usually posit that if demand is greater than supply at existing prices then the people who wish to buy at the current price, but cannot, will bid up prices or, equivalently, that suppliers will find that they can afford to raise prices and still sell as much as they want to. Therefore, prices will rise as long as demand is greater than supply. For example, in Fig. 4.2A, if the market is in a position such as P_0 then the price will rise because demand is greater than supply. Furthermore, prices will continue rising as long as demand remains greater than supply. From the point of view of this aspect of the neo-classical model, it doesn't matter whether we have excess demand because originally the demand curve was in position $d''d''$ or because originally the supply curve was in position $s''s''$ in Fig. 4.2B; what matters is that we now have excess demand and therefore the price rises. The later version of the demand-pull approach to inflation, then, is to apply this view to the economy as a whole and to say that inflation occurs when there is excess aggregate demand for goods and will continue as long as there is excess demand.

With this latter distinction cost-push is defined primarily by its denial of demand-pull, rather than as being a single theory in its own right. At its simplest it says that prices can rise even if there is excess supply.

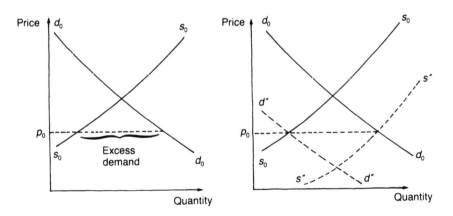

Figure 4.2 Price rising in disequilibrium

There are many versions of cost-push theory but what they have in common is the assertion that in a modern economy some markets, and some very important markets at that, do not work in the way that the neo-classical theory of competitive markets says that they should. It is this that explains one superficially anomalous aspect of modern inflation arguments: the definition of inflation typically refers to prices, but arguments about the causes of inflation concentrate on wages rather than prices. In this context as well as in those discussed earlier, the reason is that if one is looking for an important market in the modern economy that might not work in the way that the competitive theory predicts, the obvious candidate is the labour market. In this market there are institutional forces such as trade unions and employers' organisations that do not seem to accord with the competitive paradigm. Furthermore, at least since Keynes, it has been argued that the motivation of workers seeking wage rises is not the same as that of suppliers of other goods seeking rises in the prices of those goods.[5] The whole range of motivations involved is said to be very different and to lead to different forms of behaviour.

Monetary theories

One sometimes sees statements that there is a third view of the causes of inflation, in addition to the types we have classified under demand-pull or cost-push. This third view is said to be the Monetarist one. Whether Monetarism can be said to be a third view of the causes of inflation depends on whether Monetarists are prepared to give an account of the way in which money will lead to inflation or are merely content to restrict themselves to saying that there is a relationship between money supply and inflation without wanting to provide a detailed mechanism. In the literature this is sometimes called the 'black box' approach of Monetarism. Namely, that what one sees is something like a conjuring trick whereby money is put in one end of the black box and out comes inflation at the other end, with the spectators not allowed to see what goes on in between. Alternatively, it is sometimes said that this sort of Monetarism lacks a 'transmission mechanism', namely any mechanism explaining how increases in the money supply are transmitted into increases in prices.

There was something of a tendency to follow this approach amongst Monetarists in the 1950s and 1960s.[6] This tendency was strengthened by the fact that for many years Milton Friedman was the prime exponent of Monetarism and he also happened to have strong views on what constitutes a scientific explanation. His view of a scientific theory was that it needs to have good predictions, not realistic explanations and assumptions. In fact, the stronger the prediction that could come out of a simple assumption, the stronger the scientific theory. On this approach, perhaps, it was highly scientific for Monetarists to simply posit a relationship between the money supply and the general price level and for this relationship to be tested. If the theory survived the testing it was a good theory.

Nevertheless, at least in their theories, and at least since the late 1960s, Monetarists have been prepared to provide an explanation of how changes in the money supply can affect inflation. The provisos are because in works aimed at more popular audiences, the tendency to rely on mechanical linkages between money supply growth and inflation lasted much longer.[7] The influence lasted into the 1980s on both 'City' (or 'Wall Street' or their equivalents in other countries) commentators and politicians. For example, in the UK, much of the justification for the attainment of targets for control of a particular measure of the money supply as the primary aim of macroeconomic policy was that the growth of this particular measure was highly correlated with inflation 1–2 years later. Unfortunately, the correlation then broke down. However, at the time (around 1980) government ministers went as far as stating that increases in wages were irrelevant for inflation, as inflation would be reduced by controlling the money supply whatever was happening to wages. Even in 1989, two academic Monetarist economists wrote in a newspaper[8] that since inflation can only occur in an economy with money,[9] inflation must be a monetary phenomenon and therefore it depends on the money supply. This not only fails to provide any causal link transmitting the money supply changes to inflation, but seems to us to be a *non sequitur*.[10]

Once we look at the sort of explanation provided by Monetarists once they went beyond the 'black box' approach and discussed causal mechanisms it becomes quite clear that Monetarism falls within the spectrum of demand-pull theories of inflation. Where it differs from other versions of demand-pull is in the reasons given for increases in demand or the existence of excess demand. Whereas some Keynesians would say that changes in aggregate demand can result from changes in fiscal policy or from changes in investment behaviour, Monetarists might claim that prolonged increases in aggregate demand, or the prolonged existence of excess aggregate demand, depend only on the money supply. But the way in which the money supply leads to inflation is still through market forces, and therefore falls within demand-pull as we think it is usually defined. We will return to this issue of whether money is the only cause of prolonged inflation or whether other factors can be involved after we have taken a detailed look at the suggested mechanisms.

Notation

It is convenient to introduce some notation at this point. We want to have a simple way of referring to rates of change or proportional rates of growth in a variable. The notation to be used here is that of putting a dot over the variable. For example, $\dot{p}$ will be the rate of growth in prices or, equivalently, the rate of inflation. Thus, $\dot{p} = 10\%$ would mean that the rate of inflation is 10%. Similarly, if y is used as a symbol for real output, $\dot{y}$ is the rate of growth of real output. Occasionally, in the literature, the notation of a variable with a dot over it is used for the absolute change in the variable, rather than the proportionate rate of change. However, there is another perfectly serviceable symbol, namely the Δ, for the absolute change in a variable. So in this book we will be using $\dot{x}$ to mean the proportionate rate of change in x and Δx to mean the absolute change in x. In other words, Δx divided by x is equal to $\dot{x}$ in this notation.

There are a couple of properties of proportionate rates of change that will be found useful.[11] Firstly, the rate of change of a variable which is itself the product of two other variables is the sum of the rates of change of these two other variables. For example, if by X we denote the nominal value of national income, by P we denote the price level and by y we denote the level of real national output, then we have that $X \equiv P \times y$. The principle just given implies that $\dot{X} = \dot{P} + \dot{y}$. In words this says that the rate of growth of nominal output is equal to the sum of the rates of growth of the price level and of real output.

The second property is that the rate of growth of a variable that is itself the ratio of two other variables is equal to the difference of the rates of growth of these two variables. For example, if by ω we denote the value of the real wage, by W the value of the money wage and by P the price level, then $\omega = W/P$. This second principle then implies that $\dot{\omega} = \dot{W} - \dot{P}$. In words, this means that the rate of growth of real wages is equal to the rate of growth of money wages minus the increase in prices. For example, if money wages have increased by 10% over the past year and prices have increased by 8%, then the real wage has increased by 2%. That is, $2 = 10 - 8$.

THE PHILLIPS CURVE

In the introduction to this chapter, we mentioned the gap in the Keynesian approach: namely it did not discuss the determination of the degree of inflation. Since it was widely accepted that reducing unemployment could have inflationary consequences, the lack of a coherent approach integrating unemployment and inflation was a major drawback. Although many Keynesians saw unemployment as 'the' problem of macroeconomic management, it was clear that keeping inflation acceptably low was at least an important constraint on policy. Some economists and policy-makers saw low inflation as a worthwhile aim in its own right.[12] The distinction between the two views would be that on the former, provided some (possibly arbitrary) ceiling level of inflation was not breached, no further weight need be given to further reduction in inflation. On the latter view, any reduction in inflation, even if already low, would be desirable and worth pursuing. However, if at low levels of inflation relatively little weight was given to further reduction, then the two views would lead to similar results in practice. Either way, the lack of an explanation of the rate of inflation was a gap in Keynesianism.

A related issue was that the predominant form of the Keynesian approach for many years left the actual level of money wages unexplained.[13] The mainstream discussions just concentrated on the effects of downwardly rigid money wages, not on how money wages got to be where they were.

Both of these lacunae were filled following an article published in 1958 by A.W. Phillips, which claimed to show that there was a definite relationship between unemployment and the rate at which wages change. The relationship was an inverse one: i.e. that higher unemployment was associated with slower wage changes and vice versa. This is illustrated in Fig. 4.3. He claimed that this relationship was the same in quantitative terms as far back as UK data went – about a hundred years. Despite some objections to the techniques used, the findings were eagerly accepted by most economists. In honour of its originator, the relationship was soon popularly known as the Phillips Curve although others had been working on the same lines at the same time and, as usual, once the Phillips Curve had achieved widespread fame it was claimed that earlier authors had posited the same relationship many years before, even though it had not become widely adopted at the time.[14]

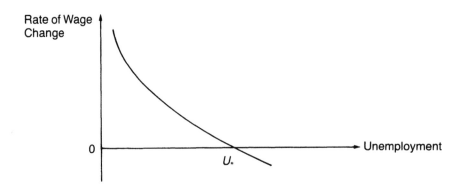

Figure 4.3 The Phillips Curve

Because in most macroeconomic models there is a relationship between wages and prices, the description 'Phillips Curve' was also applied to studies showing an inverse relationship between price change and unemployment. Similarly, because low unemployment usually goes with high employment, while high employment usually goes with high output, some economists have fitted 'Phillips Curves' which have a positive relationship between inflation and output.

Phillips' original work was presented primarily as an empirical study, with no detailed theoretical rationale provided. Indeed it seemed 'obvious' that wages would rise more during booms than in slumps. Its appeal to most economists was increased a couple of years later by an article by Professor R.G. Lipsey. Among other things, he provided an explanation of the Phillips Curve which tied it in to a market-oriented theory of inflation of the type we have described above as demand-pull.[15]

The argument can be put in words, but is also easily illustrated by diagrams.

We shall also summarise it by algebraic symbols for those who find equations helpful.

The first step is to take the standard neo-classical argument, mentioned above, about the results of excess demand or excess supply for any good, let us say apples. The hypothesis is that when the demand for apples exceeds the supply, then the price of apples will rise. Generally it is also assumed that the *greater* the gap between demand and supply, the *faster* the price will rise. Conversely, if there is an excess supply then the price of apples will fall, and the greater the excess supply the faster the fall in the price of apples. Lipsey applied this hypothesis to the market for labour as well. In the case of labour, the hypothesis means that if there is excess demand for labour wages will rise, and the greater the gap between the demand and supply for labour the faster wages will rise.

In terms of symbols and functional notation, the relation can be summarised as:

$$\dot{W} = g \left(\frac{D_L - S_L}{S_L} \right) \qquad\qquad (4.1)$$

In this equation D_L represents the demand for labour, S_L represents the supply of labour and the relationship $g(\ )$ symbolises functional dependence. In other words equation (4.1) simply says that wage change depends on the excess demand for labour. Furthermore, it is a direct relationship, namely the larger the excess demand the faster wages rise.[16] We have divided the excess demand for labour by the supply in order to express it as a proportion rather than as an absolute amount. This means that if, for example, we have an economy with a hundred million people and there is excess demand for labour of five million, we would expect the effect on the rate of increase in wages to be the same as if we had an economy with ten million people and there was a half a million excess demand for labour.

Graphically, the relationship is shown in Fig. 4.4. To the right of the origin, as we move along the horizontal axis, there is an increasing excess demand for labour; to the left of the origin, as we move leftwards, there is an increasing excess supply of labour and, at the origin, the demand equals the supply. We have thus for now included the extra standard assumption of neo-classical theory that when demand equals supply for any good the price is steady, and in the case of labour that means that when the demand for labour equals the supply of labour wages then are steady.[17]

The second stage in the argument is to recognise that we do not have figures for the demand and supply of labour and, therefore, we do not have figures for the excess demand or excess supply of labour. We cannot empirically directly relate wage changes to the excess demand for labour. However, we do have figures for measured unemployment. The second step in the argument is to posit that there is an inverse relationship between the excess demand for

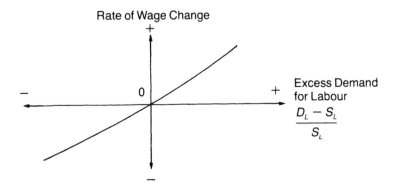

Figure 4.4 Wage change increasing with excess demand for labour

labour and measured unemployment. This is shown in Fig. 4.5. This assumption says that when we have an excess supply of labour any increase in the excess supply will be associated with a rise in unemployment. Conversely, any fall in the amount of excess supply will be associated with a fall in measured unemployment. As we move from excess supply of labour through the point where demand equals supply and into the range of excess demand for labour, unemployment continues to fall. However, measured unemployment can never be negative. The assumption, in this second stage of the argument to derive the Phillips Curve, is that as the excess demand for labour increases unemployment continues to fall closer to zero. In other words, that as the labour market becomes tighter and tighter, people who are unemployed merely because they are changing jobs, for example, can find jobs more quickly and therefore the amount of unemployment continues to fall.

Because of the last assumption, the relationship between the level of unemployment and the underlying state of the labour market, in terms of

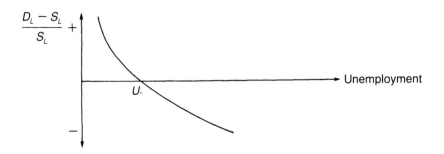

Figure 4.5 Relationship between excess demand for labour and
measured unemployment

excess demand and excess supply of labour, is a curved one rather than a straight line. In Fig. 4.5 we have denoted for convenience the point where this relationship crosses the horizontal axis at U_*. U_*, then, is that level of unemployment which corresponds to zero excess demand in the labour market, that is, which corresponds to labour demand equals supply. In the later literature, this level of unemployment is sometimes called 'the natural rate of unemployment'. It can also be viewed as the level of unemployment corresponding to 'full employment' in earlier discussions.

In terms of symbols, the second stage of the argument can be summarised by equation (4.2), where $h( )$ again denotes a functional relationship, but this time $h( )$ is an inverse relationship:[18]

$$U = h \left(\frac{D_L - S_L}{S_L} \right) \tag{4.2}$$

The final stage in deriving the Phillips Curve is to combine the previous two stages of the argument. If we combine the two preceding diagrams we end up with the Phillips Curve, Fig. 4.3. This shows that when there is high excess supply of labour, from the first relationship we would expect that wages would be falling; from the second relationship we would expect that high excess supply of labour would be associated with high unemployment; and, in the third diagram, the Phillips Curve, we do find high unemployment is associated with a fall in wages. Conversely, when we have a high excess demand for labour then the first relationship would tell us that we would expect to see wages rising, the second relationship would tell us that we would have low unemployment and this combination of low unemployment and rising wages is precisely what is shown in the Phillips Curve diagram. Furthermore, on the standard assumption, when the demand for labour equals the supply so that there is zero excess demand, the second diagram shows that the level of unemployment is that which we have denoted U_* and then in the Phillips Curve diagram, U_* is associated with steady wages, that is wages which neither rise nor fall in the aggregate.[19]

In symbols the basic Phillips Curve can be summarised by equation (4.3), where $f( )$ is an inverse functional relationship

$$\dot{W} = f(U) \tag{4.3}$$

Given our definition of demand-pull, Lipsey's explanation of the Phillips Curve is an example of a demand-pull theory of inflation. This theory seemed to have been tested and stood up to the evidence for nearly a hundred years of data. In fact, Lipsey's own testing which he performed in addition to the original work of Phillips, showed that there had been some changes in the relationship over time, but in the 1960s this was not taken as being terribly important by most economists. His work also showed that changes in prices had an extra effect on the changes in wages. The sort of order of magnitude that came out of his work and other work in the 1960s tended to suggest that every increase in prices led to an increase of about half as much in wages. That is, for any particular level of unemployment there would be some increase in wages predicted by the Phillips Curve, but there would also be an extra increase in wages (on top of that related just to unemployment) due to changes in prices, though this extra increase only compensates for about half of the increase in prices. Thus, in symbols, equation (4.3) should be modified by adding a term such as is shown in equation (4.4) where we add approximately 0.5 times the increase in prices.[20]

$$\dot{W} = f(U) + 0.5\dot{P} \qquad\qquad (4.4)$$

Throughout the 1960s the Phillips Curve provided the focus for empirical and policy work on inflation. One reason is that most economists do have a strong bias towards explaining things in terms of market forces to some extent. The Phillips Curve seemed to show that this type of reasoning could explain wages as well. In this sense the sort of demand-pull theory that has just been outlined fitted in with the prevailing economists' approach. The cost-push theory in its strongest form is that unions have grown so powerful that they can push up wages irrespective of the supply and demand for labour. The Phillips Curve showed that at least in its most extreme form, the cost-push theory of inflation was wrong. Despite the existence of unions, wages did respond to market forces. The support given for this view was one motive for economists welcoming the Phillips Curve. It might even explain why a flaw in Lipsey's argument (which will be examined later) was not widely taken up until changing circumstances led to doubts about the empirical results.

Although the kind of demand-pull theory behind the Phillips Curve relied for its appeal on extending the neo-classical market approach to the labour market, it was not seen as incompatible with the prevalent Keynesian outlook. By concentrating on the disequilibrium aspect of the neo-classical approach, it avoided the issue of whether wages quickly converge to the equilibrium. All the Lipsey theory said was that wages change in a direction that moves the wage level *towards* the level at which the demand for labour would equal the supply – i.e. towards the level corresponding to full employment. There is no necessary presumption that the equilibrium wage is automatically reached quickly enough for it to be unnecessary/undesirable to use monetary or fiscal policies to bring the economy to full employment.

Furthermore, in econometric models of the economy during the 1960s, the Phillips Curve was usually embedded in a system which embodied typically Keynesian ways of thinking about causation. The causation went from expenditure functions (such as consumption or investment), to aggregate desired expenditure, to actual output (usually set equal to desired expenditure), to employment and then to wage change and on to price inflation.[21] The econometric models incorporated estimated Phillips Curves, but did not depend on the acceptance of Lipsey's, or any other, rationale for them.

Two other relevant points might also be suggested here: *First*: although we have stressed the differences over whether all markets clear as being one of the fundamental distinctions between Keynesian and Monetarist views on the functioning of the economy and on appropriate policies, this distinction only became fully apparent and explicitly recognised during the more recent debates,[22] especially once the interlude of arguing primarily about monetary versus fiscal policy had passed. Our impression is that explicit mention of the distinction was rare until the mid-1970s, even though (in retrospect) it was implicit, and crucial, in many earlier arguments.[23]

Second: even now much textbook discussion does not integrate satisfactorily the Keynesian theory of income determination and the discussions of inflation. The former, for example, often assumes a given *level* of money supply, the latter a given *rate of growth* of money supply. Although the two can be integrated, it is not easy to do so, especially in words and diagrams, without using more mathematical techniques. One suspects that some (many?) economists still tend to keep the two blocks of the model separate in their minds when thinking about issues without writing down a rigorous and formal full model.

The Phillips Curve seemed particularly crucial for policy-making as it fitted in with the prevalent view on the correct role of economists in the policy-making process. In this view the economist was the scientific expert who could give factual guidance to elected politicians on the options available and on their consequences, but who had no greater right, or even insight, than any other citizen to say what *should* be done. The Phillips Curve summarised the advice such economists could legitimately give politicians and the options open to them. If the Phillips Curve was correct politicians had a choice – they could have low inflation or low unemployment but not both. Not only did the Phillips Curve say that there was a choice, it gave the terms of the trade-off. Allowing for productivity,[24] one could go from wage increases to price increases and the Phillips Curve would then tell officials how much inflation would result from holding unemployment down to any particular level.

A belief in the long-term existence and stability of the Phillips Curve became associated with the belief that higher unemployment was a necessary evil and the only way to beat inflation. Others took the view that we should learn to live with moderate inflation as it is a lesser evil than the level of unemployment needed to cure it. Some economists held that the terms of the policy menu offered by the Phillips Curve were too unfavourable and they supported incomes policies as a way of shifting the relationship between inflation and unemployment, that is, shifting the curve in Fig. 4.4 downwards, or at least flattening its slope, with similar effects on the Phillips Curve.

THE END OF THE SIMPLE PHILLIPS CURVE

Towards the end of the 1960s in some countries, and a few years later in others, the steady inverse relationship between unemployment and inflation seemed to break down. To the dismay of policy-makers, and of most economists, there was higher inflation simultaneously with higher unemployment in many western countries. In terms of Fig. 4.3, from somewhere around 1970 countries began to experience points to the 'north-east' of the Phillips Curve that had fitted their experience of the preceding 15–20 years. Another way of putting the same point is that actual inflation became well above that which would have been predicted by Phillips Curves fitted to data of the preceding twenty years.

In reaction to this 'breakdown of the Phillips Curve', one could, of course, have dropped the demand-pull type of theory of inflation and concentrated on trade union and other (possibly more sociological) cost-push approaches to explaining inflation. Some economists did this. However, at about the same time the accepted analysis of the Phillips Curve (outlined in the previous section) had been attacked as being faulty, from a demand-pull point of view. This attack is most commonly associated with Professor Milton Friedman and sometimes with Professor E. Phelps.[25] The amended version of the Phillips Curve is, in fact, sometimes called the Friedman–Phelps Phillips Curve relationship. In fact, there are important differences between the explanations of Friedman and Phelps, even though the resulting movement of the relationship and form of the trade-off is similar in the two models.[26] Here we shall follow the version of the trade-off that is associated with Friedman's ideas. Although the resulting 'Phillips Curve' is often described as a Monetarist one, there is nothing intrinsically Monetarist in the relationship that follows from these ideas. However, it should also be noted that these ideas are, to say the least, not inconsistent with Professor Friedman's other more obviously Monetarist ideas. It should also be noted that many, if not the majority, of Keynesians were initially extremely reluctant to accept these ideas because they did have certain policy implications that went against those typically favoured by Keynesians. In particular, as we shall see, the policy implications of the Friedman–Phelps relationship did go against the idea of successful prolonged intervention by the government to hold down unemployment.

The widely-read article of 1968, in which Friedman laid out his critique of the Phillips Curve and his own theory, turned out to admit of two different versions of his own ideas as to how wages and unemployment were related. The way in which most economists at the time interpreted his views was not that which Friedman himself later explained.[27] The latter was more clearly related to a non-Keynesian view of the way that the labour market worked. We shall first outline the majority interpretation which saw Friedman's contribution as pointing out a flaw in the Lipsey type of argument, which might have major consequences for its policy implications.

On this interpretation, the essence of Professor Friedman's contribution was to point out that there was a basic mistake in the Lipsey formulation as laid out above. The formulation above related the change in *money* wages to the level of excess demand in the labour market. However, neo-classical economic theory would say that in any market the variable which depends on the level of excess demand is the price relative to other goods' prices, not the absolute money price. In terms of the labour market, the relevant variable is not the money wage but the real wage – that is, the money wage divided by the price level. It is the money wage, relative to the price of what is produced, which determines the profitability of hiring labour. When we look at the whole economy, especially during periods of general inflation, we can look simply at the average money wage divided by some general price index. On the supply of labour side, it is the post-tax money wage divided by the general cost-of-living index which gives the return to workers from their employment, that is, what they can buy with their wages. Therefore, from the point of view of demand and of supply, we would expect *real* wages to be related to unemployment.[28]

The implications of this for the Phillips Curve can be seen either in terms of the diagrams or in terms of the equations (4.1) to (4.3).

In diagrammatic terms, a correct version of Fig. 4.4, or of the Phillips Curve, would have real wage change on the vertical axis, not money wage change. If we wish to draw a Phillips Curve with the change in *money* wages on the vertical axis, then there is no unique Phillips Curve (nor is there a unique relationship in Fig. 4.4). Instead the relationship between the change in money wages and the level of unemployment depends on the change in prices. Similarly, in equations (4.1) and (4.3) the left-hand side should not be the change in money wages, but the change in real wages. As explained above, the change in real wages is equal to the change in money wages, minus the change in prices.

It is possible to indicate more precisely how the diagrams – or equations (4.1) and (4.3) – would have to be altered if we still wanted to show explicitly what will happen to money wages. We should probably still want to show the relationship in terms of money wages because, after all, the aim is to predict inflation as well as to explain the processes involved.

In terms of the derivation of the Phillips Curve, the new version results from the replacement of the change in money wages by the change in real wages, combined with the fact that the change in real wages is itself equal to the change in money wages minus the change in prices.

If there is no price inflation, then the graph relating money wages to unemployment is the same as that relating real wages to unemployment – since the change in money wages is also the change in real wages in the absence of price changes. For example, a 2% increase in money wages is also 2% in real wages. However, if there is a 4% increase in prices, money wages must increase by 6% to give a 2% rise in real wages.

More precisely: if labour market conditions (i.e. excess demand for labour or as summarised by the unemployment rate) are such that a particular increase in real wages is required, then the increase in prices has to be added on to obtain the necessary rise in money wages. Thus, if a traditional Phillips

Curve diagram is plotted, with money wages dependent on unemployment, we obtain not one curve but a whole family of curves, each relating to a different level of price inflation.

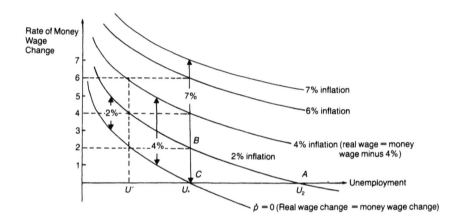

Figure 4.6 The shifting Phillips Curve

In Fig. 4.6, the *vertical* distance at any level of unemployment between the zero inflation curve (when money wage change equals real wage change) and any other curve measures the rate of inflation. In the above numerical example, if U' is the level of unemployment such that real wages need to increase by 2%, if price inflation is 2% then wage change is 4%, if price inflation is 4% then money wage change is 6% and so on. To put it another way, the money wage Phillips Curve shifts vertically up or down according to the rate of price inflation.

In symbols, the left-hand side of equations (4.1) and (4.3) should have (W/P). But $(W/P) = \dot{W} - \dot{P}$, therefore in (4.3), we should have had

$$(W/P) = \dot{W} - \dot{P} = f(U)$$

Therefore

$$\dot{W} = f(U) + \dot{P} \tag{4.5}$$

One could view Friedman's attack on the previous Phillips Curve literature as another example of the attacks on the Keynesian propensity to explain the economy by (implicitly) assuming 'money illusion' or 'irrationality'.[29] However, statistical testing seemed to have shown that workers and employers did not *fully* allow for changing prices, as was mentioned in the previous section – and is shown by a comparison of equations (4.4) and (4.5). This possible objection was dealt with by the next stage of Friedman's argument.

In practice, wages are not re-set continuously. Even where wages are not determined by formal collective negotiations, but on a one-to-one basis between the employee and the employer/manager, it is usually expected that once a wage offer has been made and accepted, neither side will attempt to alter it for some period. In many cases the convention is for a one-year wait between wage settlements. Explanations for this phenomenon are often in terms of the time costs of transacting new wage settlements, but, whatever the reason, that there is typically a wait between wage agreements is taken for granted by economists.[30]

The result is that when workers and employers agree to a wage settlement they do not actually *know* the amount of price inflation that will occur until money wages are next changed – they can only guess. Thus the relevant price change variable is not the actual inflation during the period of the wage agreement, but the expected inflation. Fig. 4.6 should be altered, adding 'expected' before inflation, and, equivalently, $\dot{P}$ in equation (4.5) should be replaced by $\dot{P}^e$ to give (4.6),[31]

$$\dot{W}_t = f(U) + \dot{P}^e_t \tag{4.6}$$

The alternatives are trivial to write, but the effects are crucial. Firstly, if people's expectations are based on the past, and if it takes them time to adapt, then during a rising inflation, they will expect less inflation than actually occurs. Hence statistical tests based on actual inflation are unreliable. Secondly, as we shall see, the policy implications of allowing for expectations may reverse those of the simple Phillips Curve.

Before we consider the policy implications of the 'expectations augmented Phillips Curve', as it is sometimes called, it is worth considering the alternative interpretation of Friedman's argument, since not only does Friedman himself favour it, but it is implicit in some of the subsequent developments (especially those to be discussed in the next chapter). Rather than focusing on the disequilibrium process of changing wages, this interpretation focuses on the level of the real wage at which the demand for labour equals the supply. However, the real wage that workers expect to receive from working is the money wage divided by the *expected* level of prices. The current money wage received is known, the current correct level of prices may not be. It takes time to learn what the price level is, following some change. The result can be illustrated as in Fig. 4.7, where D_L is the usual downward-sloping demand curve for labour as a function of the real wage, and $S_L(P = P^e)$ is the upward-sloping supply curve. As long as the price level is equal to that expected, the level of employment is given by L_0.[32] If, however, there is an expansion in aggregate demand for goods, e.g. (in the spirit of Friedman) because of an increased growth in the money supply, firms will raise their prices. As long as workers do not realise how much prices have risen, they will over-estimate the real wage they are receiving for any given money wage. In terms of the actual real wage they receive, the supply of labour curve will shift down – i.e. a lower actual real wage is required to induce any particular quantity of supply of labour when workers think that real wages are above their actual level. The greater the gap between actual prices and those expected, the greater the downward shift in the supply curve.

In Fig. 4.7, employment will be given by L_1 as long as workers mistakenly think that the price level is unchanged. Firms will raise their money wages, but by a smaller proportion than their prices. Thus workers will *think* that real wages have increased (to W_1/P_0) and therefore will be prepared to supply the extra labour. Firms will be paying lower actual real wages (W_1/P_1, where $W_1 > W_0$ and $P_1 > P_0$, but $W_1/P_1 < W_0/P_0$) and will be prepared to hire extra labour to produce more goods. As long as the increase in prices continues to outstrip the expectations of workers, employment can continue to remain above L_0.[33] Thus, for any given expected increase in prices, there will be a positive relationship between employment and the actual increases in wages and prices, since the bigger will be the gap between the actual real wage and that perceived by workers. Equivalently, for any given expected increase in prices there will be an inverse relationship between unemployment and the actual increase in wages and prices. The actual relationship will shift if there is a different expectation. Hence, on this explanation as well, we end up with a diagram like Fig. 4.6 in terms of expected inflation, and with equation (4.6).

We have outlined two possible explanations of the expectations augmented Phillips Curve, and there are others.[34] Each has its own problems. Of the two given here, the version which amends the Lipsey type of explanation of the

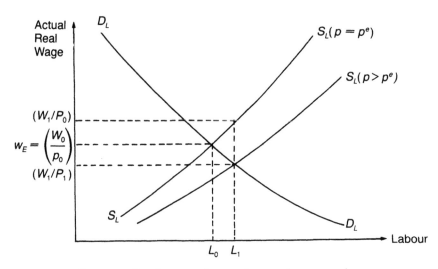

Figure 4.7 Employment changes due to price expectations

simple Phillips Curve does not fit well with the standard mark-up pricing model in which it is usually embedded. The latter implies constant real wages (if there is no growth of productivity, otherwise just growing at the same rate as productivity) – as proved in note 24. Yet the explanation of the Phillips Curve is based on a market model in which real wages are supposed to be adjusting (even if slowly) towards the equilibrium level.

The second explanation has also attracted criticisms, some of which apply also to related ideas that will be discussed later.[35] One criticism is that the process depends on asymmetrical lack of information – employers have better knowledge of the actual price level than do workers (since in Fig. 4.7 D_L either does not shift at all, or at least shifts less than S_L). This criticism can be answered, however, by noting that the real wage relevant to an employer is the money wage divided by the price that the firm charges for its own product. It surely knows this price. However, the real wage relevant to workers depends on the prices of all the goods that they are likely to buy, for example, as summarised by some sort of retail price index. This is far more difficult to know correctly and quickly. Nevertheless, the criticism has some force in so far as most countries publish retail price indices regularly and with only a short lag. For example, in those countries where the price index for each month comes out by the end of the next month, by reading the newspapers workers can know the actual level of prices 4–8 weeks ago. Unless inflation is very high, there is therefore unlikely to be a very big gap between the current actual and expected price level. Hence employment is unlikely to move far from L_0, and the approach is limited in its ability to provide a basis for discussions of how inflation varies with unemployment.

Another set of criticisms is more closely related to traditional Keynesian/ Monetarist disagreements of the sort discussed in the previous chapter. At each moment, the amount of employment is given by the intersection of the demand and supply curves for labour. The labour market 'clears' (see note 27, Chapter 3) and is, in that sense, in equilibrium, even though at times the level of employment at which it clears is based on a mistake. Thus, all unemployment is voluntary – at least in terms of what people think is going on. Quite clearly, this is not appealing to Keynesians who feel that much unemployment can be meaningfully described as involuntary.

They also feel that the notion of workers increasing or cutting down on their labour supply because they think that the real wage has altered may make sense in terms of the hours per week that employees would like to work, but not in terms of whether or not they work at all.[36] Thus, they feel that even if a diagram like Fig. 4.7 were to make sense with labour supply measured in man-hours, variations as one moves along the supply curve of labour would be by variations in the number of hours, not men. If labour supply is measured as numbers employed, it would be virtually vertical, and the Friedman argument would break down.

Even if there were sufficient elasticity in the supply of employment with respect to changes in the real wage,[37] many critics think that it is not clear why measured unemployment should change. For example, if prices are lower than workers think (so that S_L shifts up and the intersection of D_L and S_L is to the left of L_0) there will be less employment. But those who are now not working would not be expected to declare themselves 'unemployed' and 'seeking work' – which in many (but not all) countries is the basis for being included in the official unemployment figures. Instead they should consider themselves as being temporarily out of the labour force. Thus, the critics claim, even if the supply of employment were sensitive to real wages, one could not use this as part of the basis for explanations involving different levels of *un*employment and for policies towards unemployment.

There is another aspect of the first of the explanations of Friedman's argument which jarred less with traditional Keynesian accounts of the way the economy works than did the second. The first explanation is still compatible with viewing causation as going from desired expenditure, to output, to employment, to unemployment and then on to inflation. The second approach has causation going from prices to employment and output. This latter causal ordering is not only a feature of the version that, it subsequently became clear, Friedman himself advocated, but is also a feature of the 'New Monetarism' that will be discussed in Chapter 5.

POLICY IMPLICATIONS OF THE EXPECTATIONS AUGMENTED PHILLIPS CURVE

The proposition that expected price changes will be added to the wage increases that would have occurred in the absence of price inflation had important implications for the possibility of the government using the Phillips Curve to choose a point on the trade-off between inflation and unemployment. The difference can be illustrated by Fig. 4.6, and we shall consider what would happen if the government tries to choose an unemployment level below the 'natural rate' of U_*. For simplicity assume also that there is mark-up pricing and no productivity change, so that actual price inflation equals wage inflation with, at most, a very short lag.[38] For brevity we shall indicate the process only in terms of the first of the two explanations given in the previous section.

If initially the economy is at U_* and the government tries to reduce unemployment to, for example, U', where desired real wage increases are 2% per period, the effect is that money wages will rise by 2%, which will lead to a rise in prices of 2%. As long as expectations of zero inflation hold, wages and prices can continue to rise at this rate. However, eventually, workers will realise that prices are rising at 2%, and to achieve a real wage increase of 2% will demand, and get (if unemployment stays at U'), a money wage rise of 4%. But prices will then also rise by 4%, requiring, once expectations have fully adapted, a money wage increase of 6% to achieve a 2% rise in real wages. A

6% rise in money wages leads to a 6% rise in prices, and eventually to an 8% rise in money wages; and so on. As long as unemployment remains at U' the process will continue. A similar process would result for any level of unemployment below U_*. Thus, contrary to the simple Phillips Curve, any attempt to hold unemployment below U_* leads not to steady inflation but to ever-increasing inflation.[39] There is no long-run trade-off between unemployment and steady inflation. Only one level of unemployment, the so-called 'natural rate' is compatible with non-increasing inflation.

The fact that this theory denies the possibility of a long-run trade-off between unemployment and steady inflation also became known as the theory of the 'vertical Phillips Curve'. The natural rate of unemployment is compatible not just with zero price inflation, but with *any* constant (as distinct from changing) rate of inflation. For example, if we continue our assumption about mark-up pricing, the natural rate of unemployment is where any desired increase in real wages is equal to productivity change. Thus, at the natural rate, if there is an $x\%$ price inflation expected, $x\%$ will be added to a wage change that would otherwise have led to no price change. So money wages rise by $x\%$ more than the no-change amount, leading to an $x\%$ rise in prices. But this means that the actual price rise equals that expected. Expectations turn out to be correct, and so will not be changed any further. Thus there is a steady $x\%$ inflation.

This can be called a 'long-run equilibrium' : it is an equilibrium in the sense that inflation is constant (even though the price *level* is not) and like all equilibria (see Chapter 2) expectations are fulfilled. Since this argument holds for any value of x, all of the points in Fig. 4.8 are possible long-run equilibrium positions, and joining them up we have a 'vertical long-run Phillips Curve'.

For those who are happy with equations, the same argument, that there is only a single rate of unemployment which gives equilibrium, can also be shown even more directly by using equation (4.6). For simplicity take the case

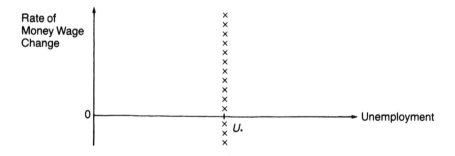

Figure 4.8 The vertical Phillips Curve

where there is no productivity change, so that $\dot{P} = \dot{W}$. Then:

$$\dot{P} = \dot{W} = f(U) + \dot{P}^e \qquad (4.7)$$

But if $\dot{P} = f(U) + \dot{P}^e$, and $\dot{P} = \dot{P}^e$ for equilibrium, we will have equilibrium if, and only if, $f(U) = 0.[40]$ The level of unemployment, which gives $f(U) = 0$, is the natural rate, U_*. Furthermore, if we have $f(U) = 0$ so $\dot{P} = \dot{P}^e$, then equation (4.7) reduces to $\dot{P} = \dot{P}$, which is compatible with any value of $\dot{P}$.

Although the name 'vertical Phillips Curve' is commonly used, it is in a sense misleading. The policy implication of the Phillips Curve was that of a trade-off between inflation and unemployment. The policy implication of the Friedman critique was that there is no exploitable trade-off. As the theory came to be more widely accepted in the 1970s, the view spread among policy-makers that, to quote the UK Labour Prime Minister James Callaghan in 1976, 'It used to be thought that we could spend our way out of unemployment ... that option is no longer available'.

The proposition that there is a unique equilibrium level of unemployment can be seen as a modern reversion to the 'classical view' attacked by Keynes. Corresponding to the 'natural rate of unemployment' is a 'natural rate of employment' and a 'natural rate of output'. The natural rate as a unique equilibrium is similar to the notion of a unique equilibrium full-employment level in the earlier literature. The difference is that whereas the earlier approach thought of equilibrium in terms of a constant wage and price level, the modern approach is in terms of a constant inflation rate. The difference may merely represent thirty years during which some (rather than zero) inflation became to be taken as normal. Since, in standard notation, the difference is between P as constant and $\dot{P}$ as constant, some have said that the natural rate theory is simply the 'classical theory with dots on'.

IS THERE STILL A ROLE FOR MACROECONOMIC POLICY?

The initial Keynesian reaction to the expectation augmented Phillips Curve theory, with its natural rate, was to try to cast doubt on the whole theory. Early testing seemed to show that expected inflation was not fully incorporated into wage change – in terms of equation (4.6) there was a coefficient on $\dot{P}^e$ which was less than unity, even though expected rather than actual prices were used. However, subsequent testing often gave results more favourable to the idea of full augmentation of money wage change by expected inflation. The difficulty with testing (4.6) is the absence of good data on the inflation expectations held by widespread groups of people. All testing therefore involves a simultaneous test of the basic theory and of assumptions used to convert data on actual inflation into figures on expected inflation, or to convert partial data on some aspect of expected inflation into full figures on expected inflation.

Other reactions were to the plausibility of the theory. As stated above, it may seem plausible. However, it was stated for the case of inflation constantly rising while unemployment was kept low. The logic of the theory also implies that if unemployment is above the natural rate for very long, then prices should *fall* at an ever-increasing rate. This seems far less plausible than the inflation aspect, and impressions of the 1930s reinforced this scepticism.[41]

Our impression is that a majority of economists currently accept that there is something like the expectations augmented Phillips Curve, though some disagree.[42] However, estimates of the expectations augmented Phillips Curve find that the natural rate has shifted. It is important to note that, as stressed in the original Lipsey approach, we do not have direct measurements of the demand and supply of labour schedules and therefore cannot directly observe the level of unemployment at which the demand and supply of labour are equal. Hence estimates of the natural rate are usually obtained indirectly by econometrically estimating an expectations augmented Phillips Curve and then using the estimated curve to see at which level of unemployment inflation would be steady. If it is found that the natural rate varies, it is always possible to provide some justification, but the feeling remains amongst some critics that the procedure is *ad hoc*.[43]

Even according to what is probably the majority view, which accepts the empirical validity of the expectations augmented Phillips Curve, the policy implications are not necessarily as straightforward as suggested by the above 1976 quote by the UK Prime Minister. As put by those who feel that the 'vertical Phillips Curve' rules out any attempt to reduce unemployment by *macro*economic policy (as opposed to microeconomic policies to shift the natural rate), it would seem that any such attempt will lead simply to higher inflation without any benefit to employment and output. However, the speed with which inflation rises depends on two factors: (i) the slope of the short-run Phillips Curve; (ii) the speed with which expectations of inflation alter. If the short-run Phillips Curve is relatively flat, then an expansionary monetary/fiscal policy will have relatively little immediate impact on the rate of wage increases. If expectations of future inflation adapt only very sluggishly to actual inflation, then the short-run Phillips Curve will not quickly shift up very far. Thus the mere existence of an expectations augmented Phillips Curve does not in itself mean that runaway inflation will soon result from any attempt to reduce inflation. There could still be something of a trade-off between permanently higher inflation and a temporary reduction of un-employment, and the length of time that the 'temporary' reduction lasts may not be trivial. (Again, we have purposely used vague words like 'relatively' and 'some' in this paragraph, as these are matters of judgement.)

It remains true that if there is an expectations augmented Phillips Curve, in the long run any expansionary macroeconomic policy taking employment above the natural rate will be fully crowded out by inflation, unless the government is prepared to accept higher and higher inflation by providing more, and faster, increases in the money supply. The increases in the money supply are needed to stop the cumulative price rises reducing the real value of money balances, and hence raising real interest rates.[44] In the absence of ever-increasing monetary growth the crowding out is similar to that occurring in the older classical model, in the way that aggregate demand is reduced back to the natural rate of output (corresponding to the 'full employment' level). Here, however, the mechanism does not need to concentrate on the real wage returning to its full-employment equilibrium level (though this does happen in the Friedman version). In the modern model, the mechanism also says what determines how quickly there will be a return to the natural rate.

Although the idea of the expectations augmented Phillips Curve does not have to specify that the explanation is in terms of an equilibrium real wage to which the labour market returns once expectations are correct, and at which the demand for labour equals the supply, this is certainly the notion behind Friedman's theory. The terminology of 'natural' rate itself seems to carry with it the suggestion that it is the normal position of the economy, and (possibly) that it would be 'unnatural' to try to shift the economy away from it. As we have suggested in the previous chapter, some economists do seem to react to the emotive force of terminology, and those economists who reject one or more of the apparent implications have argued that the 'natural' rate may not really be natural in all of the standard connotations of that word. As a result, alternatives have been proposed. A widely-used alternative is NAIRU – which stands for Non-Accelerating Inflation Rate of Unemployment. Those who prefer this expression feel it is more neutrally descriptive than 'natural rate of unemployment'. From now on we shall use both, but with no necessary committment to the connotations attaching to either.

There are various approaches which predict that in the long run inflation will continuously rise if unemployment is kept below a particular level, and which therefore incorporate the existence of a NAIRU, yet which differ in various aspects from the Friedman approach. Many of these incorporate what could be called cost-push elements, and will have different policy implications.

One such alternative is to consider that the existence of trade unions, and other imperfections (itself an emotive term) in labour markets, means that in the labour market, even if there is a balance between the demand and supply of labour, there will still be pressures on real wages to rise. In terms of the diagrams, the effect of trade union pressure is that in Fig. 4.4, the locus relating wage change to excess demand for labour is displaced upwards, even if $\dot{W}$ is replaced by (W/P^e).[45] Real wage change is still positively related to the excess demand for labour, but to choke-off wage increases, and get steady desired real wages, requires not a balance of demand and supply but supply exceeding demand. The hypothesis is that what are normally taken as equivalent equilibrium notions do not coincide in the labour market; 'constant price' (here wage) and 'demand equals supply' are not the same condition with labour. On this approach, the NAIRU in Figs 4.6 and 4.7 corresponds to an excess supply of labour. Proponents of this sort of approach would often couch their differences by saying something like 'the NAIRU is not a reasonable balance in the labour markets but represents massive excess supply and unacceptable unemployment'.

Other theories which are Keynesian in the sense of seeing labour markets as different to the neo-classical market paradigm may similarly imply the existence of an augmented Phillips Curve and NAIRU. For example, some economists feel that workers (and their trade union representatives) bargain for some notion of a target real wage, where the target is based on the sort of rises in real wages that they have got used to. However, they will adjust the extent to which they push for the target according to the level of unemployment.[46] In fact, many cost-push theories will include the assumptions: (i) wage setting is not completely insensitive to the state of the economy (so that the short-run Phillips Curve is not completely horizontal); (ii) workers and their representatives are not completely incapable of realising that their real wage depends on inflation; and (iii) workers and their representatives are capable of eventually revising their expectations about inflation. These conditions will imply the existence of a NAIRU.

However, the views on policy will often be related to views on the extent to which labour markets are 'typical' markets and on how smoothly or sluggishly they react to changes and disequilibria.

A non-interventionist macroeconomic policy stance will be most appealing if the natural rate is also thought to represent full employment and if it is felt that any divergence from it will be quickly corrected – in other words, that steep short-run Phillips Curves and quick alteration of expectations ensure that in the absence of misguided economic policies, the economy is always close to the natural rate. In this sense, belief that divergences from the natural rate will be automatically limited and of short duration fits in well with what we described in the previous chapter as the Monetarist belief that the economy is stable. Furthermore, with such beliefs, the government does not even need to know the NAIRU – the economy will itself quickly converge on the natural rate.

Such an argument is reinforced by a stress on inevitable uncertainty and on risk aversion. Given that all econometric estimates are uncertain and subject to error, the economists who advise the government can never be sure of exactly what rate of unemployment constitutes the natural rate. The theory of 'accelerating inflation' can then be taken as strengthening the case against using macroeconomic policy to alter output and employment. If attempts are made to expand the economy because current unemployment is above the estimated natural rate, but the estimates may be wrong, there is a danger that inflation will increase explosively. It would seem that to avoid this risk, expansionary policies should be eschewed even if unemployment is thought to be 'high'.

Conversely, if it is believed that the economy would only very slowly move towards the NAIRU if monetary/fiscal policy were kept steady, these latter views imply that the inflation cost of 'misguided' policy may not be very high – since, as explained above, they follow from flat short-run Phillips Curves and sticky expectations. Furthermore (again as in the discussions of the previous chapter), with very slow convergence the unemployment cost of inaction will be high if unemployment could have been reduced by more expansionary policies.

Economists who accept theories which have a NAIRU that is not a reasonable balance of supply and demand for labour will also often want to hold unemployment below the NAIRU for as long as possible – if it were possible, indefinitely. At a fundamental level, with the opposite view (i.e. that the natural rate is where demand equals supply) it is not only likely to be costly to try to reduce unemployment by macroeconomic policies, it is also undesirable. In a theory with a 'vertical long-run Phillips Curve', to move the level of unemployment away from the natural rate involves fooling people. Only if expectations are wrong ($\dot{P}$ not equal to $\dot{P}^e$) will unemployment not be at the natural rate. But it is a standard proposition in welfare economics that if all markets, including labour markets, work 'properly' and everybody has full information then the result is optimal. Therefore, in the type of theory summarised in Fig. 4.7, it is suboptimal, i.e. inefficient, to try to reduce unemployment since it can only be done by inducing mistakes. Higher employment only occurs because workers mistakenly think that they are earning higher real wages when they are not. The supply-curve of labour represents the results of utility maximising behaviour by individuals; it is not optimal to fool them into supplying more labour than they would wish to if they had correct information.[47] In the opposing, more Keynesian viewpoint, some markets, especially (but not necessarily exclusively) the labour markets, display 'imperfections'. Hence optimality is not ensured by the 'invisible hand', and sensible government intervention to increase employment may increase welfare.

Although much of the policy debate is posed in terms of whether governments should attempt to move unemployment below the NAIRU, and of the eventual complete crowding-out by increasing inflation if it does, it is of course also possible that the economy can experience a rate of unemployment above the NAIRU. Under these circumstances, expansionary government policy will not necessarily lead to runaway inflation, but could merely stabilise inflation at the expected rate, provided that unemployment is not reduced beyond the NAIRU. Expansionary policy would speed up the return to the NAIRU, rather than waiting until expectations of inflation had declined enough to bring the economy back to the natural rate. An example is shown in Fig. 4.6. If the economy were initially at point A, with unemployment of U_2 and zero inflation, one could wait until expectations of inflation had also declined to zero and the economy would then be at point C. Alternatively the period of going through unemployment above U_* could be avoided by increasing aggregate demand by enough to move the economy to point B, with 2% actual inflation. It remains true, and not just in our particular example, that although there will not be explosive inflation (provided employment is not increased too far), nevertheless the end result will be higher inflation than would have occurred if unemployment had been allowed to stay above the natural rate for longer.

Because inflation is often seen as the strongest counter-argument to expansionary policy, some Keynesians have tried to provide alternatives to accepting 'high' unemployment as the only way to avoid increasing inflation.[48] There are various forms of incomes policies that have been suggested.[49] They are typically opposed by non-Keynesians (as well as by some Keynesians) and the division between proponents and opponents is often based on the split we have claimed is fundamental. Any incomes policy is going to include some attempt to hold down money wage increases which would have taken place otherwise. But holding down aggregate wages involves limiting individual wage rises (since the aggregate percentage wage increase in the economy is the average of all individual increases) and thus intervening in the wage-setting process – usually at the same time freezing the *pattern* of wages or at least limiting the circumstances in which individual wages can change by more than the norm.

From what we have described as a Monetarist perspective, incomes policies are both unnecessary and undesirable. They are unnecessary because if there is a sensible steady growth of the money stock then the economy will settle down at the natural rate and reasonable inflation (if the economy has some long-run growth of output, a growth of the money supply equal to output growth would give zero inflation). Incomes policies are undesirable because they stop changes in relative wages – since, on this aspect of the Monetarist view, labour markets work well if there is no intervention, relative wages are signals to induce correct allocation of labour resources. Thus freezing wage differentials in the face of the inevitable changes that occur in technology and consumer demand will lead to a misallocation of resources and be inefficient.

From the converse point of view, incomes policies are both necessary and fairly innocuous. They are necessary because the NAIRU may not represent a reasonable balance of demand and supply, but an unacceptable level of involuntary unemployment, and there may not even be any guarantee of a quick return to the NAIRU following some disturbance. They are innocuous because the freezing of the pattern of wage differentials may not be particularly inefficient if, anyway, wages are set largely by forces other than supply and demand. If wages are largely governed by inertia, demands for 'comparability' and 'fairness' or other 'non-economic' factors, they do not perform an important role as signals for resource reallocation. Therefore there is no harm in stabilising wage differentials, at least in the short run. Not all Keynesians go so far as to say that a permanent wages policy would have no efficiency costs, but many do see incomes policies as at least a way of dealing with particular surges of inflation that might otherwise accompany desirable expansions of expenditure. Some do see permanent incomes policies as a necessary, and not too costly, adjunct of active attempts to control unemployment by monetary and fiscal policies.

Even if incomes policies were desirable, this would not in itself guarantee their feasibility. Once one starts to consider more interventionist incomes policies, with governments playing a role, there are strong disagreements over whether such policies can work or have ever worked. At the time of writing, the mood in many countries is probably against any sort of formally imposed incomes policies. They do not fit in with the fashionable key phrase and approach of 'de-regulation'. However, any widespread reversion to Keynesian policies in countries where wage bargaining is currently largely decentralised would probably bring with it a serious re-appraisal of mechanisms designed to influence wage-setting towards less inflation than would occur in their absence.

MONEY AND INFLATION

An often repeated statement, usually attributed to Professor Milton Friedman (in Schultz and Aliber, 1966, p. 25) is that 'inflation is always and everywhere a monetary phenomenon'. In this section we examine in what senses the statement may or may not be correct – in particular is it tenable to claim that inflation will occur, and can only occur, if there is a prior increase in the growth of the money supply? To put the same question in more formal terms: is growth of the money supply both a necessary and sufficient condition for inflation?

As discussed on pages 55–6, 'Monetary theories' are sometimes simply assertions of empirical regularities – the rate of growth of the money supply affects inflation with a 1–2-year lag. As also indicated there, this approach requires picking on some particular measure of the money supply (since the different measures do not always move closely together). Even then, however, it is not always clear whether it is being asserted that money supply changes are the only thing that affect changes in the price index or whether other things may change inflation, but so will changes in monetary growth. The context of the assertions often implies the former, but it is frequently not explicit. The distinction is important for policy assessment – especially whether holding down the growth of 'the' money supply would always avoid inflation.

Traditionally, what is often called the 'classical quantity of money theory' may or may not have provided an explanation of the transmission mechanism by which changes in money led to changes in prices, but in its popular form money growth was both a necessary and sufficient condition for inflation. This can be seen by looking at equation (2.3) in Chapter 2 and using the rules about rates of change mentioned in the section entitled 'Notation' earlier in this chapter (pp. 56–7) They give:

$$\dot{M} + \dot{V} = \dot{P} + \dot{Y} \qquad (4.7)$$

The quantity theory assumed velocity to be constant[50] – since V does not change it follows that $\dot{V} = 0$ in equation (4.7). It was also taken to assume that real output is determined by real forces and is independent of monetary factors – often expressed as the view that 'money is a veil'. Thus money and prices move together. Algebraically, using (4.7), if real output and income are exogenous, while $\dot{V} = 0$, then there is a one-to-one relationship between inflation and the change in money. For example, if output were steady, so that $\dot{Y} = 0$, then equation (4.7) would reduce to $\dot{M} = \dot{P}$. It was assumed that causation went from $\dot{M}$ to $\dot{P}$.[51] Sometimes it was only in the longer run that output was assumed exogenous, and determined by long-run forces of technology and accumulation. The one-to-one relationship between money and prices would then only be applicable to the longer-run, but not to shorter-run, inflationary episodes.

The modern, simplified approach which simply asserts an empirical regularity could then be based on equation (4.7) with the extra assumptions that velocity is constant and output exogenous over a two-year period. It remains, however, a 'black-box' approach if left at this level.

If one starts to examine causal mechanisms by which changes in money supply can lead to inflation, there is no difficulty in seeing that since money can affect aggregate demand (whether or not velocity is constant), it can move the economy along a short-run Phillips Curve.[52] In this way, it is a demand-pull theory – in equation (4.7) an increase in $\dot{M}$ will lead to an increase in $\dot{P} + \dot{Y}$, with the exact split between $\dot{P}$ and $\dot{Y}$ determined by the Phillips Curve.[53] Furthermore, if we just compare equilibria, so that the economy is at the natural rate, then $\dot{Y} = 0$ (with no long-run growth, or equal to an exogenous constant if there is natural growth), and then $\dot{P}$ is dependent on $\dot{M}$. Thus in any theory in which money can affect expenditure and in which the state of the economy affects inflation, changes in the rate of growth of money supply would be expected to change inflation.

The much more controversial issue is whether inflation can change without changes in the rate of growth of money. For simplicity in this discussion we shall take the case where the *level* of the money stock is constant, and where we start with zero inflation and growth (so that $\dot{M} = \dot{P} = \dot{Y} = \dot{V} = 0$), but the conclusions would be similar if we started in a steady state where money, output and prices were all growing at constant rates.

If we have a demand-pull theory, and if we are not in the special 'quantity theory' Monetarist case (where V is constant because there is no responsiveness of money demand to interest rates), then a change in fiscal policy could lead to a change in output. Thus it would seem that, given a short-run Phillips Curve, there could be an increase in inflation. Similarly in various cost-push theories, one can conceive of an autonomous increase in inflation – for example, an upward shift in the short-run Phillips Curve because of an increase in trade union militancy or of unrealistic worker demands for real wages in the face of a fall in the affordable real wage.

Under these circumstances the question is whether inflation could take off and continue in the absence of increases in the stock of money. If velocity were strictly constant, equation (4.7) would imply that $\dot{P} + \dot{Y} = 0$ if $\dot{M} = 0$. Thus any increase in prices ($\dot{P} > 0$ for some period, however short) could only occur if output fell ($\dot{Y} < 0$). But the Phillips Curve implies that as output falls, and unemployment rises, inflation must fall. As a result, if the special extreme

Monetarist case is a good description of reality, an inflation (defined as a process of continually rising prices) cannot get under way if the money supply is held constant.[54] How quickly the rise in prices will be halted or reversed depends on the steepness of the Phillips Curve and on its shifts. With a very steep short-run Curve, even a small fall in output will stop any inflation.

If, however, as most economists now think, the special case of strictly constant velocity is not a good approximation to reality, then velocity is variable. Thus from equation (4.7) inflation can be positive, even if the money supply is constant, without falling output, as long as velocity is increasing. In the special extreme Keynesian case of the liquidity trap this can occur indefinitely as long as the liquidity trap continues. More generally, however, in the 'standard' case where there is some response of money demand to interest rates, there are likely to be limits to the increase in the velocity of circulation, as increases in velocity will require increases in interest rates. If there are limits to how far velocity can rise (which is equivalent to saying there are limits as to how far the demand for holding real money balances can fall), then eventually the rate of increase in velocity must slow down (i.e. $\dot{V}$ goes towards zero). Eventually, then, we reach a situation similar to that discussed in the previous paragraph for the case where velocity was constant from the beginning. Therefore, eventually any further inflation must be offset by falling output and the Phillips Curve implies that inflation will decline. In terms of the mechanisms, as prices continue to rise while the nominal money stock is held constant, eventually the fall in real balances could be expected to raise real interest rates and reduce real expenditure.

The conclusion would be that most economists accept that in the end an inflationary process could not continue indefinitely without sufficient increases in money. How long it would take to reach this stage would depend on a whole series of factors: on the initial increase in inflation, the speed with which inflation rose (the short-run Phillips Curve shifted up with increases in expected inflation), the limit on velocity (how soon $\dot{V}$ would have to start declining towards zero) and the slope of the short-run Phillips Curve (how soon a fall in Y, and therefore $\dot{Y}$ negative, would slow down inflation). Many economists, but by no means all, and not even all who might otherwise be termed Keynesians, would judge that prices might continue rising for long enough for one to legitimately consider that there could be inflation even in the absence of an accommodating increase in the money stock.

For all those economists who think that there can be autonomous cost-push pressures, the government is always faced with a choice sooner or later. Either the government can 'validate' (as it is often called) the initial price rises by increasing the money supply, or it can refuse to allow inflation to continue and accelerate by holding tight on to the money supply – but this may require a rise in unemployment above the NAIRU to bring inflation to a halt, if the inflationary process has become embedded in expectations.

Only if one either refuses to admit the possibility of any sort of cost-push pressures[55] or considers that velocity is so close to constant that price rises could never even begin to translate into an inflationary process would it follow that money is a necessary as well as a sufficient condition for any sort of inflation. As stated, however, most economists would accept that *eventually*, however long 'eventually' might be, monetary growth is necessary for inflation to continue indefinitely. In this case, the stress placed on always controlling monetary growth in order to avoid inflation will depend on the importance given to the shorter- versus the longer-run effects of policies.

CONCLUSIONS

During the past fifty years, the policy discussions among economists moved from treating the inflation that might result from a policy to keep unemployment low as a worry, but with no strong foundations, to seeing it as a cost which might have to be borne. This cost, however, was manageable – there was a well-defined trade-off, and whatever level of inflation was decided on as the maximum acceptable was sustainable and determined how low unemployment could be kept. The terms of the debate were then completely changed by the theory that there is no sustainable trade-off between inflation and unemployment.

The economists' debates over the prediction that explosive inflation would result if governments attempted to reduce unemployment came into the more general political consciousness just when there was increasing worry about the pervasiveness of high and increased inflation in Western developed economies in the 1970s. It is, of course, quite likely that the public worries also affected the issues that economists debated, and the terms on which they debated them.

As far as current policy is concerned, it seems clear that in many countries the fear of inflation is the main brake on expansionary economic policies. Some economists may feel that the fear is overdone and that it would be possible to expand employment, for some time at least, by macroeconomic policies without setting off an explosive acceleration in prices. Others may feel that the current levels of unemployment are well above the NAIRU, and that therefore some reduction in unemployment could be undertaken before even running the danger of getting into accelerating inflation. Yet others may feel that well-designed incomes policies could play a role in enabling a long-run expansion of employment to persist. However, there are many economists who support the position that all attempts at expansionary monetary/fiscal policies would be ill-advised and that steady macroeconomic policies, with low rates of monetary growth, will ensure the emergence of steady low inflation and reasonable, natural, levels of unemployment.

Typically, behind the various views, lie the theories discussed in this chapter, the positions taken on them, and the econometric (or more casual empirical) estimation of the relationships involved. ·

81

5

FORESIGHT, RATIONALITY AND THE EFFECTIVENESS OF POLICY

INTRODUCTION

In Chapter 2 we mentioned the 'Treasury View' of the 1930s: that fiscal policy cannot alter aggregate demand. The Keynesian theory outlined in Chapter 2 led to the opposite view: that policy can alter aggregate demand. As explained there, generally the effects of fiscal policy will be reduced by crowding-out of some investment due to rises in interest rates but, except in the special case in which the velocity of circulation of money is completely constant, there will be some effect of fiscal policy on aggregate demand in a closed economy. The rise in interest rates and the crowding-out which results could, of course, be avoided by a judicious use of monetary policy.

In Chapter 4 we discussed the view that although fiscal and/or monetary policy can alter nominal aggregate demand, the effect on real output and employment may be reduced by the induced increase in inflation.

In the long run, it could be that the non-accelerating inflation equilibrium implies a single level of output and employment which cannot be affected by policies which work only through aggregate demand. At least in the short run, however, there will be still some effect from policies which act on aggregate demand.

Recently both of these propositions have been subject to critical debate. It has been claimed that fiscal policy may have little or no effect on aggregate demand even if there were no rise in interest rates and therefore no crowding-out of investment expenditure. This is a result of the 'Ricardo–Barro equivalence theorem' which will be explained in 'Taxation and bond equivalence'. In 'Rational expectations and policy ineffectiveness' we will explain the view that even in the short run monetary/fiscal policies cannot work because of the induced effect on inflation. This latter view is called by various names: 'policy ineffectiveness', 'new-classical macroeconomics' and, after its initial proponents and popularisers, the 'Lucas–Sargent–Wallace proposition'.

The common factor in these two criticisms of more conventional macro-economics is that both rely on individuals having (and being able to act on)

82

very full information about current events, including policies, and foresight about their implications for the future. Those who accept the type of reasoning behind these criticisms are also sometimes called 'New Monetarists' and their approach has important differences from the older Monetarism that we have discussed up to now.

In 'Credibility and consistency' we consider a further argument which has been advanced against using expansionary policies to increase employment and output. This is that as people begin to expect expansionary policies whenever unemployment is 'high', these expectations will affect their behaviour in ways that have undesirable consequences for the economy. This argument is sometimes called the 'credibility' argument against using monetary/fiscal policies, as it is related to the issue of whether governments will be believed on those occasions when they want to damp down inflationary pressure.

TAXATION AND BOND EQUIVALENCE

Although often not stated explicitly, analyses of pure fiscal policies imply that any resulting change in the government budget deficit/surplus is made up by changes in the sale of bonds to members of the public. Only in the case where there are simultaneous changes in government expenditure and taxation which exactly offset each other in their effects on revenue, the so-called 'balanced-budget multiplier' case, will there be no changes required in financing. Effects on the economy from changes in bond-holdings are usually ignored in short-run Keynesian analyses, even where financing by bond sales is required.[1]

It has been alleged that we are not justified in ignoring changes in bond-holdings. The changes in bond-holdings may themselves alter private expenditure. The theorem, which is traced back to Ricardo,[2] says that an increase in sales of bonds to the public means that in future taxes will have to be higher so that the government can pay the interest on the extra bonds. Individuals will realise that they will have to pay extra taxes in future, and if they base their consumption not just on current disposable income but also on expected future incomes,[3] they will cut back their consumption. Under suitable assumptions, a tax-reduction which is financed by increased sales of bonds will have no effects at all on consumption. The increase in consumption due to the current increase in disposable income will be completely offset by the decrease in consumption due to the expected reduction in future disposable income of taxpayers.

Complete offsetting, so that bond-financed changes in tax have no effects, or (equivalently) that increases in bonds are exactly opposite in their effects to an equal decrease in current taxes, and vice versa, requires that individuals can correctly foresee the future tax implications of current bond sales and take these into account in their decisions. This is sometimes called 'super-rationality'. It also requires that individuals are worried about their future tax liabilities over the whole life of the bonds. Given that some government bonds have no maturity date ('perpetuities', in the UK called 'consols'), in its original form the proposition assumed infinitely long-lived individuals. Robert Barro (1974) showed that mortality makes no difference provided that people care in a particular way about their descendants' welfare, and each has descendants.[4] They will then cut back on consumption now in order to increase their bequests to make up just enough of their heirs' future tax liabilities. In effect people have vicarious infinite lives via their descendants, under Barro's assumptions.

Another assumption needed for complete offsetting is called 'perfect capital markets'. This means that all individuals can borrow at the same rate of interest at which they can lend, and that 'the' rate is the same for each individual as it is for the government. The need for this last assumption is more subtle. We shall explore several ways of seeing its reason. One way is that if it holds, any individual faced with a current tax bill could always borrow a lump sum to meet it and, furthermore, the interest payments on this personal debt that would be needed in subsequent years would be exactly the same as the tax payments the government will have to raise to pay the interest on its borrowing. In this sense, if there are no capital-market imperfections, when the government increases its debt by issuing a bond instead of levying a current tax, it is merely doing on each individual's behalf what the individuals could do for themselves to avoid paying the tax out of current income.[5] Conversely, knowing that they will have to pay more tax in future when faced with government bond sales now, individuals could, if they wanted to, lend money now and use the interest receipts on their lending to pay their taxes in future.[6]

For those who have done an intermediate-level microeconomics course, another way of seeing the requirement for perfect capital markets is that if they exist, consumption decisions depend only on the present value of disposable income. The present value of a current tax payment is equal to the payment itself, and is also the same as the present value of the future tax payments to finance the interest on a bond which replaces the current tax payment. Thus the individual's present value is unaffected if the government replaces current taxes by bond sales, and therefore their consumption will be unaffected also.

We have so far discussed the fiscal policy implications of the Ricardo–Barro theorem in the form that changes in taxation financed by bond sales will have no effect. The theorem has been explained in the form that an increase in bonds is exactly equivalent in its effects to an increase in taxation, and therefore offsets the actual reduction in current taxes, and conversely for a reduction in bonds. The bond/tax equivalence proposition also has implications which weaken a fiscal policy of changing government expenditure. It does not mean (as is sometimes stated) that a bond-financed change in government expenditure has no effect on aggregate demand. It does mean that a change in government expenditure financed by government selling more or less bonds to the public has the same limited effect as if it were financed by a change in taxation. It is well known (see any introductory textbook) that the 'balanced-budget' multiplier is less than the multiplier when the financing is by bonds (and when bonds are assumed to have no effects), but the balanced-budget multiplier is not generally zero.

This weakening of the impact of government expenditure because of the concomitant changes in bond-holdings can be linked with both another way of seeing why the assumptions mentioned above are necessary and another implication of them. Bonds have a value because of the payments which will accrue to the owners. In fact it can be shown that, ignoring any expected capital gains, the price of the bond equals these future receipts discounted by 'the' rate of interest. But these future receipts equal the future taxes necessary to pay them. Therefore, one can similarly treat the present value of the future taxes, also discounted by 'the' rate of interest as the value of the current debt equivalent to these future tax payments. Since we are discounting the same payments (viewed as future receipts on ownership of the bonds and as future taxes) by the same rate of interest if there are perfect capital markets, the value of the debt-equivalent equals the value of the bonds. Thus if we add the negative debt-equivalent to the positive worth of the bonds, they add to zero. If it is helpful, one could think of the debt-equivalent of each bond as a kind of 'anti-bond', analogous to the concept of anti-matter, which exactly equals the actual bond in value when there are perfect capital markets.

We can conceptually split the economy into two groups: those who buy government bonds and get receipts from them and those who pay the taxes to finance the payments on the bonds (some people will fall into both groups and could be counted twice, once in each group). Or, more simply, we can think of the 'representative person' who both buys bonds and pays taxes. Either aggregating over the two groups or adding together the different transactions of the representative person, the bonds and the debt-equivalent or 'anti-bonds' will cancel each other out. Therefore we end up with the important conclusion of the Ricardo–Barro theorem that 'government bonds are not net worth'.

This implication helps to reinforce the view that it makes no difference whether changes in government expenditure are financed by changes in taxation or by changes in bond holdings. Consider an increase of government expenditure in the current year, which divided by the number of households amounts to £x per household. If financed by bond sales, then the 'representative' household pays £x to the government this year, and receives pieces of paper called bond certificates in return. If financed by taxation, the 'representative' household pays £x to the government this year and receives a piece of paper called a tax receipt in return. The only difference between the two situations is the name given to the piece of paper.[7] There will only be a difference in behaviour if people react differently to ownership of bond certificates than to ownership of tax receipts. But nobody considers mere ownership of a tax receipt as wealth. Therefore bond-financed government expenditure change will only be more effective than a tax-financed 'balanced-budget' expenditure change if government bonds are net wealth.

So far no empirical testing of the implications of the equivalence theorem has been widely accepted as conclusive. Assessment and criticism have therefore centred on the 'reasonableness' of the assumptions and the sensitivity of the implications to variations in these assumptions.[8]

One very popular attack is on the fundamental concept of super-rationality, viz. that individuals can foresee the future tax implications of current bond sales. It is claimed that people do not have, or do not bother about acquiring, the relevant information. However, this attack is not as powerful as it might seem. If the gap between the initial sale of the bond and the date of the first interest payment is not long (typically a maximum of a year), then taxpayers will soon be paying the first of the regular increased taxes to finance the interest payments. Under these circumstances, even people who use fairly crude 'rule-of-thumb' methods of guessing at their future disposable income *will* soon take account of the taxes needed to finance the bond interest payments. The majority of economists now accept that expectations about the future, and wealth, do affect consumption, which is therefore not dependent only on current disposable income, even though there are still disagreements on details of consumption function theories. Some Keynesians, following Keynes himself, still see a more rigid divide between a known present and an uncertain future (or between current income and financial wealth) than would allow the eqivalence theorem to hold.

Quite clearly, the infinite life version of the assumptions is untenable. Without the replacement by the Barro assumptions, if the bonds have a long maturity, let alone an infinite one, then mortal individuals will in the aggregate treat bonds as net wealth. This follows from the determination of bond prices since the positive wealth effect of bonds reflects the market's discounting of the interest payments over the whole period to maturity, while individuals' negative wealth effects (the 'anti-bond' above) only reflects the discounted tax payments over their expected lifetime, which will be shorter than the time to maturity for at least some people. Equivalently, they will allow for the future tax payments only over their lifetimes while the interest receipts from owning bonds are discounted over the whole of the period to maturity, since bonds can be sold on the market even by elderly owners. The factual importance of finite lives if people do not worry about their heirs will depend on the typical maturity of government debt, average life expectancies, and laws concerning tax payments in retirement. It is difficult to generalise.

There is strong disagreement on whether the Barro assumptions about people's concern for posterity are reasonable enough to overcome the finiteness of human lives. Introspection does not leave economists agreeing over whether people are more likely to be concerned with the average standard of living of each of their heirs or the total resources available to all their heirs, and therefore over whether family size matters, nor over whether they take account of the fact that (since procreation requires two partners) their infinite stream of heirs will receive resources from other families. It is claimed that behaviour of those with no children is not likely to be exactly offset by the behaviour of those with larger than average family size. It is also possible that some people would prefer to end their lives leaving debts, not assets, to their heirs – if only it could be arranged – either because with economic growth our descendants will anyway be better off than we are, or because of selfishness: 'What has posterity ever done for us?'

Disagreement over whether perfect capital markets exist approximately enough for the theory to hold tends to split rather more on Keynesian/Monetarist lines. Keynesians (to varying degrees within the group) are more sceptical about the easy applicability of the neo-classical, perfect competition, market paradigm to current economies. This has already been discussed in Chapter 3 in the context of labour markets. The stress on the importance of establishing long-run personal relationships and the difficulty of acquiring knowledge about non-identical people also carry over to the capital market. If combined with the inability to sell oneself into legally binding slavery, it leads Keynesians to stress that it is expensive or impossible to borrow against future earnings. The implication is that the government can borrow at a much lower rate of interest than can private individuals, and therefore individuals discount future tax payments at a higher rate than the market uses in valuing government bonds. The future taxes will weigh less heavily in people's decisions, and they will not cut back consumption now because of the future taxes by as much as they would if they had to pay current taxes equal to the market value of bonds being sold by the government. A cut in current taxation financed by bond sales will therefore be expansionary, and similarly an increase in government expenditure financed by bond sales will be more expansionary than one financed by an increase in taxes.

In terms of one of the explanations above for the theorem, if governments and private individuals cannot borrow at the same rate then individuals could not counter government actions by their own financial transactions. They could not pay their current tax bills by borrowing on the same terms as the government can. They are therefore better off if the government borrows rather than if they do, and will thus increase their consumption.

Another way of putting the point, in terms of an alternative explanation given above, is that if individuals discount future taxes at a higher rate than the market uses in discounting future interest payments to determine the price of a bond, the value of the negative debt (or 'anti-wealth') corresponding to future tax liabilities is less than the value of the positive wealth attaching to ownership of the bond. Therefore bonds *are* net wealth, leading to the expansionary tax reductions financed by bond-sales and to the greater multiplier on bond- (as compared to tax-) financed increases in government expenditure.

This objection to the theorem is strengthened if some private individuals find it completely impossible to borrow long term for consumption purposes.[9] They may be at a stage in their life-cycle where they would like to consume more than they earn (e.g. when raising a family on an income which is expected to increase as they gain promotion in the future), but cannot borrow to do so. They will then have no discretionary saving which can be cut back if current taxes are raised. Conversely, any increase in disposable income will be partly spent now. People who buy bonds are typically saving anyway, and are therefore not constrained by an inability to obtain credit, which is irrelevant to them. Under these circumstances we cannot amalgamate and offset bond-owners and tax payers, nor is the 'representative' household who both buys bonds and pays average taxes a legitimate method of analysis. Instead, a reduction in taxation leads to an increase in current consumption by credit-constrained households despite any expectation of future taxes to eventually pay for bond interest payments. From this angle as well the bond-tax equivalence theorem breaks down.

The Ricardo–Barro equivalence theorem might at first sight seem more palatable to Monetarists than Keynesians – Barro himself is one of the leading members of the 'New Classical' school of modern monetarism (to be explained in the next section). As already mentioned, the necessary assumption of perfect capital markets does not fit in with a typically Keynesian view of the world. In addition the theorem weakens the multiplier effect of bond-financed government expenditure changes and completely destroys that of taxation changes.[10,11] However, on a deeper analysis the theorem also has some unpalatable implications for some economists and politicians who might otherwise be called Monetarists and some palatable ones for some Keynesians.

The implication of the theory which worries some who are opposed to government budget deficits is that so long as they are financed by issuing bonds, even continuing large deficits will have no cumulative long-run effects. The budget deficits resulting from tax-cutting ('supply-side' economics in the popular usage) have no macroeconomic effects and are thus of no concern if the theorem holds. As debates in the 1980s in the USA made clear, this conclusion is welcomed by some who might be termed anti-Keynesians, but definitely unwelcome to others. In the UK in 1980, the 'new-Right' government of Mrs Thatcher placed great stress on reducing the budget deficit. However, when a Committee of the House of Commons (1980) sent a questionnaire to various prominent economists asking for their views on UK policy, Milton Friedman replied that he could see no reason for worrying about the deficit provided that it was financed by issuing bonds rather than money.[12]

From a Keynesian viewpoint, the theorem also has its attractions. The multiplier on bond-financed government expenditure may be weakened and only be the same as the 'balanced-budget multiplier', but it is still non-zero. Furthermore, by removing any worries about the cumulative effects of the continuing bond-sales needed to finance deficits, the theorem also removes one of the main objections to continued expansionary government expenditure policies. In particular, if the theorem holds, the bond-sales will not raise interest rates (since they have no effects in aggregate) and therefore this will not be a source of crowding-out of private investment.[13] This implication, that a deficit has no effect on interest rates, constitutes one of the important differences between 'old' and 'new' Monetarists.

At the time of writing, the empirical relevance of the bond-taxation equivalence theorem has not been conclusively settled. It has aroused much interest and debate among economists concerned with macroeconomic policy, but its implications for policy can be used to support opposing positions. Most economists would see it as weakening the expected effects of fiscal policies, but it also weakens some of the objections to them.

RATIONAL EXPECTATIONS AND POLICY INEFFECTIVENESS

It is clear that the level of many variables which affect output, e.g. investment, are affected by people's expectations about the future. One of the major problems in economics has been how to model satisfactorily the way that people form their expectations about future events, such as future inflation. In the previous chapter, when explaining the expectations-augmented Phillips Curve and how the short-run trade-off between inflation and unemployment altered and eventually vanished, we implicitly assumed that expectations of inflation adapted with a lag to actual levels of inflation. However, this has unsatisfactory aspects, such as the implication that people make systematic errors in their forecasts during periods of steadily changing inflation.

Recently a way of modelling expectations, initially proposed for micro economics by Muth (1961), has been applied to macroeconomic models. The theory is called by the name of 'rational expectations' – the latest in the long stream of economic concepts officially value-free but given normatively persuasive names: who, after all, would want to be accused of having 'irrational expectations', or be patronising enough to attribute them to others?

Basically the approach assumes that people optimally use all available information when making the forecasts that enter into their decisions. This information includes not only the most recently available data series, but also the best available knowledge of the structure of the economy (i.e. 'the' best model of the economy, or the part of it under consideration). The information will take account of government policies themselves if they are known or can be deduced. It will include a knowledge of any past forecasting errors, and if these showed a systematic pattern then this pattern itself could have been used to improve forecasting. Thus individuals will not make systematic errors in forming their expectations, since such errors would be inconsistent with 'rational expectations'.

When combined with some other assumptions about macroeconomic behaviour, powerful and surprising results follow. The particular proposition we shall concentrate on is due to Lucas (1972) and emphasised by Sargent and Wallace (1976).[14] In the context and level of this book the easiest way to see the proposition is to use the full expectations – augmented Phillips Curve developed in Chapter 4. The argument will be put both verbally and using symbols.

In that chapter, the result was that money wage changes were related to unemployment and to expectations of price inflation – in the strong version of the model wage changes reacted fully to price inflation expectations. If there is also, as is often assumed, a systematic relation between actual price changes and wage changes, it follows that actual price inflation will be related to unemployment and expected price inflation. Furthermore, long-run equilibrium was defined as when actual inflation equals that expected, and then unemployment is at its 'natural' rate or NAIRU. Thus only if actual price inflation is not equal to expected price inflation will unemployment be different from its natural rate or NAIRU. (For the rest of this section we will assume that the NAIRU is the natural rate where demand equals supply.)

In the initial treatment it was assumed that wage changes, and therefore actual price changes, depended on unemployment and expected inflation, but the implicit direction of causation can be reversed. (In the Friedman explanation in Chapter 4, pages 67–70, this is clearly so.) In this case the level of unemployment, and thus of output, depends on the gap between actual and expected price inflation. Unemployment will only differ from the 'natural rate' if expected inflation differs from actual inflation. Policies will only be able to affect unemployment if they can affect the gap between actual and expected inflation. But *with rational expectations* people will be able to foresee the pattern and the effects of any systematic government policies. Thus if governments respond systematically to events, rather than erratically, they will not be able to drive a wedge between actual and expected inflation. Therefore they will not be able to affect output and employment, which will be at the natural rate except for unforeseeable random shocks.

The argument can also be summarised using the notation of Chapter 4. We had equation (4.6):

$$\dot{W} = f(U) + \dot{P}^e \tag{5.1}$$

If $\dot{P} = \dot{P}^e$, then $U = U_*$, the natural rate.

Again, for simplicity, assume an economy with no growth and also conventionally (though not unproblematically in this context) assume that wage increases are fully passed on into prices. With these assumptions $\dot{P} = \dot{W}$ so that (5.1) becomes, as in (4.7):

$$\dot{P} = f(U) + \dot{P}^e \tag{5.2}$$

And for $\dot{P} = \dot{P}^e$, $U = U_*$ or $0 = f(U_*)$.

Equation (5.2) can be rewritten as:

$$f(U) = \dot{P} - \dot{P}^e \tag{5.3}$$

Which can be rewritten (since the short-run Phillips Curve of Chapter 4 is always downward-sloping) as:

$$U = j(\dot{P} - \dot{P}^e) \tag{5.4}$$

with $U_* = j(0)$, where $j(\ )$ denotes another functional relationship. The implications are even clearer if (5.3) or (5.4) are rewritten as:

$$U - U_* = k(\dot{P} - \dot{P}^e) \tag{5.5}$$

with $k(\ )$ also denoting a functional relationship. Thus government can only affect U if it can affect $\dot{P} - \dot{P}^e$, which it cannot do by systematic policy if there are rational expectations. Furthermore, except for random shocks, with rational expectations $\dot{P} = \dot{P}^e$, therefore $U = U_*$.

This conclusion could be rephrased as saying either that with rational expectations there is no short-run trade-off between inflation and unemployment or that the Phillips Curve is vertical even in the short run. Under such conditions not only is systematic policy powerless, it is also unnecessary, as all unemployment is natural (except perhaps for some unforeseeable mistakes due to purely random shocks). In addition, as will be detailed later, if deflationary policies are foreseen they can be used to reduce inflation without any harmful effects on employment – an attractive prospect for a government.

As has been stated, the proposition that systematic government policy is impotent to change output and employment refers to the macroeconomic effects of both monetary and fiscal policy.[15] There might be microeconomic side-effects, popularly called 'supply-side' effects, from particular instruments of fiscal policy but these are a separate issue – they change the natural rate of unemployment itself rather than controlling movements around an existing natural rate.[16]

Various extensions of the model have been made (e.g. to deal with the empirical reality of business cycles, which are inconsistent with the original form[17]) but provided that output, or changes in output, can only be altered by affecting the gap between actual and expected prices the basic proposition holds, i.e. macroeconomic policy is ineffective.

The policy ineffectiveness proposition has been attacked from two main directions. One points to the requirements of rational expectations. In its simplest form there is a questioning, largely based on introspection, of whether people do form the best possible unbiased forecasts using all the information possibly available to them. However, the requirements of rational expectations can be weakened slightly and yet still retain the essentials of the policy ineffectiveness proposition, if all the other assumptions hold. Unbiased forecasts, with no systematic errors, are sufficient even if they are not the best possible forecasts. The ability to form such forecasts (which are on average correct) may be easier, and if the world moves smoothly enough then some unsophisticated 'rule-of-thumb' forecasts may also be unbiased. Furthermore the proposition does not require every single person to have rational expectation forecasts about every single variable in the economy, only about those which may affect their actions. For example, an individual worker whose earnings are fixed by collective bargaining and who is old enough not to be contemplating changing his or her employer, let alone occupation, does not need to trouble gathering information on as many aspects of the economy as the trade-union official engaged in the collective bargaining.

The assumption that everybody has full information on the structure of the economy (or at least as full as is needed for their own decisions) is attacked by pointing out that even 'experts' differ in their forecasts – as is apparent from reading the macroeconomic forecasts published by different institutions. Therefore it cannot be true that everybody knows the 'true' model of the economy, otherwise there would be unanimity. At its simplest: can believers in rational expectations and the policy ineffectiveness proposition also believe that advocates of Keynesian demand-management policies use the fullest and most correct information on the structure of the economy?

The idea that people have full information on the structure of the economy is also attacked as being implausible once one considers an economy which is occasionally subject to major structural changes. It may be possible to infer correctly the quantitative structure of a static economy by using accepted statistical techniques, but there are unsolved problems in how one can learn about changes – especially since each individual's behaviour will depend on (rational) expectations about how other people alter their (rational) expectations following a change. The actual path of the economy will itself therefore depend on expectations about expectations of how the path will evolve.

It should be noted that the attack on the realism of the rational expectations and widespread full-information assumption comes also from the adherents of older Monetarism. As explained in Chapter 3, pages 42–9, their disagreement with Keynesian stabilisation policy centred on the lack of knowledge by the government. They opposed stabilisation policy because it was powerful and effective, but likely to be wrongly used. This is the complete opposite of the policy ineffectiveness proposition.

The other main line of attack on the policy ineffectiveness proposition has been on the extra, sometimes implicit, assumptions needed for the proposition to hold. Yet again, the main argument reverts to the issue of whether wages and prices move smoothly enough for all markets to clear, including the labour market. If, for institutional or other reasons, wages and prices do not adjust smoothly and continuously there may be room for governments to affect output. For example, if wages are set for a year at a time, while governments can change their monetary policies more frequently, then monetary policy can be revised to take account of events which were not foreseeable at the time that most of the wage agreements currently in force were set.[18] In those countries (as contrasted with the USA) where the Executive is not elected separately, so that the government can command an almost automatic majority in the Parliament/Assembly, fiscal policies can also often be adjusted at shorter intervals than the typical duration of wage agreements. Thus fiscal policy can also react systematically to new events that could not have been rationally expected when wages were agreed. A wedge can thus be driven between actual price change and that expected when wages were set.[19]

On a more traditionally Keynesian view, wages (especially) are sticky over longish periods and do not respond smoothly to equilibrate supply and demand either as they are at the time of new bargaining, or as they are foreseen for the next year at the time of bargaining. In terms of symbols, once rigidities of this type are allowed for, then the functions (5.4) or (5.5) are no longer adequate representations of the determinants of unemployment and output.

Some defenders of the policy ineffectiveness proposition have retorted that wage and price rigidity in the face of unexpected changes would be sub-optimal for the parties involved – in the sense that both parties could gain from more flexible behaviour – and therefore there will not be such rigidities.[20] As discussed in Chapter 3, some Keynesians have defended the 'rationality' of rigidities, and others have said that whether or not a consistent microeconomic theoretical foundation can be found for rigid wages/prices they are simply a fact, and therefore cannot be ignored in a realistic analysis.

Although the flexibility of wage/price movements and their responsiveness to market forces of excess demand and supply has probably been the extra assumption most often found unacceptable by economists who oppose the policy ineffectiveness proposition, there have also been attacks on other assumptions to which the proposition is sensitive. The proposition does also seem vulnerable to some of these attacks,[21] but others have strong answers.

The latter include the suggestion that the government may have superior information to the private sector, which it can use to stabilise in response to events about which the private sector does not yet know. The answer to this is that if the government has such information, it would be more efficient to simply publicise it to the private sector which could then utilise it in its own decision-making. Similarly, the basic reasoning above which led to the ineffectiveness proposition was couched in terms of systematic policy being ineffective. The implication is that erratic policy, e.g. systematic policy jumbled-up with a purely random component, could fool people, who would not be able to forecast policies, and thus it would have real effects. However, within a standard neo-classical microeconomic framework, with the normative 'optimality' of a full-information market economy, purposely fooling people must reduce efficiency – individuals will come to the correct decisions if they know all prices (and therefore relative prices, including real wages). This retort basically reiterates the points made earlier: with rational expectations and flexible wages and prices the economy is at the natural rate except for unforeseeable shocks, and (as discussed in the previous chapter) the natural rate under assumptions of perfect competition, flexible wages/prices and full information is also the optimal rate. Even though it could have real effects, purposefully erratic policy, therefore, cannot improve the economy since fundamentally there is no macroeconomic problem to be solved by such policy.

The second line of attack could be summarised by saying that if embedded in a model which is not of the smoothly functioning neo-classical, monetarist type, then rational expectations on its own does not invalidate activist policy. For example,[22] if expectations are rational, but we have a rigid wage Keynesian world in which investment depends on expected output or growth in output, then an announcement of government intentions to run a stabilising fiscal policy if necessary, itself makes the economy more stable and the policy less necessary. Because firms expect output to be more stable, they will keep a steadier path of investment which will not fluctuate in response to temporary shocks to aggregate demand – they have confidence that shortfalls in demand will be rectified by the government. The stabilising of investment will lead to a more stable level of demand and output than if investment fluctuations reflected and thus amplified other fluctuations. In this way government fiscal policy has stronger stabilising properties when there are rational expectations in an otherwise typically Keynesian world.

Although, as already indicated, the older Monetarists and the New Classical school also do have important differences, the points analysed here indicate some of the areas of continuity. There is the stress on market clearing and equilibrium – the more detailed reasoning given by some proponents for equations like (5.4),[23] fit in well with the explanation in Chapter 4 that we stated is held by Friedman himself. There is also the implication that policy to affect economic activity is wrong because it can only work by fooling people and therefore is suboptimal. Finally, for here, both groups are against activist attempts at macroeconomic stabilisation policy.

There is a considerable literature on empirical testing of the policy ineffectiveness proposition. Our own subjective (biased) impression is that rational expectations seems to stand up to testing better in explaining behaviour in some well-structured particular asset markets, such as the Stock Exchange, but that as far as the full policy ineffectiveness proposition is concerned, the results go more against the proposition than in favour of it.[24]

A final comment on the implications of the policy might be called the 'Pascal's Wager Argument'. Pascal, the mathematician/philosopher, wrote that one cannot find conclusive proof whether God (he assumed only a Christian one) exists or not. However, it is worthwhile betting on the existence and acting as if one could be sure. Pascal's reason is that if God does not exist, and one acts as if He did, then the only loss is a relatively minor one of some inconveniences and passing-up of opportunities for occasional pleasurable activities. Conversely, however, if God does exist, and one acts as if He did not, then the gain is the minor one of avoiding some inconveniences and obtaining occasional pleasures but the loss is immense: eternal suffering through damnation. If one acts as if God exists and He does, then there is the corresponding immense gain. It is therefore prudent to always act as one would if one were sure of God's existence.

If the policy ineffectiveness proponents are correct, and everybody has full information about government policies and can correctly foresee their impact on prices, then a mistakenly systematic activist policy has little effect. It will not affect output and employment, but only change the price level. However, in a flexible price world where everybody knows fully about the price changes, inflation only has trivial costs for the economy.[25] Thus if the world is really that of the model of the policy ineffectiveness proposition, the mistaken use of monetary/fiscal policies does little harm.[26] If it really is Keynesian there are great gains available from using such policies. Conversely, if governments do not try to stabilise and the world is a rational expectations and flexible price one then the gain is trivial, but if the world is really Keynesian the loss from abstaining from stabilisation policy is very large. Thus in the face of not knowing whether the world is really Keynesian or whether it is really close to that of the ineffectiveness proposition, governments should wager on it being Keynesian and actively try to stabilise employment and output.

The last paragraph does assume that the government has enough information and sense to avoid destabilising policies. The policy conclusions of the current section would be disagreeable to a Monetarist of the older persuasion.

However, Monetarists who still believe that lack of information may lead to inadvertently destabilising policy now seem to be relatively few in number. One could, very contentiously (and unsympathetically), put the 'rational expectations revolution' into historical perspective by arguing that it came just when Keynesian economists were claiming that simulation of statistically-based quantitative econometric models showed that we do have enough information to avoid inadvertent destabilisation from activist policies. The argument against such policies then switched from being based on the assumption of insufficient information to being based on the assumption that very full information is available to everyone.[27]

CREDIBILITY AND CONSISTENCY

In addition to the above formal analysis of rational expectations models, the basic approach has been used to attack activist policies aimed at increasing employment from another angle, which is not limited to the formal models (though not incompatible with them either). This attack concentrates on the public's expectations of government policy. Although it has been strongly advocated by some economists who are associated with a belief in the rational expectations/market-clearing hypothesis, it can also be found in the writings of economists not of this persuasion.[28] It will be explained here in a context which is not limited to a world in which the policy ineffectiveness proposition holds. The crucial point it has in common with the full rational expectations models is the assertion that when people make their own decisions they will take into account their expectations of what the government is likely to be doing and its presumed effect on the economy.

For example, if the government frequently takes action to expand aggregate demand because it wants to expand employment, people will come to expect 'buoyant' aggregate demand and build this into their own wage/price-setting behaviour. There will be large increases in money wages (and therefore prices) because people expect the government to be increasing nominal aggregate demand, e.g. by increases in the money supply. Once such increases in money wages have occurred the government has an awkward choice – it can either 'validate' the wage increases by further increasing the money supply or it can refuse to do so. If it makes the former choice then it also proves people's expectations of its policies correct and they will then continue to act on the assumption of further expansionary policies. If it makes the latter choice there will be a shortfall of real demand (nominal aggregate demand will not increase as much as money wages and prices) and output will fall, or at least not increase as much as it otherwise would, and therefore the unemployment situation will deteriorate.

One way of putting this kind of dilemma is that there may be a 'time inconsistency' with otherwise optimal policies.[29] Considering in isolation any one period in which employment is likely to be lower than the government wants, e.g. because of a contractionary shock (whether from abroad such as a rise in oil prices, or at home such as a particularly high rise in wage settlements), the correct policy would be to have an expansionary monetary/ fiscal stance. But because of its effects on public expectations about future policies, the expansionary policy is inconsistent with the long-run aims of the government, especially its desire to avoid an inflationary spiral. The government would like people to believe that it will not 'bail out' the economy if there are contractionary shocks, so that wage/price behaviour will be moderated, but then reflate if there is contraction anyway. However, it cannot fool people indefinitely.

Another aspect of the dilemma can be seen when governments want to reduce inflation. This can be most easily seen by using the expectations-augmented Phillips Curve diagram. Consider an economy in which people expect $x\%$ price inflation. For simplicity, in the diagram again assume an economy with no natural growth in productivity, though again this is not at all essential to the argument. Also to keep the treatment most straightforward assume that the velocity of circulation of money supply is constant. Thus this economy would remain at the natural rate of unemployment U_* and price inflation $x\%$ (= money wage increases of $x\%$) if money growth were held steady at $x\%$, i.e. at point A in Fig. 5.1.

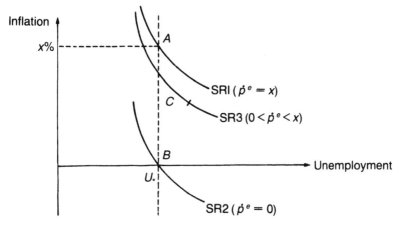

Figure 5.1 Credibility influence on inflation/unemployment split

If the government announces that it aims to reduce or get rid of inflation, and to achieve this it will reduce the growth of the money supply below $x\%$, what it would like to do is to move straight to lower inflation with no rise in unemployment, e.g. from A to B in Fig. 5.1. But if people think that it will not stick to its policies, they will not expect inflation to fall and the short-run Phillips Curve will remain the same (at curve SR1 in the diagram).[30] At the least they will not expect inflation to fall much, and the Phillips Curve will remain close to its original position (e.g. shift only to SR3 in the diagram). If the government goes ahead and reduces money supply growth anyway (perhaps fully to that consistent with point B, which in our simplified case is a constant *level* of money, i.e. zero growth), then the economy will move to a level of unemployment greater than the natural rate (somewhere like point C in the first period). Only if the government is fully believed when it announces its anti-inflationary policy could it move straight to zero inflation without going through a period of high, i.e. above natural rate, unemployment. If it were believed, it could announce that from now on the money supply would be held to a level consistent with no inflation and immediately expectations would alter and the whole short-run Phillips Curve would shift down (to SR2 in the diagram) so that the economy could remain at the natural rate with no inflation.

The more quickly the government is believed, the more quickly people will change their expectations and therefore the more quickly will the short-run Phillips Curve fall. Therefore the shorter will be the period for which the economy has to have unemployment above the natural rate.

If when the unemployment increases (e.g. to point C in the diagram) the government becomes alarmed at the cost of its policy and reflates the economy, not only will it fail this time to achieve its aims of the full reduction of inflation (to zero in our example) but it will increase the unemployment costs of future anti-inflationary policies. Next time round its anti-inflation policy will be less credible, therefore people will be even less willing to accept that any initial reduction in monetary growth will be sustained and therefore there will be less of a fall in their expectations of inflation. Therefore there will be less of a moderation in money wage increases. Diagrammatically, there will be less of a drop in the short-run Phillips Curve. Because of its effects on future credibility, each time the government adopts an easy policy not only is there a cost in immediate inflation, but there is a longer-term cost on future inflation and a longer-term cost on employment of future attempts at reducing inflation.

This sort of mechanism has also been used to explain why in some countries, such as the UK after 1980, tight monetary and fiscal policies were associated with large increases in unemployment but only slow reductions in the rate of money wage rises. The suggestion is that because over the preceding few decades governments had never stuck to a tight policy in the face of (what would have been transitory) increases in unemployment, people expected a weakening of the restrictions once again. This explanation seems to have appealed particularly to supporters of politicians who fought elections claiming that by reducing monetary growth, inflation could be painlessly cured,[31] but when in office found that the drop in inflation was not smooth and that it involved unemployment costs. The fact that it has been used in this way does not itself mean that it is false as an explanation of the events. If the other assumptions behind the policy ineffectiveness proposition are relevant, this explanation of actual events seems the best defence available. Once people do correctly realise what the government is doing, the proposition would hold again.

These general arguments about the possible long-run inconsistency of expansionary policies and the need for governments to retain credibility for anti-inflationary policies were stated earlier to be compatible with varying views on macroeconomics. Despite their formal consistency, they do not seem to us to fit very well into a belief that people have rational expectations and that markets clear quickly because of wage/price flexibility.

To start with, if wages and prices are flexible over relatively short periods, the government intentions that are relevant are also only over relatively short periods.[32] Credibility over such short periods should be easier to establish – especially in the early years of a new government when elections are not in the offing. In addition, the type of account just given when discussing credibility seems in some ways closer to an account of the expectations formation process in which expectations adapt slowly to past events.[33] In the spirit of rational expectations based on full current information one might want instead to posit that people have a good idea of government determination. This latter point is related to the one mentioned in the previous section as one of the problems with the rational expectations model, viz. the lack of a well-founded way for people to change their expectations following a structural change.

As far as the version dealing with the time inconsistency of optimal policies is concerned, if the full policy ineffectiveness proposition holds it hardly matters – whatever pattern of policies is used over time it will have no effect on employment. The notion that it would be helpful if only people could be fooled comes from a view of the world which is very different to that underlying the rational expectations/flexible wages and prices/market-clearing approach.

A related aspect of the credibility/time inconsistency argument that does not fit into the policy ineffectiveness paradigm is that the reason for worry is because expansionary policies, even in response to a shock which leads to a period of unemployment above the natural rate, will eventually lead to more inflation or to greater costs of reducing inflation. However, as already mentioned,[34] in a world of unbiased forecasts and price flexibility inflation is not a particularly serious problem.

The tone of the discussions about why governments should stick to tight policies implies that the public will tend to see the government as an either/or in its approach. *Either* always expand demand *or* always worry only about inflation. From the tone it seems to claim that not only possibly governments, but also the public assessing their policies, are too unsophisticated to be able to handle the notion that there may be more than one objective, with trade-offs between them, such that more precedence is given to control of inflation the higher it is (for any given level of unemployment) and more precedence given to employment the lower it is (for any given level of inflation). Any alleged inability of the public to comprehend anything but the most simplistic policy pattern seems to be at the opposite pole from the assumption which has typified recent rational expectations modelling, i.e. that all individuals are very well informed and capable of intelligent decision-making.

In fact, it seems to us that even those economists who do not accept the rational expectations approach in its technical meaning, but do accept rationality in its everyday meaning should be chary of the 'time incon-sistency' argument for *always* eschewing expansionary policies. It does not require immense sophistication for governments, or the public, to realise that there is a likelihood of multiple objectives, and that different policy stances may result from different relative levels of the actual variables involved.

Despite all our own caveats, it remains true that various economists from a variety of other inclinations share a worry about the long-run inflationary effects of expansionary policies. Some are always against such policies, but some who would otherwise favour such policies if applied when unemploy-ment is high nevertheless take the worry seriously. Many of these latter would advocate an incomes policy as a way out of the dilemma of time incon-sistency. If an adequate incomes policy is not achievable, then even the analysis of the last two paragraphs supports the view that there may be times of already high inflation when fears of fuelling further inflationary expectations will inhibit action, despite unemployment being at levels considered too high. This is not the same as saying that these fears should always inhibit expansionary policies.

CONCLUSION

The main part of this chapter has considered two arguments which would weaken the effects of macroeconomic policies aimed at altering output and employment. The first, the Ricardo–Barro theorem, if the assumptions were close enough to reality to be applicable, would weaken fiscal policy, though not monetary policy. The second, the Lucas–Sargent–Wallace policy ineffectiveness theorem would render both monetary and fiscal policies ineffective and also make them unnecessary.

The two arguments have several things in common. They both assume a great deal of knowledge and forward-looking behaviour which are claimed as rational – indeed the former argument is sometimes referred to as 'super-rationality' and the latter incorporates the concept of 'rational expectations'. On closer inspection they both also depend crucially on markets with no rigidities and institutional constraints – the former requires what are called perfect capital markets and the latter argument requires full price/wage flexibility. At the time of writing it seems that neither of the arguments has been used directly in popular discussions of the economy and politics, but they have been much debated by economists and (given the usual lags between professional economic theory and political influence) are likely to be used in the future to justify policies on stabilisation. Finally, and importantly, both arguments have in common that they not only weaken the effects of macroeconomic policies directed at changing employment but also weaken the objections to them and the risks of pursuing such policies.

The third argument considered has in common with the two preceding ones a basis in the importance of people's expectations. It concentrates on expectations of future government policies, and their feedback on to current decisions. Although often linked with the rational expectations approach, it is possible to argue that it is less powerful if embedded within the full set of assumptions of the policy ineffectiveness proposition. For some Keynesians it is an extra argument in favour of an incomes policy. If both governments and the public are capable of understanding macroeconomic policy rules that incorporate trade-offs between desirable objectives, then those who favour active use of monetary/fiscal policies can still advocate that expansionary policies should be used when appropriate. However, in the absence of effective incomes policies, the influence of expectations about future macro policies may further limit the conditions under which expansion of demand is considered appropriate even by the proponents of active macroeconomic intervention.

6

INTERNATIONAL LINKS

INTRODUCTION

So far we have followed most of the academic literature and much of the more general discussions in considering the possibility of government policy affecting employment and other macroeconomic goals, while ignoring the influence of relations with other countries. In this chapter we shall consider the way that the existence of trading and financial linkages with other countries can influence both the possibilities for demand management in any one country and the appropriate mix of monetary and fiscal policies. In the literature, allowing for these linkages is called 'open economy' analysis, while treating them as negligible, as we have implicitly done so far, is the 'closed economy' case.

The importance of these linkages will vary from country to country – some economies are much more open than others. A measure of the importance of trade could be the proportion of National Product which is exported, or the ratio of imports to National Income (the two are typically quite close for most countries), and these vary from country to country. For example, among the developed capitalist countries it is now (at the time of writing) about 10% for the US, about 15% for Japan, about 20–35% for the large EEC countries, and over 50% for some of the smaller countries such as Belgium. The degree of openness to financial flows, and their influence, is more difficult to measure. What will often be important is the extent to which an individual country (whose exchange rate is expected to be steady) can allow its interest rate to diverge from rates in other countries without inducing large capital flows.[1] This ability will depend both on formal controls over capital movements and on the extent to which its financial institutions are integrated into world markets. In many cases there are different opinions as to the margin of divergence in interest rates that a country could achieve.

After an initial brief review of the concepts and terminology to be used, we shall have to consider two aspects of the relationship between employment policies and the external links of the economy, which are closely interrelated. It is expositionally more convenient to deal first with what many would think is the less fundamentally important of the two issues: the effects of monetary as compared to fiscal policy in an open economy, and therefore the best choice of either policy alone or combination of them. This is discussed on pages 108–17. External constraints (pages 118–21) deals with the interrelated issue of whether the existence of trading and/or financial market links with other countries rules out any attempt of macroeconomic management aimed at unemployment.

In the section on pages 121–3 we move on to consider the effects on employment of exchange rate changes occurring for reasons other than monetary/ fiscal policy aimed primarily at employment itself. There is also a brief discussion of the role of external events as possible explanations of recent increases in unemployment.

The analysis of these sections has implications for the desirability of co-operation between countries, and this is dealt with on pages 123–8.

CONCEPTS AND TERMINOLOGY

The basic concepts needed for this chapter are dealt with in the standard introductory textbooks. We shall just very briefly review them here. We shall also set out our terminology as this sometimes differs between sources. This section is only a brief review and is unlikely to suffice for those who have never looked at the foreign trade/balance of payments/exchange rate material in a textbook.

Definitions and types of system

One particular definition which varies between texts reflects a variation in national practice. In many countries the exchange rate is defined as: number of units of domestic currency per unit foreign currency – e.g. in Germany it would be so many DM per $. In a few countries, including the United Kingdom, the reverse measurement is used: units of foreign currency per unit domestic currency – e.g. so many $ per £. We shall use the latter definition, not only chauvinistically because we live in England, but also because it fits in better with standard economists' practice in other parts of economics. Under this definition, if there is an excess demand for a currency in the foreign exchange markets then the exchange rate (as measured) will tend to rise, which is what is normally expected to happen to a price when there is excess demand. Thus when we talk about a rise in the exchange rate we mean that the currency appreciates or is revalued. When we talk about a fall in the rate we mean that it depreciates or is devalued.

Although there is not a definite consensus, we shall follow what seems to be the common practice of using the terms 'devaluation' and 'revaluation' to describe discrete movements in exchange rates when governments are attempting to run a fixed-rate system. Conversely, we shall tend to use the terms 'depreciation' and 'appreciation' for movements within a floating-rate system.

The analysis of whether monetary or fiscal policy in an open economy will affect output at all, and if so, by how much, will turn out to require consideration not only of the degree of openness but also of the extent to which governments are simultaneously trying to control movements in exchange rates by direct intervention in foreign exchange markets. The two polar cases considered in textbooks are floating exchange rates and fixed exchange rates. The latter is usually defined as where the government announces and attempts to enforce a particular exchange rate, with only a very narrow margin of fluctuations around the 'central rate'. The margin is also made public. In analysis we usually ignore the margin and treat fixed rates as exactly fixed. In this context the government usually acts through the Central Bank – we shall lump the two together in this chapter and not worry about the relationship between them in those few countries in which the Central Bank retains independence. Often the two bodies are jointly referred to as 'the authorities'.

However, in the past two decades there has often been an intermediate state of affairs. Sometimes this is called (in a value-laden term) 'dirty floating', as compared to 'clean floating' where the authorities do not intervene at all in the foreign exchange markets. Sometimes the recent situation is called (less emotively) 'managed floating', which is the phrase we shall adopt. What has happened in these cases is that the authorities have not explicitly announced a target exchange rate which they will defend, but nevertheless they do have a fairly narrow range in which they try to keep the exchange rate. However, if they cannot do so, they will allow market forces to push the rate outside their preferred range, often again without any open statement. In addition, sometimes the authorities will not have any particular target, but will simply intervene to slow down exchange rate movements when they think that the movements are too sharp and may be developing too much speculative momentum.

For the purposes of analysing the role of demand-management policies aimed at altering employment in an open economy, the relevant distinction will mainly be whether the authorities are holding the exchange rate close to some target or not. Thus we shall generally distinguish between explicitly fixed rates and managed rates with an unannounced target on the one hand, and on the other hand 'clean' floating and managed floating which attempts to slow down movements but not to prevent them.[2] For simplicity we shall call the former 'fixed' and the latter 'floating'. The latter will also include the cases of attempted management, where governments would like to stick to a target rate and occasionally have some limited intervention but where in the face of much pressure, they are unable (or do not want) to regularly commit enough reserves to intervention to keep rates at the target. Obviously in practice it may sometimes be difficult to distinguish full-hearted but unsuccessful intervention from half-hearted and unsuccessful intervention, but the analysis will (we hope) clarify which factors to consider within our context of macroeconomic policy.

When a group of countries fix their exchange rates against each other, but float as a bloc against non-member countries, a member should be treated as on fixed rates if its own rate does not individually dominate the bloc rate *vis-à-vis* the rest of the world. This applies to the members of the exchange rate mechanism of the European Monetary System (though some commentators feel that the Deutschmark sometimes can pull the whole of the ecu behind it at times of major movements against the US dollar or Japanese yen).

Policies to affect the balance of payments and exchange rates

As well as direct intervention in foreign exchange markets, governments may take domestic monetary and fiscal policy actions in order to support or influence exchange rates. Actions which raise interest rates compared to those abroad tend to raise exchange rates by encouraging capital inflows/discouraging outflows. Actions which squeeze domestic income and spending will tend to discourage imports, and therefore improve the current account of the balance of payments. In most cases,[3] if the level of interest rates were simultaneously held constant, the improvement in the current account would be expected to raise the exchange rate, all other things equal, and to force the authorities to intervene in the foreign exchange market if there are fixed rates. The same direction of pressure on the current account would occur if changes in incomes occurred without prior government action.

If we assume that home demands for imported goods and foreign demand for exports are elastic enough,[4] then a rise in the prices of domestically produced goods as compared to those produced overseas will lead to a deterioration of the current account of the balance of payments. Conversely, a fall in the relative price of home goods will improve the current account. As in the previous paragraph, *ceteris paribus*, the changes in the current account will tend to affect the exchange rate. Note also that changes in relative prices occur if domestic prices are constant, and those overseas change.

The short-run elasticities (of home demands for imports and overseas demand for exports) may be much less than the long-run ones, which can lead to the phenomenon known as the 'J-curve'. For example, a rise in domestic prices relative to overseas ones will then initially improve the current account because of the inelastic demands – in the short run the higher prices of exports are not offset by reductions in the volume of exports or increases in the volume of imports. In the longer run (typically after a year to two) as the quantities demanded do adjust to the changed prices, the current account deteriorates.

The name 'J-curve' comes from the case where a change in relative prices occurs from a devaluation and therefore domestic prices fall relative to foreign ones, and is illustrated in Fig. 6.1 If there is a devaluation at time t_0, the short-run lack of elasticity initially leads to a fall in the current account, eventually because of the greater long-run elasticities, the current account rises, relative to the position before t_0. With some imagination the graph can be seen as a tilted letter J.

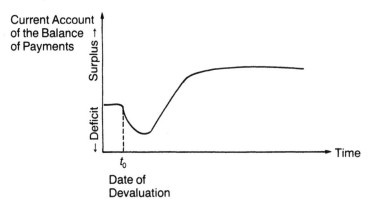

Figure 6.1 The 'J'-curve

Similarly, overseas changes in income will also affect our exports and hence the current account.

As well as these traditional channels for the way that domestic policies (and changes for any other reasons in relative interest rates, prices and incomes) affect the balance of payments and exchange rate, another channel has been suggested since the early 1970s. This is popularly known as 'the monetary theory of the balance of payments'.[5] It concentrates rather more on the capital account of the balance of payments, and says that if the supply of money in a country is increased (relative to that abroad) then the excess supply of money will result not only in people spending extra on goods including imports, which worsens the current account, but also in their demanding overseas as well as domestic assets, and hence to a capital account deficit.[6] Conversely, if the domestic money supply is reduced below demand, then as people try to build up their money balances they will not only cut back on consumption, but also sell other assets (including overseas ones) thus improving the capital account.

One way of summarising and extending the discussion so far in this section is to list the various factors that are often thought to lead to a change in the overall balance of payments when there are fixed rates, or, equivalently, to a movement of the exchange rate when there are floating rates. (In the Appendix we try to clarify the equivalence between balance of payment surplus/deficits and exchange rate appreciation/depreciation for those who are still uncertain after reading a standard text.) Different economists tend to place more stress on different factors out of the list we shall consider, and which factor is stressed can explain differences in views on the likely impacts of policies to increase employment in open economies, and on the relevant constraints on policy-makers. For simplicity [!] in this list of factors, we shall discuss them as those which lead to a 'deterioration' in the balance of payments, i.e. decline in surplus or increase in deficit,[7] or, equivalently, to a depreciation of the exchange rate. Obviously reversing the direction of change of the causal factors would imply an improvement in the balance of payments or, equivalently, a rise in the (UK definition) exchange rate.

The factors are (i) a rise in domestic real income, (ii) fall in overseas real income, (iii) rise in home prices as compared to overseas prices, (iv) fall in home interest rates and (v) rise in overseas rates. These would tend to lead to deterioration in the balance of payments/exchange rate depreciation. These influences could have changed as a result of government monetary/fiscal policies or for some other reason. It is important to note that the government policies may have been expressly undertaken to 'improve' the balance of payments or 'protect' the exchange rate. In addition on the 'monetary' theory, a rise in domestic money creation relative to demand for money would have its effect, without having to consider the possible channel of interest rates or income.[8]

Since 1973, and its dramatic rise in oil prices, attention has also been paid to the effects of an overseas price rise in a product for which the domestic import demand is inelastic. In such a case the overseas price rise harms the balance of payments rather than improving it.

There may be changes in exchange rates or in the balance of payments not because the factors listed above have changed, but because they are expected to change in the near future. If changes are anticipated, future exchange rates will be expected to be different from current values. But a changing exchange rate alters the attractiveness of holding domestic as compared to overseas assets. For example, unless offset by a sufficient rise in domestic interest rates compared to those abroad, if a depreciation is expected people will find it more profitable to switch now out of domestic assets into overseas ones. They can then switch back later on, when they can get more domestic currency from the sale of foreign currency because of the drop in the exchange rate which has occurred in the meantime. (If domestic currency is 'cheaper' on the exchange market, more of it can be bought for any given amount of foreign currency.)

With floating rates, expectations of future rate changes are likely to start to alter the rate immediately. In this sense the foreign exchange markets are sometimes described as 'forward looking'. There are strong disagreements over whether there are likely to be jumps in exchange rates because of unjustified swings in expectations – unjustified either in the direction of the switch in expectations or in its magnitude, with people overreacting to small changes in what should be the underlying determinants of the rates. There are also disagreements over whether exchange rate changes often develop their own momentum, leading to explosive movements,[9] or at least to vastly excess volatility.[10] In the recent literature these disagreements are related to ideas about 'rational expectations', as discussed in the previous chapter. In the earlier literature they are expressed as notions about speculators' motives and behaviour.[11]

Effects on income

To understand the implications of the openness of an economy for its level of employment, we have to consider not only the impacts of domestic variables on the balance of payments or exchange rate, but also the reverse causation from changes in the balance of payments or exchange rate on to domestic activity.

One effect can be seen most easily from the standard National Income definitions.[12] Any increase in exports of goods and services will count as increased earnings and hence raise National Income. Similar results come from a decrease in imports. Thus any improvement in the current account will, *ceteris paribus*, increase Income and a deterioration will reduce Income. Furthermore, an increase in the volume of exports will typically increase employment in the industries supplying the goods (assuming they are not simply diverted from the home market).

In a Keynesian framework, a change in the current account of the balance of payments will also have multiplier effects on the economy in addition to the size of the initial impact.

The domestic price of imported goods can change if their price changes in the currency of the originating country or if there is a change in the exchange rate. For example, the price of imports will increase if there is a devaluation (provided that the suppliers do not cut their own price to our market by enough to offset the devaluation).[13] The size of the impact effect on prices will depend on the openness of the economy. For example, a country importing 20% of its goods which has a 10% fall in the exchange rate could expect a 2% extra rise in its overall domestic price level from the direct effect on import prices. If workers then obtain 'compensation' for the increased cost of living there will be greater effects on prices as the price of domestic production increases.[14]

If we assume that most governments usually like increases in output, at least at times when they do not feel that demand is too high, but dislike rises in prices, then we see that a change in the exchange rate has ambivalent results for a government. A fall in the exchange rate helps output and employment (assuming there is no absolute full-employment constraint) but harms the limitation of price rises. Conversely an appreciation harms output and employment but helps limit price rises.[15]

Furthermore, there is likely to be a clash between the interests of those who remain in employment throughout, and those who gain/lose jobs. If money wages move sluggishly and there is not full compensation for cost-of-living changes, then those who remain in employment increase their living-standards when consumer prices fall as compared to money wages because of an appreciation, whereas living standards are squeezed when prices rise because of an exchange rate fall.[16]

The final influence to be considered here from the balance of payments on to domestic activity and policy variables is the effect of the balance of payments on to the money supply. If there is a balance of payments surplus, then there will be pressure for the money supply to increase,[17] conversely for a balance of payments deficit. In this sense we have an expansionary 'monetary' impetus from a balance of payments surplus, working in the same direction as the income linkages stressed by the Keynesian analysis above.[18]

With both the monetary and the income channels, governments can try to offset the impacts on to the domestic economy. With the latter channel the impact can be offset by changing the fiscal budget balance in the same direction as the balance of payments – an increase in a balance of payments current account surplus is expansionary and offsetting requires an increase in the budget surplus (or reduction in budget deficit), and so on. The effects on the money supply may be counteracted by open-market operations aimed at altering the domestic-based components of the money supply – a balance of payments surplus increases the money supply and offsetting it requires a sale of government bonds so as to mop up the extra money base,[19] and so on.

The offsetting of the monetary effects of the balance of payments is usually referred to as 'sterilisation'. There is considerable debate over whether sterilisation is always, sometimes, or never, possible.[20] It seems likely to us that the possibility of sterilisation will vary with the size of the flows needing offsetting and will vary between countries according to the structure of their financial markets and degree of financial openness.[21]

As shown in the Appendix, with 'cleanly' floating rates there is no effect on to the domestic money supply, since the balance of payments is always in balance.

MONETARY AND FISCAL POLICIES IN AN OPEN ECONOMY

As is apparent from the material reviewed in the previous section, there are a large number of ways that domestic events can affect the components of the balance of payments. The overall effect of any particular policy on the total balance or on the exchange rate will depend both on the relative strength of the different impacts that it has on such variables as income, interest rates, or prices (or money supply if this has a role independently of the interest rate), and also on the relative strength of each impact on to each component of the balance of payments. In addition the feedback on to the domestic economy from any change in the balance of payments or exchange rate will vary with the degree of sterilisation of monetary effects and degree of openness to trade. Where different writers end up with conflicting results in this area, the cause will often be that they have chosen different assumptions as the ones they think most relevant.

An exhaustive taxonomy of all possible cases, according to all theories/ assumptions ever suggested and for both fixed and floating rates, would be exhaustingly long and tedious in our context.[22] We shall restrict our treatment to some of what we judge to be the more commonly used analyses and empirically relevant assumptions. To some extent the notes show the sensitivities of the results to the assumptions. We shall also deal with expansionary policies – contractionary ones will have symmetrically opposite results.

Wages and prices unresponsive to external events

The framework which is still probably most used by economists is the Mundell–Fleming model.[23] It fits very neatly into the basic IS–LM model, and can be straightforwardly (and diagrammatically) incorporated into that model.[24] In its common form, the Mundell–Fleming analysis also assumes fixed money wages and domestic prices, and ignores any feedback from exchange rate changes on to the domestic price level. It is thus very much in the Keynesian approach to employment and output discussed in Chapter 2, and fits best into a view in which full employment is not the virtually continual norm. As with that Keynesian approach, flexible prices can be incorporated into the Mundell–Fleming model and typically do not make too much difference to the results as far as output is concerned, provided that nominal wages are still assumed to be exogenous.[25] We will stick to the fixed price version.[26]

In building up analyses in this framework, note that increases in income always lead to increases in imports and to a decline in the current account of the balance of payments. Increases in interest rates, *ceteris paribus*, lead to an improvement in the capital account. Thus the open economy effects of an expansionary fiscal policy may be ambiguous. In a closed economy there would be a rise in income *and* interest rates (for a 'pure' fiscal policy holding the money stock constant, and therefore where a rise in the transactions demand for money requires a rise in interest rates to restore equilibrium in the money market).

For convenience we will outline the process of adjustment as if the economy tended towards its closed economy configuration and then, subsequently, the external forces moved the economy to its final equilibrium. We do not claim that this sequence is necessarily realistic. Alternative sequences would alter the dynamic adjustment process, but not the final equilibrium described. We will also start the analysis with an initial balance of payments/ exchange rate equilibrium.

The overall effect of fiscal policy on the balance of payments at this stage depends on the relative strength of the current and capital account effects. If international capital movements are small relative to the trading account there will be a balance of payments deficit (*ex ante* only, with floating rates); if there is substantial capital mobility in response to interest rate differentials then there will be a balance of payments surplus.[27] We deal with this latter case, as it is now thought to be more realistic for virtually all countries. What then happens depends on which further cases are relevant for the particular country.

If there are floating rates: then the incipient balance of payments surplus (which is equivalent to an excess demand for the domestic currency on the foreign exchange markets)[28] leads to an appreciation. The appreciation leads to rise in imports/fall in exports and hence, eventually at least, to a fall in output and income back from the initial expansion.[29] In the limiting case of 'perfect' capital mobility, where any international interest rate differential at all leads to overwhelming capital flows, the exchange rate has to appreciate so far that the level of income returns to its initial level (so that domestic interest rates can return to their initial level, as the transactions demand for money declines back to its initial level). Thus, in the case where capital movements are sufficiently responsive to interest differentials and so dominate changes in the current account, the effects of an expansionary fiscal policy are partially crowded out by the effects of the induced appreciation. In the limiting case of perfect capital mobility, there is complete crowding out, and pure fiscal policy is completely ineffective.

If the country is keeping its exchange rate fixed: (and continuing with the case where the rise in interest rates induces a capital account surplus that outweighs the current account deficit due to the initial increase in income) then the results of the overall balance of payments surplus depend on whether the country can sterilise the monetary effects of the balance of payments surplus. If they can, and do, then the expansionary impact of the fiscal policy can continue.[30] If the authorities cannot sterilise the domestic money supply, but have to allow an increase because of the balance of payments surplus, the induced money increase will not only lead to a reduction in interest rates down toward the initial level, but also to a further increase in income. Thus with fixed rates an expansionary fiscal policy has its initial impact on domestic income and output reinforced by the feedback from the external sector.

The open economy thus provides another route for the 'crowding-out' of a purely fiscal expansion – if there are floating exchange rates and high capital mobility then output and employment are crowded out by the fall in exports and the rise in imports arising from the induced appreciation. Many commentators have suggested that this form of crowding out can explain, for example, both the dramatic rise in UK unemployment in 1980 and the slowdown of the US boom in 1985. In both cases a fiscal policy that was relatively loose compared to monetary policy led to large rises in interest rates and to major appreciation of the exchange rate.[31] Obviously, not everybody accepted this diagnosis. In both countries various other explanations were preferred, some of which are dealt with elsewhere in this book.[32]

However, it is important to note that those who use the assumptions of the floating rate open-economy world with strong capital mobility as an argument against using expansionary fiscal policies to reduce unemployment cannot consistently also refer to the older 'crowding out' reasons for opposing such policies. As discussed in Chapter 2, the mechanism for the older crowding out is the rise in interest rates which chokes off private investment in new capital goods. In the case of the open economy, the crowding out occurs precisely because interest rates cannot rise appreciably in the new equilibrium because they are ultimately pegged by the forces of international (financial) capital mobility. Thus the two forms of crowding out cannot occur simultaneously.

In the closed economy case, the crowding out of investment can be avoided by using monetary policy instead of fiscal policy, or at least sufficiently in conjunction with it, to stop interest rates rising. We now therefore examine the use of monetary policy in an open economy to see if similar conclusions hold.

If there is an expansionary monetary policy (for symmetry, we analyse the 'pure' case with an unchanged fiscal policy) then in a closed economy income would increase and interest rates would fall. Thus there will tend to be a deficit in both current and capital accounts under fixed exchange rates – under floating rates the rate would depreciate.

As above, we distinguish the various further possibilities.

With fixed rates: if the authorities can sterilise the monetary effects of the balance of payments deficit, then the deficit will continue and income will remain at its new, higher, level. However, the continuance requires also that the authorities can continue to finance the drain on the foreign currency reserves. This may be impossible after a time. Reserves will run out and eventually any overseas borrowing ability will also probably dry up unless there is an indication that the balance of payments deficit will be rectified. The government will then either have to reverse its initial monetary expansion or else devalue. If it cannot run a balance of payments deficit for a long period and yet it resists devaluation, then monetary policy cannot be used to expand an open economy, even with sterilisation.[33] If the Central Bank cannot sterilise the monetary effects of the balance of payments deficit, the money supply will automatically decrease until it returns to its original (pre-monetary policy expansion) level. This will reverse the increase in income which will also return to its initial level, as will interest rates.

If there are floating rates: the decline in the exchange rate will encourage exports and discourage imports. The current account will improve, leading to a further increase in income. There will also be an increase in interest rates back towards their initial level as spending increases further, with the money supply fixed at its new, post-initial monetary expansion, level. In the extreme case of perfect capital mobility, the depreciation will continue until the induced extra income (and transactions demand for money) is sufficient to bring interest rates fully back to the initial level.

In general then, if exchange rates are fixed pure monetary expansion will not be a viable way of increasing employment. If, however, exchange rates can vary, then the fall in the exchange rate will reinforce the initial expansionary effect of the money supply increase upon employment.

We stated above that it was precisely in the case of fixed rates that fiscal policy works effectively in an open economy, whereas with floating rates and high international capital mobility fiscal policy is less effective – in the limit, with perfect capital mobility, fiscal policy is completely nullified. However, if there are floating rates then monetary policy can be used to increase income.[34] Thus at least one of the two types of policy can always be used to expand income even in an open economy.[35]

Less sluggish wages and prices. Inflation and crises

Once we allow for some flexibility in nominal wages and in prices of domestically produced goods, there are more possibilities in the effects of monetary and fiscal policies. We shall continue to assume that prices and wages are *not* so flexible that they would ensure continuous full employment (except for any very short random shocks).

Many of the formal models used to discuss monetary and fiscal policies in open economies which have flexible wages and prices continue to incorporate purchasing power partity (PPP) as a property of long-run equilbrium. PPP states that the same homogeneous traded goods have to sell at the same price in all countries. The simplest forms of PPP ignore differentiated goods, goods which are not traded and also changes in transport costs. They therefore simply say that price levels in different countries have to be the same in equilibrium.[36] Therefore changes in the domestic price level when adjusted for changes in the exchange rate have to match overseas price changes. If we denote the domestic price level by P; the index of the rest of the world's price level as denominated in their own currencies by P_W; the exchange rate (UK definition) by e; and use the 'dot' notation of Chapter 4; then purchasing power parity says:[37,38]

$$\dot{P} + \dot{e} = \dot{P}_W \tag{6.1}$$

If PPP relationships such as equation (6.1) only apply to the long-run equilibrium they may not tell us too much about the short run, this depends on how quickly prices/exchange rates adjust, and in response to what forces. If we also assume that wages/prices react to excess demands and supplies, even if sluggishly, then long-run equilibrium will also be a position of full employment. As in the discussion of Chapters 3 and 4, the long-run equilibrium, if it is ever closely approached, would then anyway not be particularly relevant for purposeful government employment policy.

Because the exchange rate market is a market for an easily traded asset, in the absence of exchange controls it is likely to move quickly in response to changes in demand/supply in that market. The demand and supply themselves will depend on expectations about the future. This means that the effects of monetary/fiscal policies will depend on how they affect expectations. In this way the effects of the policies may be speeded up and/or amplified, or else may be retarded, as compared to the effects which would occur if expectations were not altered by the policy.[39]

For example, an expansion in the money supply may lead to a quick fall in the exchange rate, even if incomes only react to the expansion with a lag and domestic prices also do not increase immediately. This could happen because people expect that eventually price levels will rise,[40] and, by PPP, the exchange rate will eventually have to fall. However, because people will not want to make avoidable foreign exchange losses they will start to sell (or postpone buying) the home currency on the exchange markets, driving the exchange rate down. There will therefore be an immediate depreciation. The same result would also follow directly from the 'monetary theory'.[41,42] But the depreciation has two further effects on the domestic economy. It adds to the increase in demand created by the rise in the supply of money (or the fall in interest rates engineered by the Central Bank to increase the money stock).[43] The depreciation also raises the domestic consumer price level because of the rise in the price of imports. Overall domestic prices therefore rise faster and further than they would in the absence of the quick exchange rate repercussions. Therefore the 'cost' of unemployment reduction (the rise in prices) is felt more quickly.

If some people who deal in foreign exchange tend to simply extrapolate recent changes as a guide to what is likely to happen in the near future, the depreciation can develop its own momentum.[44] The resulting 'exchange rate crisis' and spiralling 'imported inflation' as the rate plummets (leading to further prices rises, and further depreciation) can cause governments to reverse the monetary expansion in a bid to stop the 'crisis' and halt the induced cost-of-living rise.[45]

If there are fairly fixed exchange rates, or managed floating, speculators may predict the possibility of future devaluation because of the price rises expected to result from the initial monetary (and/or fiscal) expansion. They will sell the currency on the foreign exchange markets. This leads to a balance of payments deficit on the short-term capital account,[46] possibly well before the rises in income and domestic prices send the trading account into deficit. The deficit encourages further expectations of a devaluation. As the capital outflow momentum builds up, the government is forced to squeeze the economy to 'reassure the market'. It may even have to concede a limited devaluation and yet introduce contractionary monetary/fiscal policies to convince people that there will be no further devaluations. Part, at least, of the French experiment of 1981–3 can be seen in these terms (note that France was part of the fixed exchange rate mechanism of the European Monetary System). The failure of the French experiment has been widely cited in Europe as a cautionary tale by those who believe that expansionary policies are either unwise or impossible within a single country.[47]

Returning to the case of floating rates, these depreciation effects of an expansionary monetary policy, even without speculators naïvely extrapolating recent changes, are reinforced once we allow for international capital mobility in response to interest rate differentials. Because the monetary policy is typically accompanied (or achieved) by a quick drop in interest rates, the exchange rate depreciates for this reason – as with the Mundell–Fleming assumptions. However, the interesting possibility arises of 'overshooting', that is, that the exchange rate actually jumps too far down and depreciates further than its new equilibrium level and then gradually appreciates back up to the new equilibrium level (which is still below the original level).

The key to the 'overshooting' model[48] is that if there is very strong capital mobility, and we assume that asset markets, including the foreign exchange markets, clear very quickly, then there must be a relationship between expected exchange rate changes and interest rate differentials. The relationship is simplest in the case of perfect capital mobility. Then along an equilibrium path,[49] where the demand for internationally traded assets denominated in each currency must match their given supply, any differential in interest rates must be offset by an expected appreciation/depreciation. For example, if the UK £ is expected to depreciate over the next year by 5% against the US $, people will only willingly hold sterling assets if the return on them is 5% higher than on dollar assets. The formal models also often assume rational expectations (as defined in the previous chapter) and an absence of random shocks, which together imply that there are no mistakes, so that expected exchange rate changes equal actual changes. Thus, again using the dot notation to represent percentage changes, letting e be the exchange rate, i the home interest and i_w the 'world' interest rates, the implication is that:[50]

$$\dot{e} = i_w - i \qquad\qquad (6.2)$$

If an expansionary monetary policy is announced, and is expected to continue, i will fall and be expected to remain below its initial value (which for simplicity we take as equal to i_w) for some time – because domestic producer prices only rise sluggishly, the increase in the nominal money supply will not be immediately eroded by a price rise and therefore interest rates have to fall to equate the demand and supply of money. For a while, at least, $i_w - i$ is positive, therefore so is $\dot{e}$. That means the exchange rate is appreciating during this process. However, as stated earlier, the final equilibrium point must be with the exchange rate below its initial, pre-monetary expansion, level. If the rate is to appreciate up over a period before it reaches its final level, it must be below the final level during this period. Therefore it must have jumped down and depreciated *too far* immediately after the monetary expansion. Hence the 'overshooting'.

On the assumption that domestic wages and producer prices move slowly, the overshooting and excess depreciation mean that the economy goes through a period where its competitiveness is higher than it will eventually settle down to be. This extra competitiveness leads to an extra improvement in the balance of trade and hence a boost to output and employment in the short run.[51]

Later on, using this analysis, we shall return to what happens in the reverse situation of a monetary squeeze, when we discuss reasons for the increases in unemployment in some countries. That is, if governments try to impose tight targets to reduce inflation, there will be not just an appreciation of the exchange rate, but an excess appreciation soon after the tightening is announced (if it is believed). This appreciation helps to immediately control inflation, as the price of imported goods is reduced below trend, but at the cost of increasing the unemployment associated with the squeeze, due to the loss of international competitiveness. When the appreciation is partially reversed, competitiveness may start to recover, but governments concerned about inflation may be tempted to try to limit the depreciation by raising interest rates further, harming any return to full employment.

Despite the reasoning so far, there have been many occasions in recent years when an unexpected increase in the money supply has triggered a rise in the exchange rate, not a fall. The most likely explanation in these cases is that in a country where the authorities are known to have monetary targets, they may want to reverse, or at least limit, any undesired breach of the money supply. Exchange market participants therefore expect the authorities to implement a rise in interest rates, which will lead to a rise in the exchange rate.

Real wage bargaining

Although our concern in this chapter has been primarily with *employment policies* in the open economy, so far we have followed the literature in being rather cavalier about behaviour of firms and workers in the labour market. The Mundell–Fleming approach usually simply follows the first generation type of Keynesian model and assumes both nominal wages and prices constant. As stated in Chapter 3, more recent analyses of the same assumptions point out that the underlying behaviour of such rigid wages/prices is that workers and firms are 'off' their 'normal' supply-and-demand schedules. Workers will take jobs, even though real wages do not rise, and firms will offer jobs and sell the product even though real wages have not fallen (and price/wage margins have not risen). It is possible to adapt Mundell–Fleming to allow for firms only to offer more employment if real wages fall (money

wages fixed, prices rising), provided that workers are involuntarily unemployed in the sense that they would take jobs even at a real wage which is
lower than the going one. The standard analyses of quick movements of
exchange rates together with sluggish wages/prices implicitly also assume
either that workers will take jobs irrespective of what happens to real wages in
the short run or that firms'/employees' expectations happen to lag behind
reality in a way that allows the goods demanded to be produced.[52]

There is another group of analyses, often applied to post-1970 experience,
which makes an alternative assumption which is claimed to be realistic for
many developed economies.[53] The assumption is that money wages *closely*
follow prices, in such a way as to keep real wages constant. The justification
for this assumption looks at one of two types of institution. *First*, those
countries with strong trade unions, where union wage claims aim at constant
(or steadily increasing) real wages – this is the 'real wage resistance', or 'real
wage target', approach mentioned in Chapter 4.[54] *Second*, some countries
have formally indexed wages to prices. That is, wages in between bargaining
rounds, are automatically increased if the cost of living (usually measured by
the Retail or Consumer Price Index) increases.

The details of the argument vary between authors. Some, but not all, have
firms producing more, and taking on more employees, only if the real wage
drops. The general results on the use of monetary and fiscal policy, on this
assumption, depend on an important distinction in the meaning of the term
'real wage', which was mentioned in Chapter 4. As far as workers are
concerned, the real wage which matters is the money wage relative to some
overall measure of consumer prices, or cost of living. For a firm, what matters
is the money wage relative to the price at which the product can be sold – it is
this which determines whether it is worthwhile hiring more labour. The
former measure is usually called 'the consumption real wage' or 'consumer
real wage'; the latter is the 'producer' or 'production' real wage. In a closed
economy, at the aggregate level the two indices will coincide. In an open
economy the two may diverge if the prices of imported goods change relative
to the prices of home-produced goods.[55]

In a closed economy, if money wages and prices are highly flexible, but real
wages are fixed, then full employment cannot be achieved by monetary or by
fiscal policies.[56] In an open economy with floating exchange rates, however, it
is possible to change employment. As before, we consider that the realistic
case is where there is some capital mobility. A monetary expansion would
simply lead to an equal percentage increase in nominal wages, in home
producer prices and in the domestic price of imports (via an equal depreciation). There would be no change in real wages, and therefore no change in
employment or output. However, a fiscal expansion would lead to an
appreciation of the exchange rate. Although this will harm exports and
increase imports, nevertheless there will be an overall increase in output. The

mechanism is that the appreciation reduces the price of imports relative to that of home-produced products. The overall cost of living or Consumer Price Index, which reflects both imported and home product prices, falls relative to the home producer price (both may rise, but the latter rises more than the former). Since money wages are linked to the cost of living, they therefore fall *relative* to producer prices. As a result the production real wage falls, even though the consumption real wage has remained constant. The fall in the production real wage encourages firms to hire more workers.

The result is that by leading to an appreciation, and driving a wedge between consumption and production real wages, fiscal policy can have an expansionary effect. This result applies to floating rates with high capital mobility. It was precisely in this case that fiscal policy did not work at all in the case of fixed money wages and fixed prices.

Conclusions

The last sentence leads to one of the conclusions of this section. In general, in an open economy with less than full employment, it will be possible to expand employment and output by the appropriate use of monetary and/or fiscal policy. The correct choice of whether to use monetary, fiscal or some combination of policies is difficult. It will depend very much not only on why one thinks there is unemployment but also on the related issue of one's views about wage/price flexibility and on how one thinks exchange rate market participants will react. In an economy in which trade and capital flows were small enough to be ignored, we pointed out that, except in very special cases, either monetary, or fiscal policies, or both together could be used to expand aggregate demand. In the more open economy the policy mix is much more important.

Another conclusion is that the timing of results of policies may be even more uncertain in open economies. It will partly depend on how quickly, and by how much, expectations change. Movements in expectations may not be very predictable and may vary irregularly according to extraneous swings of confidence, rather than being precisely triggered by the authorities' actions. In many countries it is believed that changes in exchange rates may take a while before they change export and import prices, with a further lag before there is a strong effect on volumes.[57] It becomes a difficult matter of judgement to assess whether policies are working as planned in the presence of such long lags.[58] It may also mean that the price effects of exchange rate changes will be felt before any employment effects. Especially when the policies entail a devaluation/depreciation, the undesired price rises may give pressure for policy reversal if it seems that the 'cost' of price rises are not being compensated for by the 'benefit' of employment gains, simply because the latter are slower to appear.

EXTERNAL CONSTRAINTS ON EMPLOYMENT POLICIES

Using the discussions of the previous section we can examine the validity of one set of arguments commonly used by those opposed to expansionary employment policies: that the repercussions on the balance of payments and/ or the exchange rate are unacceptable.

In the fixed rate world of the 1950s and 1960s (and for countries in a bloc like the EMS) such an argument would only seem to be valid in special circumstances, on the standard assumptions. It requires that the balance of payments is only negligibly responsive to interest rate differentials. If the capital account is so unimportant, or subject to such strict controls, then any attempt to use either monetary or fiscal policy will lead to a balance of payments deficit, and therefore eventually will either reverse itself (via automatic, unsterilised money supply contraction) or have to be reversed as reserves become exhausted.

This may have been a valid description of the 1950s. Nowadays, most countries can be taken to have capital accounts which are responsive to interest rate changes. As discussed above, it will then always be possible to expand income by the use of fiscal policy. Only if governments simultaneously try to stick to inconsistent monetary targets might there be a problem – even then for most countries, which have capital accounts very responsive to interest rates, the 'problem' would be that of a balance of payments surplus, not deficit.[59]

It must be admitted that the above is a short-run analysis, in the sense that if the process starts from balance of payments equilibrium, then after the expansionary policy there is a current account deficit (due to the increase in income, reinforced by any rise in prices) offset by a capital account surplus.[60] The capital account surplus implies borrowing from abroad and/or a run-down of domestically-owned overseas assets. Such a situation may be considered untenable if it has to continue indefinitely. It would then eventually be necessary to try to take measures to stimulate competitiveness, e.g. encouraging productivity growth,[61] price restraint to keep home inflation below overseas inflation, or any other way of reducing the domestic propensity to import. Differences over the importance of worrying about long-run effects as compared to the legitimacy of ignoring them bring us back yet again in the fundamental split in outlook between those who reject and those who accept the relevance of Keynes' dismissive phrase: 'In the long-run we are all dead'.[62]

Even those who think that at least 'moderate' current account deficits can continue to be financed by capital account surplus for a 'reasonably' long time,[63] might feel that the consideration places some limits on expansionary policies. *First*, for many countries it will require some rise in interest rates above those of competitors (the closer to 'perfect' is capital mobility, the less is the interest rate differential required). There will thus be some, though only partial, crowding out of domestic real investment.[64] *Second*, speculators may look at the current account and also at any price rises or money supply increases, depending on their own views. They may decide (whether correctly, in the absence of speculation, or not) that the position is untenable, thus precipitating an outflow on the short-run capital account.

The second factor, that of arousing unfavourable expectations, can act as a serious constraint on governments. We discussed this problem in the previous section, and gave as an example the French experience of 1981–3. How serious a constraint it is will vary from case to case. Sometimes 'symbolic' acts, such as raising interest rates higher than would otherwise be considered desirable, may 'reassure the market'. In other cases the support of authorities in other countries or in the IMF may suffice – assuming that they are themselves sympathetic to the expansion and do not impose contractionary conditions for their loans and exchange market intervention, which they often do. It may be, however, that an individual country cannot completely overcome the external constraint unless all the major countries with which it is trying to maintain fixed exchange rates simultaneously have expansionary policies.[65]

In general, the importance of the balance of payments constraint of the last two paragraphs will initially depend on how great, if at all, would be the current account deficit if the economy were to reach what is considered to be full employment.

In the 1960s the belief spread that a solution to the balance of payments constraint on policies to attain full employment would be to switch to floating exchange rates. As stated above, much discussion at that time ignored capital flows and concentrated on current account deficits stemming from expansionary monetary/fiscal policies. This view of floating rates as a panacea for governments wishing to increase employment, was one (though only one) of the factors leading to the abandonment of the fixed rate system in the early 1970s.

However, experience has largely changed this view, and worries about exchange rate crises have replaced worries about balance of payments crises as a constraint on expansionary policies. The crucial point is that governments do not feel that they can be indifferent towards a dropping exchange rate: despite the favourable impetus to employment, the increase in domestic cost of living is of concern. Any circumstances which would give rise to an overall balance of payments deficit (not just a current account one) with fixed rates, will lead to a depreciation with floating rates and hence to an increase in domestic prices.

As discussed in the last section, in the basic Mundell–Fleming analysis an increase in output can always be achieved with floating rates by the correct choice of monetary/fiscal policies.[66] If one can rely on money wages remaining unaffected by the cost-of-living rise,[67] and if there are no problems arising from expectations of future exchange rate changes, then the Mundell–Fleming results could be applicable – provided governments are prepared to put up with the effects of the rise in the price of imports when a depreciation is involved. As also dealt with in the last section, an expansion with suitable use of fiscal policy can lead to an appreciation rather than depreciation, at least in the short run, though the appreciation limits the rise in employment as compared to a closed economy policy impetus of the same amount. As with fixed rates, however, there may also still be long-run problems due to the current account deficit.

If a more strongly expansionary monetary policy is the whole, or part, of the package[68] then a depreciation will occur. However, as also discussed already, the world may be different enough from the simple Mundell–Fleming assumption for the initial depreciation and rise in import prices to give rise to further price rises and depreciations. Governments may therefore be faced with what they feel to be an unbreakably strong constraint on expansionary policies. At the very least, floating rates may lead to increasing the price rise/inflation cost of a reduction in unemployment. At the time of writing, governments in many developed countries have, compared to the past, stressed the 'evils of inflation' as compared to those of unemployment. Depreciation, especially if likely to be sharp and continuing, is therefore even less acceptable, despite the fact that the depreciation itself will help output and employment.

How crucial and realistic the fear of cumulative depreciation and its effects is for any particular country depends therefore on a series of factors. These include whether a rise in interest rates, as a result of a relatively more expansionary fiscal than monetary policy, can actually induce an appreciation, or whether the expectations of the future will soon lead to a fall in exchange rates anyway.[69] Another factor is the sufficiency of reserves and sources of loans available to the authorities if they decide to drop 'clean floating' but to try to manage any depreciation so as to limit its extent. This ability to manage the rate itself depends on both the actions and the (if credible) pronouncements of other countries' authorities. Finally, in this summary, whether a cumulative momentum develops also partly depends on the willingness of workers to accept any erosion of living standards caused by a rise in the prices of imports, without seeking to compensate by a rise in money wages. This brings us back once again to the fundamental theme of the functioning of the labour market and to another reason why some Keynesians advocate incomes policies as an adjunct of expansionary policies.

There is thus no clear-cut case that the fear of uncontrolled depreciation should invariably inhibit expansionary domestic policies in an open economy. If it is considered worthwhile to limit the employment effects of expansionary policy and to worsen the current account associated with any particular level of output, then it may or may not be possible to hold, or even raise, the exchange rate for quite a long time. It will depend on the circumstances facing the country. For example, the US expansion of the mid-1980s combined a large increase in the budget deficit with an initially tight monetary policy. During the initial period the dollar appreciated at the same time as employment increased.

DIRECT EXTERNAL LINKS TO EMPLOYMENT

If they are not afraid of continued unacceptable momentum developing, countries worried about unemployment may even devalue, or purposely engineer a depreciation. Such an attempt at achieving 'export-led'[70] employment increases can only work for a single country at the expense of others' employment. If too many countries simultaneously try to achieve increased employment by 'beggar-my-neighbour' devaluations, the attempts are self-defeating. All countries cannot reduce their exchange rates, since the exchange rate is the relative price of one country's currency for another's.

Similar comments apply to the open economy justification for the claim that if inflation is reduced then employment will automatically increase. As we discuss elsewhere,[71] it is not at all obvious that a reduction in inflation will itself increase employment in a closed economy. In an open economy, however, a reduction in inflation will increase international competitiveness, or at least reduce any deterioration that would otherwise occur. As discussed on pages 107–8, by increasing exports and reducing imports, the improvement in competitiveness will increase employment. Since the level of competitiveness depends on countries' relative prices in domestic currencies multiplied by the exchange rate, the mechanism is the same as in the previous paragraph and it is subject to the same proviso – employment cannot be increased in all countries at the same time via reduction in inflation leading to all of them simultaneously improving their competitiveness.[72] In addition, if a reduction in a country's inflation is to increase its output, either the exchange rate has to be fixed or at least it has to respond to factors other than relative prices. If purchasing power parity holds, then any reduction in relative prices due to a decline in inflation will be offset by an equal appreciation in the exchange rate, leaving competitiveness unaltered.

In the next chapter we shall try to assess the various explanations for the increase in unemployment in the 1970s and 1980s. A couple of the reasons sometimes suggested fit in to the discussion of this chapter on the open economy and so will be introduced here. They are also relevant to the relationships between changes in employment/output and other aims of macroeconomic policy.

Countries which are worried about a deficit in their balance of payments or about a decline in their exchange rate may introduce contractionary macroeconomic policies. One aim of such policies is to reduce imports by squeezing income (and possibly to improve competitiveness if a fall in employment leads to a reduction in inflation or even price levels). Furthermore, a monetary squeeze involving a rise in interest rates is likely to lead to an improvement in the capital account. Often a major intended result of contractionary policies is to affect the capital account by influencing expectations – people are supposed to be reassured that the authorities will take whatever action they think necessary in order to keep the exchange rate at the desired level.

Obviously such an explanation for *widespread* increases in unemployment requires that many countries are simultaneously worried about balance of payments deficits/exchange rate declines. Normally (given our earlier remarks about the relationship between different countries' exchange rates and balances of payments) such a situation would seem unlikely. However, there may be periods when one large country has an appreciation and many other countries have a depreciation against it that they find worrying. Such a situation could be claimed for the depreciation of most other countries against the US $ in the first half of the 1980s. Similarly, the non-oil-producing countries might all be concerned about sharp deteriorations in their current accounts following the sorts of rises in oil prices engineered by OPEC in 1973–4 and 1980.

The other open economy explanation for increases in unemployment is the obverse of the attempt at beggar-my-neighbour devaluations dealt with at the beginning of this section. If a government is worried about inflation and thinks that it is in a situation where the cost of an increase in unemployment is a worthwhile one to reduce inflation, it may attempt to squeeze the economy in such a way as to appreciate simultaneously the exchange rate. An extra impetus is given to the anti-inflationary policy by the depression of import prices due to an appreciation of the exchange rate. In the simple models this involves at least enough of a monetary squeeze to keep interest rates from falling too much. By actually raising interest rates the exchange rate will appreciate even further. In a world involving expectations, such as the overshooting model of the section on pages 114–15, the appreciation may be further amplified. But any appreciation not only helps reduce inflation, it also adds to the unemployment associated with the initial squeeze.

The unemployment is on the assumption that domestic money wages do not respond immediately to price changes stemming from exchange rate changes. However, it has sometimes been claimed that because a monetary contraction leads to an exchange rate appreciation, reduction of inflation in an open economy may be smoother and involve less unemployment than would be anticipated by those who ignore this channel for the effects of money supply reductions and high interest rates. The argument depends on the alternative assumption that money wage settlements respond quickly to changes in prices and potential loss of competitiveness, but only slowly to unemployment. If this assumption were correct the appreciation would quickly feed through into domestic wages and prices, leaving unaltered both the 'real exchange rate' (i.e. competitiveness, which is the change in the nominal exchange rate adjusted for any change in relative prices) and unemployment.[73] Those who accept this line of argument as realistic would therefore be keener on strong anti-inflationary policies, particularly those involving reductions in the growth of the money supply over a long period.[74]

Whether or not the argument about the relative painlessness of anti-inflationary policy is accepted, it is still clear that any appreciation of the exchange rate will increase the deflationary effect on the domestic cost of living. However, once again, reliance on the channel of appreciation stemming from tight monetary policy to help to reduce inflation cannot be justified if all countries try to use this route simultaneously. But if each country in turn worried about the effect on its domestic anti-inflationary aims were its exchange rate to depreciate (which, as already stated, is the arithmetic implication of other countries' appreciations), and *a fortiori* if instead it tries to appreciate its own rate, then there may be a series of 'beggar-my-neighbour' appreciations. Each attempted appreciation is accompanied by a tight monetary policy involving a rise in interest rates. Even though the attempted appreciations are each nullified by similar attempts elsewhere, the result will be that all of the countries enter a spiral of rising interest rates and tight money. Thus in this way, open economy considerations might help to explain a widespread lack of demand and high unemployment.

SPILLOVERS AND INTERNATIONAL CO-OPERATION

The discussion in the last section indicated that a country's attempt to consciously use its external links to achieve domestic policy changes, may be frustrated by other countries' own policies and reactions. If many countries are attempting 'beggar-my-neighbour' policies they may all end up no better off, or possibly worse off, because of the disruptions caused by the movements in exchange rates as each attempts to outbid the other. This would apply both to widespread devaluations in order to achieve gains in employment, or widespread appreciations in order to try to reduce inflation by reducing the domestic price of imported goods. The situation may be even worse if the attempted means of increasing output and employment consists of raising trade barriers. Widespread use of this method can lead to a dramatic and undesired fall in total world trade. Some commentators see such attempts at 'beggar-my-neighbour' tariff and trade barrier policy as part of the reason for the collapse of trade during the Great Depression.

Even where the effects on other countries are not a deliberate part of the policy, many domestic policies will have effects on other countries. In some cases, the country initiating its own domestic policies may not have any trading/capital movement partners with whom its relationships are large enough to make an appreciable difference to the latter. However, in many cases, individual countries are not small enough for others to be unaffected by their actions. To take the most obvious example, any United States policy which leads to a depreciation of the dollar is unlikely to be viewed as unimportant by most other countries, whose trade with the United States is a non-negligible part of their total exports. Similarly, a recession in the United States will also have a non-negligible effect on other countries' exports, and, therefore, their own output and employment.

Another important form of 'spillover' occurs when countries are unwilling to see their exchange rate depreciate, even if formally exchange rates are floating. As already discussed, this is most likely to be because of fears about the effects of a depreciation upon domestic consumer prices. The most discussed case in recent years is when a country which is important in world capital markets raises its interest rates for some domestic reason. It may do so intentionally because of an attempt to tighten monetary policy in order to squeeze domestic income, or it could be as a result of running a large budget deficit because of an expansionary fiscal policy. Whatever the reason, if a country such as Germany or Japan raises its interest rates other countries may feel compelled to do the same, in order to avert the depreciation/devaluation that would be necessitated by the large deficit on their capital account should their interest rates drop below those in the major economies. Similar considerations apply to any other policy actions taken elsewhere that leave a country with a choice between seeing its exchange rate depreciate or trying to prevent this by taking domestic policy actions that would otherwise be undesired. For example, a country which is broadly satisfied with its current balance between unemployment and inflation may find itself in a position where it has to take contractionary actions in order to stop a depreciation of its currency (induced by overseas actions) from adding to its prices.[75]

One way of summarising the sorts of considerations we have just outlined is to say that a country cannot determine its exchange rate or its balance of payments on its own.[76] This is obviously true for an exchange rate: for example, the exchange rate of sterling against the dollar is by definition the obverse of the exchange rate of the dollar against sterling. It is also true for the balance of payments: for example, British exports to the United States are the same as United States imports from Britain. Because countries are concerned about their exchange rates and/or balance of payments (since changes in these result in changes that concern them within their domestic economies) they must care about economic policies and events in other countries. The more they trade with these other countries, or the more that capital flows with these other countries are mobile, the greater the impact of the other countries upon them. Because of the growth in importance of capital movements as compared to the balance of trade, and the growing mobility of international capital movements (and therefore the increased sensitivity to interest rate differentials, given any particular expectation about future movements of exchange rates) particular attention has been paid in recent years to the interrelationship of countries' interest rate policies.

The implication of all of the above is that on the whole countries may be better off if their policies are mutually consistent and reinforcing. At the very least they should not negate each other. For example, with a system of managed floating, countries should not be aiming at inconsistent exchange rates against each other. Another example would be for two countries who are major trading partners and currently fairly happy with their exchange rate, then one should not tighten its monetary policy at a time that the other is relaxing by increasing its money supply and reducing its interest rate.

There is another set of reasons for international policy co-operation, which is related to ideas discussed in the previous chapter and earlier in this one. These ideas are those relating to credibility and expectations. They particularly concern international co-operation over managing exchange rates, or supporting fixed ones.

The volume of mobile financial capital in the modern world is such that it is very difficult, and probably impossible, for any one country to be able to stop a depreciation/devaluation in its exchange rate once there is a widespread feeling in the 'market' that such a drop in the exchange rate is likely to occur in the near future. The fear of making losses if one holds assets denominated in the currency, and the chance of making capital gains by selling the currency and then rebuying it when the fall in the exchange rate occurs, lead to such large deficits on the short-run capital account, and therefore such a large excess supply of the currency on the foreign exchange markets, that the Central Bank will soon run out of foreign reserves and be unable to continue to mop up the excess supply. However, if several large countries are jointly prepared to attempt to peg their exchange rates, or to co-operate in ensuring that any movements in their exchange rates are relatively slow and do not develop too much momentum, their joint holdings of reserves may be enough to be able to counter the excess supply of the currency under pressure.[77] The ability to stop the undesired fall in the value of the currency under pressure by joint co-operation will be even greater if much of the demand for other currencies (which is a counterpart of the pressure on one currency), is a demand for one of the currencies of a participating country in the joint action. The Central Bank of that country can always meet a demand for its currency by increasing its own supply.[78]

An example, or rather, a series of examples, of such co-operation has been the attempts by the major economies (in particular those of Germany, Japan and the United States) to ensure that the decline of the dollar after 1985 was a controlled one. By that time 'everybody' knew that the dollar would have to fall, the danger was that when it began to fall it would go into a precipitous decline. How far the avoidance of such a panicky collapse was due to the efforts of the participants in the set of agreements, and how far it was just luck, is obviously something that can never be known with certainty. However, many participants do believe that the concerted Central Bank interventions did play an important role. The mere fact that the largest Central Banks were co-operating in this way was itself enough to give speculators reason to hesitate.

The last point mentioned is important. If the agreements to manage exchange rates are credible to those who buy and sell foreign exchange, then that alone reduces the scale of intervention necessary by the authorities. In this area, as in others that we have discussed throughout this book, expectations can be largely self-fulfilling if enough people share them. If people are confident that the authorities of the major countries intend to intervene if necessary, and have the reserves and political determination to do so, then they will expect that exchange rates will not move very much. But if they are confident that exchange rates will not move very much, then they will not undertake speculative buying or selling. But then there will be far less pressure on the exchange rates to move.

There is another aspect of credibility which can stem from the commitment of a country to join with other countries in maintaining the exchange rate. This credibility concerns the effects of the fixity of the exchange rate on people within the country. Because the government is joined with others in an agreement to maintain the exchange rate, that commitment may be more credible than a unilateral announcement by the government that it intends to peg its exchange rate. To see why such credibility is important for domestic policy-making, one needs to look at the role that a fixed exchange rate commitment can play in the domestic economy.

Most economies are sometimes subject to inflationary 'shocks' of the sort mentioned in the previous chapter, such as a rise in oil prices or a particularly high wage settlement.[79] Then, again as in the last chapter, the government has the choice of 'validating' such a shock by increasing aggregate demand so as to attempt to leave output unchanged but accept higher prices, or it can attempt to hold down the rise in prices but at the cost of increasing unemployment. If the exchange rate is to be held constant, then the government cannot simply allow aggregate demand to increase, particularly if this means not just a rise in the price level but the beginning of an inflationary process. The resulting loss of competitiveness is incompatible with a fixed exchange rate.

The impact of a fixed exchange rate is thus rather similar to that of a fixed monetary rule in situations where an economy is subject to disturbances. If they are to be followed then the government must be prepared not to 'accommodate' any rise in costs. Both policies also have credibility and 'time consistency' problems, as in the previous chapter. The government would like people to be convinced that it will not accommodate rises in costs – hence discouraging inflationary wage settlements and other behaviour. However, if there has been a rise in prices, the way to prevent an increase in unemployment would be to increase the level of aggregate demand. But any such increase would reduce future credibility. In the exchange rate case, the government would like people to believe that it will not allow the exchange rate to fall, but if domestic prices have risen then a fall in the exchange rate would avoid deflationary pressure. But if it takes place then future credibility will be harmed. A commitment to other countries that the exchange rate will be pegged will increase the credibility of the government's commitment, as contrasted to a unilateral declaration.

The aspect of a fixed exchange rate that is being considered here has, as stated, a strong similarity to a constant money growth rate rule.[80] Both are what has sometimes been called 'intermediate targets'. That is, the constancy is not desired for its own sake, neither the constant growth of the money stock nor the fixed exchange rate are necessarily good things in themselves, but by keeping them constant things which are desired may be achieved: here non-inflationary behaviour. The arguments just discussed amount to saying that the fixed exchange rate may be a preferable, because more credible, intermediate target than a monetary rule by itself.

There is another way of seeing the relationship between fixing the exchange rate and other domestic policy instruments. Ultimately, if a fixed exchange rate is to be adhered to whatever else is happening in the economy, then this implies that other domestic policies may have to be subordinated to the fixed exchange rate. As shown in the Appendix, in the end a fixed exchange rate can only be achieved if a country can avoid a continuing balance of payments deficit. Because the balance of payments depends on domestic income, prices, and interest rates amongst other things, this means that monetary and fiscal policies cannot be used just to achieve what would otherwise be the domestically-desired levels of these variables. In a group of countries with fixed exchange rates, either they all agree to co-operate in setting monetary and fiscal policy stances, or if the group is to continue to have a fixed exchange rate, at most one country can have freedom to decide its own policies, and the others have to subordinate their policies to keep their exchange rates fixed *vis-à-vis* the independent country. For example, it is widely accepted that in the European Monetary System during the 1980s West Germany was the country which decided independently on its monetary and fiscal policies, and the other members had to 'passively' fit their domestic policies so as to maintain exchange rate fixity against the Deutschmark.[81]

The requirement to subordinate domestic policies to the fixed exchange rate, for countries which participate in a fixed exchange rate system, may or may not be seen as desirable. In some cases, such as the arguments of some of the proponents of the United Kingdom joining the European Monetary System in the late 1980s, this is seen as an advantage. In particular, if one member of the EMS is seen as having the enviable ability to run a successful low-inflation policy, by fixing the exchange rate other countries are forced to adopt policies which will be compatible with it. What this comes down to is the feeling that some other country's monetary authority is more successful than one's own and one really wants it to effectively determine one's domestic policy. It could be seen as a way of transferring effective sovereignty without admitting it.

The situation becomes more difficult if the requirement to subordinate one's other domestic aims to the fixed exchange rate involves a level of aggregate demand (and therefore income, unemployment and prices) with which one is unhappy. There is then a clash between the different aims, and choices have to be made. The clashes may be somewhat reduced, if it is possible to have genuine co-operation at an international level over the setting of monetary and fiscal policies – as mentioned above, this applies particularly to interest rates.[82] However, such co-operation will not always solve the problem and with any international policy agreements there may be, and typically will be, clashes of interests that have to be resolved somehow. This applies not just to the balance of domestic macroeconomic policy tools, but also to the levels of exchange rates in a fixed or managed exchange rate agreement. It is somewhat like a 'time consistency' problem: countries have to be prepared to subordinate what they would like to do at any one moment for the longer-run gains of a continuing agreement. Similarly, if exchange market intervention is required at some time, each country would gain if the others were to bear the burden of intervention by using *their* reserves and having *their* Central Bank acquire the weak currency into its reserves. To keep the agreement going, countries have to be prepared to forgo the short-run advantages that would ensure from not playing their part in the co-operative action.[83]

If interests are too divergent, and if links are not strong enough for the longer-run gains to be apparent, there is unlikely to be any sort of lasting international co-operation over either aggregate demand policies or exchange rate management.

CONCLUSIONS

The long discussions of alternative views in the sections on pages 108–21 have probably reinforced our initial statements about the greater diversity of opinions once we allow for considerations of the links between countries, as compared to restricting attention to the closed economy. In general, however, the fact that an economy has strong trading and/or financial links with other countries does not itself mean that macroeconomic policies to affect employment cannot work. Only if one adds other assumptions is such a conclusion likely to be true. In most cases, the other assumptions are those of very flexible wages and prices, which would also mean that macroeconomic policy directed towards employment is unnecessary or undesirable, even in a closed economy.

One exception, where neither monetary nor fiscal policies work, is nowadays usually considered unrealistic: the case of a country on an unalterably fixed exchange rate where capital flows do not respond at all to interest rate differentials. A more commonly expressed worry comes from fears about the overreaction of speculators, using this term in its widest sense. Typically, such a worry would be incompatible with views of rational expectations and equilibrium usually held by some of the opponents of macro-employment policy, discussed in Chapter 5.[84]

If, however, such fears are well founded in reality, and if even a 'reasonable' rise in interest rates cannot overcome outflows of 'hot' money, then the cost of policies to reduce unemployment will be considerably increased. In particular, if the authorities cannot intervene with sufficient funds from reserves and borrowing to offset the speculative pressure, there will be a much greater and faster increase in the domestic price level, which may lead on to an acceleration of domestic money wage settlements. If these can be resisted, then there will be an erosion of living standards for those whose wages do not keep pace with the cost of living. In the extreme, governments may feel that the extra problems resulting from a rapid, uncontrollable, decline in exchange rates are enough to make it necessary to forgo any expansionary monetary/ fiscal policies. For countries which are part of a fixed exchange rate bloc, the cost would include having to leave the bloc.[85]

Under such circumstances the only way to use macro policies to increase employment would be for several 'large' countries to simultaneously expand their economies – sometimes known as the 'convoy' approach. At the very least, those countries with comfortable current account surpluses should first expand – sometimes known as the 'locomotive' approach. The expansion in the surplus countries would have both a direct expansionary effect on those countries who export to them, and allow them room to undertake their own monetary/fiscal expansions. If countries are closely linked by trading and capital markets, and have very strong inhibitions about exchange rate move-ments (whether because of formally fixed rates or fears about any movements getting out of hand), then effectively they only have a joint sovereignty with respect to monetary and fiscal policies. Each national government's apparent sovereignty is illusory – they can officially take actions on their own, but can only actually take them together.[86] Those who believe that, in a closed economy, macro policies can affect employment, would have to switch their focus to actions taken on a wider level than the nations as determined by historical 'accident'.[87]

Of course, those who anyway feel that macroeconomic policy aimed at the level, or stabilisation, of economic activity is unnecessary or undesirable, will see less need for concerting monetary and fiscal policies. They will feel freer to argue against the loss of sovereignty involved. Particularly if they also think that flexible exchange rates and a steady domestic monetary policy will also provide insulation against 'imported inflation',[88] then they see no economic reasons for international decision-making. For example, in the UK in 1990, the most prominent group opposing both further monetary union and political supernationalism (which were widely accepted as linked issues), was primarily a group associated with support of the earlier 'monetarist' and 'anti-interventionist' policies of the Thatcher government. Many also opposed British entry into the EEC fixed exchange rate mechanism. Simultaneously most were strongly in favour of the removal of the final remaining trade and capital movement barriers in the EEC. It seems to us that there is consistency of the two sets of economic ideas (for trade/capital integration, against macroeconomic policy integration) for those opposed to 'interventionist' macro policies. On the other side, many of those in favour of EEC political integration saw it as being a necessary result of the already agreed completion of trade and capital market integration among the Member States. Implicitly or explicitly, such a linkage accepts that macroeconomic policies both matter and are heavily influenced by policies in countries with which one has close trading and capital market links.

It is also possible that in many (most?) cases the openness of the economy would not lead to overwhelming costs from expansionary policies. As discussed in the section external constraints pages 118–21, it may well be that no depreciation at all ensues, or that it is containable. Even if the fear of runaway depreciation has some foundation, very often a single country could still manage to obtain some increase in employment before the risk becomes very strong – some decrease in involuntary unemployment would be desirable for those who believe that it exists, even if one cannot go all the way to what would otherwise be considered as full employment. In many cases the claim that external constraints inhibit any expansionary action at all, seems to be made by those who for other reasons would anyway not favour expansionary monetary and fiscal policies directed at unemployment.

7

WHY UNEMPLOYMENT HAS INCREASED

INTRODUCTION

We have so far looked at the issue of whether governments can control unemployment and other macroeconomic variables. In passing we have at times mentioned the question of why so many developed countries have seen a large increase in unemployment levels since 1970, as compared to the levels during 1950–70 (see Table 7.1 for some details). In this chapter we consider directly some of the reasons given, and whether the causes themselves are independent of government actions.[1]

There are various ways of classifying the possible causes. One useful distinction comes from using the framework of the approaches to the unemployment/wage nexus discussed in Chapters 3–6: viz. to distinguish factors which could have caused a shift in the 'natural rate' of unemployment (or the rate corresponding to 'full employment' in the older jargon) from those factors which can be thought of as movements away from the natural rate. For this chapter, we shall not bother about whether the term NAIRU is preferable or not to 'natural rate', except in the section on pages 145–8.

An alternative classification is to distinguish between changes in employment due to changes in aggregate demand from those due to other causes.[2] In general this classification would coincide with the distinction between movements around a natural rate and shifts in the natural rate. We shall follow the natural rate terminology and approach.

Readers may be familiar with the split of unemployment into the categories of frictional, structural and cyclical. Traditional distinctions (pages 132–3) relate this split to the split between the actual and natural rate unemployment.

In the following sections we consider some of the reasons why the natural rate might have increased. Competence in econometrics and other statistical theory is required to appraise adequately the tests that have been made of the quantitative importance of the various suggestions as to why the natural rate might have increased. As such competence is not assumed for this book, we limit ourselves to a discussion of the coherence of the arguments, supplemented by occasional casual empiricism – by their nature such casual

Table 7.1 Unemployment rates 1961–90*

	USA	W Germany	France	Italy	UK	Japan
1961–64	5.6	0.9	1.4	4.4	2.0	1.3
1965–68	3.8	1.3	2.0	5.5	2.1	1.3
1969–72	4.9	0.9	2.6	5.6	3.3	1.2
1973–76	6.6	2.4	3.5	6.0	4.0	1.7
1977–80	6.4	3.3	5.6	7.3	6.0	2.1
1981–84	8.5	6.5	8.4	8.6	11.5	2.5
1985–88	6.4	7.1	10.3	10.5	11.1	2.7
1989–90	5.3	6.3	9.2	10.4	7.6	2.2

* OECD standardised definition unemployment rates

references to data and events cannot be conclusive refutations or strong confirmations of the views examined.

TRADITIONAL DISTINCTIONS

Traditionally, textbooks classify unemployment into frictional, structural, cyclical – sometimes cyclical is replaced by demand deficient – and, in some books, real wage unemployment. However, there is a tendency nowadays to disregard much of this classification. To start with, frictional unemployment may itself be affected by aggregate demand, within the 'search theory' approach to unemployment.[3] In this view, the amount of time between jobs is often dependent on choices made by employers and employees. For example, employers have to decide how much to spend on advertising vacancies and whether to offer a job to the first potential worker who turns up. Similarly, employees make decisions on which jobs to apply for and whether to take the first job offer they receive. Both sets of decisions will depend on the actual and the expected state of the job market, and on the wages expected in other firms. Similarly the degree of mismatch between the occupational/regional structure of job opportunities and that of the labour force may depend on the perceived incentives to retrain or migrate.

Those who keep the traditional distinctions, perhaps, keep them as indicators of the different sorts of policies which might be used to reduce unemployment. The typical remedies suggested to ameliorate structural and frictional unemployment, e.g. improved provision of information, are 'microeconomic', in the sense that they are not macroeconomic. In our terms, they are primarily means of shifting the 'natural rate'. Some may also have implications for the slope of the short-run Phillips Curve, but this aspect is usually ignored. We shall similarly limit our consideration of the factors often mentioned in connection with structural and frictional unemployment to their effects on the level of unemployment corresponding to full employment.

132

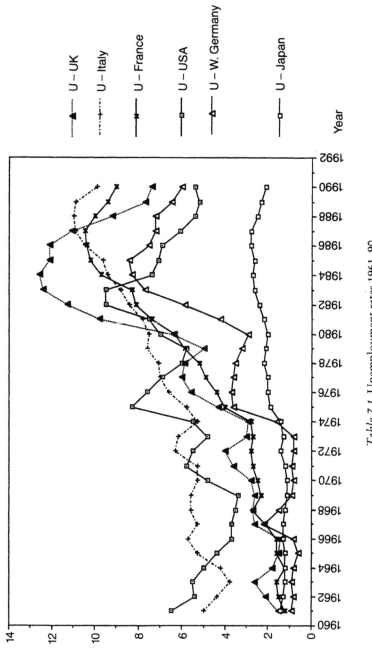

Table 7.1 Unemployment rates 1961–90

Source: OECD standardised definition rates, linked across breaks and extended by national definition rates.

SOCIAL BENEFITS, EMPLOYEE PROTECTION AND TRADE UNIONS

Many economists have suggested that a major reason for the increase in unemployment after 1970 has been well-intentioned but misguided attempts to help workers. Relevant attempts by governments include both those to protect employees and those to help the unemployed. The two need separate consideration when examining how they might raise the natural rate of unemployment. Another suggested reason, popular with some economists and with sections of the media, is the activities of trade unions in attempting to improve the earnings of their members.[4] Because trade unions in most countries have less than 100% coverage of the labour force, they also require separate consideration.

Employer responsibilities

The policies of employee protection often mentioned in this context include measures giving employees security against unfair sacking, redundancy payments to employees who lose their jobs,[5] increased statutory leave (e.g. for pregnancy/maternity), tougher safety-at-work measures and increased employer contributions to health and other social security funds.[6] Increases in the late 1960s in these measures are often lumped together and blamed for having raised the natural rate of unemployment. This blame is commonly used to explain high West European unemployment, both by some European economists and by some US economists who contrast the mid-1980s' fall in US unemployment and the continued high levels in Europe, but do not want to attribute the contrast simply to looser fiscal policies in the US (i.e. who do not want to say that European unemployment levels have stayed well above natural rates).[7]

Although these measures are usually lumped together, there are important differences in them which are too often ignored when assessing their credibility as causes of increases in unemployment. If we first consider the employment protection measures (including redundancy payments[8]), the sort of mechanism by which they might increase the natural rate is as follows. If employers can easily sack a worker who turns out to be unsuitable, they will not be too fussy about offering a job to an applicant. If, however, it will be difficult and possibly involve costly (in terms of time, at least) appearance before a tribunal or labour court, then they will, if necessary, wait longer till somebody comes along who they are sure will be a reliable worker with the right skills and attributes. Thus, on average, vacancies will last longer, and – since employment is the total number of jobs available minus unfilled vacancies – the level of employment will be lower.

In addition, if a firm faces an increase in demand for its products which it is not 100% certain will last indefinitely, it has various choices. It can simply allow order books to lengthen or it can increase output. In the latter case production can be increased by either or both of two ways (in addition to installing new capital): existing employees can work longer hours or new workers can be hired. The firm will be more willing to pay any overtime premia to get employees to work longer and be less willing to increase employment if it knows that, should demand later decline, it will be difficult to bring its labour force back down again, and/or involve redundancy payments. As a result those firms who are growing will have less employment than otherwise, hence the natural rate of unemployment will be higher.[9]

The argument that the introduction of employment protection measures may have helped existing employees, but will have reduced the employment prospects of those not yet employed, seems plausible. Its quantitative importance has not been established. One extra theoretical point should also be noted, which links employment security to other policies intended to help employees. The discouragement of hiring is because employment security measures are equivalent to raising the potential cost to the firm of hiring new workers, since it might have to incur the costs (explicit for redundancy payments and implicit for going through other procedures) of sacking the new workers after a short period. However, if it were possible to hire the currently unemployed and for a limited period pay them lower wages than experienced employees, employment protection legislation could simply reduce the wages of new entrants to firms, and not necessarily raise unemployment.[10] The assumption that such differentials cannot be paid has been noticed in other areas of economics, and is accepted by many economists, but is by no means uncontroversial. Interestingly, in the other contexts in which this assumption has been made, it tends to be advocated particularly by those who are sceptical about the efficacy of market forces in solving unemployment, even in the absence of government regulations.[11]

The other measures to help employees that were listed above are also supposed to have reduced the amount of labour that firms will employ. They all raise the cost of labour to the firm, hence reducing the demand for it. Again, for the effect to be appreciable depends on assumptions that may be correct, but need to be spelled out and examined. If wages are flexible downwards (or can rise less rapidly than prices), although the initial introduction of the measures raises the cost to firms of employing labour, the ultimate incidence will be at least partly on labour, and may be completely on labour. The argument is illustrated in Fig. 7.1.

On the standard market assumption, there is a downward-sloping demand curve relating labour demanded by firms to the real wage they have to pay. Forcing firms to bear the costs of measures which are supposed to benefit employees, shifts the demand curve down, where the vertical gap between D_L and D_L' represents the cost to employers. For example, if initially real wages paid directly to employees were to remain at w_0, firms would wish to reduce employment to L_1. At this point, the extra costs to employers are equivalent

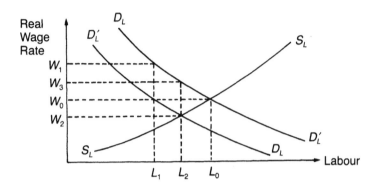

Figure 7.1 Effect of rise in employers' costs on employment

to $w_1 - w_0$ per employee per period, so that the total cost per worker per period is

$$w_0 + (w_1 - w_0) = w_1$$

If the labour market acts like any other market, eventually real wages received by employees will fall to w_2, and employment will be L_2.[12]

With normally-sloping supply and demand curves, the rise in average labour costs to employers ($w_3 - w_0$) will be less than the extra government-imposed costs ($w_3 - w_2$). If the supply of labour is very insensitive to the real wage (S_L virtually vertical), virtually all of the extra cost will actually fall on employees, and there will be very little fall in employment.[13] As mentioned in Chapter 3, many economists think that (at least for full-time primary employees) the supply curve of labour is very inelastic. If so, these measures cannot lead to a large fall in the full-employment level of the labour force. Even were the supply of labour to be elastic, then, as in Chapter 4, since this kind of fall in employment (such as from L_0 to L_2) is a move down the supply curve, it will not be 'involuntary' unemployment. Whether it shows up at all as a rise in the natural rate of unemployment will depend on whether changes in L represent changes in numbers of people or mainly in hours per person, and, in the former case, on whether those who drop out of the labour force because of a fall in wages are measured as unemployed.

The empirical testing has tended to focus on the more easily quantifiable aspect of these policies, which is the employer contribution to social security funds. Unlike the other aspects, such contributions have also increased in the 1980s in many countries – either because of continued rise in unemployment benefit/health costs (in those countries where the contributions are closely linked to the calls on the funds) or as a form of taxation which can be raised by governments who have promised to reduce direct taxes and feel that taxes which can be called contributions to national insurance funds will not attract the same opprobium.[14]

Although some studies have found that employer contributions have had an effect on unemployment,[15] little attention has been paid to an anomaly in many of the results. If the mechanism by which employer contributions have reduced the equilibrium level of employment is according to a theory of the sort illustrated in Fig. 7.1 and just outlined, then increases in income taxes, or any other taxes paid by households,[16] should have had exactly the same effect,[17] by the following reasoning. Income taxes will shift the supply curve of labour upwards by the amount of the tax. In Fig. 7.2, if workers were to continue to receive a post-tax real wage of w_0 (and therefore still to supply L_0 of labour) wages paid by employers would have to rise to w_6, where $w_6 - w_0$ is the extra tax paid by each employee per period. But at a wage of w_6, employers would only demand L_3.[18] As in the discussion of employer taxes, under standard market assumptions the wage rate will end up at w_5 and workers will receive post-tax w_7, where $w_5 - w_7$ is the tax per employee per period. If the tax in the case of employer contributions ($w_3 - w_2$ in Fig. 7.1) is the same as the tax on employees ($w_5 - w_7$ in Fig. 7.2), the level of employment is the same in both cases (L_4 is the same as L_2). The rest of the preceding discussion on whether measured unemployment will rise by much applies here too. Despite the equivalence of employee and employer taxes, much discussion, including econometric testing (see note 12), which attributes some of the rise in the natural rate of unemployment to employer contributions does not consider employee taxation to have had the same effect.[19] This casts doubt on the role of government policies which raised employer costs as a major cause of a rise in the natural rate of unemployment.

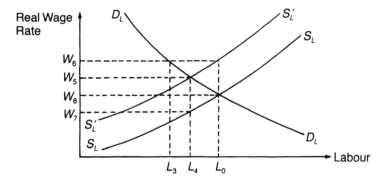

Figure 7.2 Effect of rise in income tax on employment

Social benefits paid to the unemployed

Earlier in this book (especially in Chapter 3), we have examined the question of whether there is a sense in which unemployment may be involuntary. Both in popular talk about 'scroungers' and for many academic economists who claim that all unemployment is best defined as voluntary, a crucial role is played by unemployment benefits. They are also, however, relevant for the analyses of those economists who do not want to get embroiled in the voluntary/involuntary dispute.

We shall use the term 'unemployment benefits' to include not only payments made under such a title, but all payments made to those who are unemployed, even if officially made under some other section of social welfare spending, such as more general poverty support schemes. Whatever the source of these payments, the crucial notion is that which is often called the 'replacement ratio'. This is the ratio of the income which an unemployed person (or a household where somebody is unemployed) receives while the person is unemployed, as compared to the income that would be received if at work. The phrase 'if at work' is ambiguous here – it could refer to the last job the person had (if any) before becoming unemployed or it could refer to the best job which could be had immediately – on the assumption that there is always some job, even if miserably paid, which could be taken: in some countries economists who think this assumption relevant tend to use dish-washing as an example, in others selling shoe-laces and matchboxes on street corners. For analyses which incorporate the replacement ratio it is usually the income in an available, if inferior, job which is relevant for the denominator of the ratio. However, it is very difficult to obtain data on such potential income, and empirical work tends to use either the previous income or even average earnings for all workers, as a proxy.

The simplest way that a rise in the replacement ratio can lead to a rise in the natural rate of unemployment is if people feel better off not working, but receiving benefits, than when working. It might be that they are actually better off financially, i.e. a replacement ratio greater than one, or that even if they are financially worse off without a job, the avoidance of the disutility of work is worth more than the loss of income. Obviously if unemployment is viewed as unpleasant (social stigma, isolation etc.) the disutility of unemployment also enters into the calculation. People for whom a high replacement ratio leaves them preferring unemployment to available jobs, have effectively dropped out of the labour force, but may continue to be measured as unemployed.[20]

The replacement ratio also plays a crucial role in more complex models of the way labour markets work. Just a couple of examples will be given here. In models incorporating union bargaining, the level of income of union members who might become unemployed helps to determine the union's wage demand – at its simplest, the higher the unemployment benefit, the less unions will be deterred by the probability of making more of their members unemployed as a result of obtaining higher wages. Therefore the higher the level of unemployment benefit, the higher the wage level is set, and the fewer the number employed.[21]

Another example is the 'search theory' approach to unemployment mentioned above. The higher is the replacement ratio, the less is the cost to a worker with a job offer of turning it down, in order to continue searching for a better job. A similar argument also applies to the choice of quitting an existing job to search for a new one. Thus a rise in the replacement ratio will lead, *ceteris paribus*, to longer spells of unemployment per person, and therefore to a rise in the total number unemployed at any one time.

There has been considerable testing of the role of benefits as an explanation of the rise in unemployment. Many studies find some role, but there are strong disagreements over its quantitative importance.[22] In many countries, although there was a sizeable rise in the replacement ratio in the late 1960s/early 1970s, there has been no such further rise, and in some cases a fall, since the early 1980s. This casts doubt over how much of the more recent rise and then plateauing in unemployment can be attributed to unemployment benefits.[23]

Trade unions

The attempts by trade unions to raise the real wages of their members could lead to an increase in the natural rate of unemployment by two routes. The most obvious is if they succeed in raising their real wages and the demand for labour by employers is sensitive to the real wage level. However, this is not the end of the matter. Not all workers belong to trade unions. Even if allowance is made for those workers whose earnings indirectly depend on unions of which they are not members (e.g. because the wages set by the collective bargain apply to all workers in the group whether or not they personally are members of the union), there are sizeable sectors in many economies in which unions play little or no role. If unions raise wages in sectors where they have power, and employment falls in those sectors, standard micro theory would suggest that the displaced workers would move into the more competitive sectors and find work there, by driving down the wage in the competitive sectors till it reaches its new, lower, equilibrium.

To explain how unions can cause a rise in overall unemployment, one has to explain why the fall in employment in some sectors is not offset by a rise in others. There are various candidate explanations. One is, yet again, that some workers are discouraged from working by the lower wage, but still show up as unemployed – this is subject to the provisos made in the previous section. Another is that wages in the non-union sectors do not fall because of government policies – minimum wages in some countries, or unemployment benefits providing a floor below which wages cannot be driven as people will prefer to be unemployed rather than work for less money. There are other possibilities we need not spell out here,[24] but all have the same result that increased union pressure on wages could lead to an increase in overall unemployment.

As a matter of terminology, it could be argued that an increase in unemployment caused just by this route is not a decrease in the level of employment corresponding to full employment, and should therefore not be described as a shift in the natural rate of unemployment. Instead it is simply a movement to below full-employment equilibrium because the real wage is too high, and is no different to the issues discussed in the 1930s and later, as examined in Chapter 3. Conversely one could argue that because the new level of unemployment could have zero, or steady, inflation it is a natural rate. Essentially, for unemployment which is due simply to too high a real wage, but where no dynamics of money wage setting has been postulated, it is possible to ignore the notion of a natural rate which is also a NAIRU and to sever its link to 'full employment'.[25] This issue is bypassed if the aggregate demand versus supply classification is used instead (see the section on pages 131–2 above). However, the issue of terminology and classification is one of convenience here, and not one of substance, so we shall ignore it in the rest of this chapter.

Whether or not the demand for labour in the union sector is particularly sensitive to the real wage may be irrelevant for a second possible route for the effect of unions on unemployment. If unions push for higher real wages, but firms wish to protect their profit margins, the firms may give higher money wages, but raise their prices. As unions then try to obtain compensation for the rise in prices (possibly unexpected at first), they push for still higher money wages and the process is repeated.[26] The result is higher inflation, and, if unions learn to expect the rises in prices, probably accelerating inflation. The only way to reduce inflation, or stop it accelerating, is for the government to allow (or force) unemployment to increase to the point where it chokes off the push for higher real wages – on the assumption that unions care enough about the effects of unemployment on their members for desired real wage increases to vary inversely with unemployment.[27] Essentially the argument just outlined says that increased union pushfulness can mean that the NAIRU increases – so that a level of unemployment previously consistent with zero, or steady, inflation is now inconsistent with it.[28]

Although some studies do find that unions have effects on the natural rate of unemployment, again the quantitative importance varies significantly between studies.[29] There is also a widespread (if not universal) consensus that although trade union strength and militancy may have increased in the late 1960s and 1970s, in most countries unions have been weakened in the 1980s – hence their existence may be one of the determinants of the natural rate but, on its own, it will not help to explain the rise in unemployment in the 1980s.

It should be noted here, however, that if unions have not pushed for increases in real wages above previous trends which were due to productivity growth, but have merely tried to maintain previous trends (or even just previous levels) then this may be part of the reason for an increase in the natural rate if combined with other changes in the economy. Any of the factors suggested in previous or succeeding sections which would require a fall in real wages to return to equilibrium, will lead to an increase in unemployment, by the routes mentioned, if unions try to resist the fall and maintain what is now an inappropriate level of real wages. Once the factor has become operative, from then on the effect is the same as if there has been no such change in the other factor but unions had autonomously pushed for higher wages. Under the new circumstances, unchanged union behaviour is incompatible with the simultaneous maintenance of both the same level of unemployment as before and steady inflation.

Some studies (though not all)[30] have estimated that in West European countries there is considerable inertia in real wages as compared to the US (where it is nominal wages which are sticky). This difference has been used, together with the other labour market rigidities mentioned in the subsection on pages 134–7 above, to explain the different unemployment records in the 1980s. However, it should be noted that in some West European countries, e.g. Italy, which previously formally indexed wages to the cost of living, the indexation was broken in the early 1980s, which should reduce the real wage inertia. Nevertheless unemployment has not been reduced.[31]

STRUCTURAL CHANGES

On the basis of some very casual surveys (talking to friends and reading letters/ articles in newspapers) it seems that if one had asked the typical (mythical?) man-or-woman-in-the-street during the 1980s why unemployment increased and remained high, the most popular answer would be: 'because of computers'. By this they would mean not just computers, but that all the automation in offices and factories that has recently been introduced has had the effect of reducing the number of people needed to produce goods and services. The second most popular answer would be: 'because of cheap imports from the Far East'.

On the whole, these explanations have not been popular with economists, despite some exceptions.[32] We briefly examine why most economists do not stress these two types of structural change, and then look at a third type which has been taken more seriously within the profession, viz. the rise in the price of oil in 1973–74 and in 1979–80.

Automation

Obviously, a person who has seen his or her job disappear, as the task he/she previously did is now done by an electronically-controlled machine, will attribute the subsequent unemployment to the technical change embodied in the machine. Nevertheless, economists have tended to deny that technical change can cause widespread unemployment. The tension between the experience of individuals who feel threatened by the redundancy of their skills and the dismissal of such fears as unfounded goes back to at least the beginning of the Industrial Revolution. 'Luddite' has been a term of scorn by most economists, historians and other commentators.

There are various strands in the standard economists' view. To start with, machines themselves have to be made, and it is not obvious *a priori* that the making of the new equipment requires fewer workers than are replaced once the machines are in place. Provided that there are always new machines to be made, and serviced, aggregate employment can be provided.

Furthermore, if technical changes make it possible to produce goods or services with less labour per item produced, this does not mean that fewer people must be employed providing the good or service. It is also possible to keep employment unchanged and produce more of the same good. Even if output does not rise by as much as productivity per person in some particular industry, a rise in productivity in a country means that potentially the country is richer and people could buy more. The pattern of demand may change as income rises, but unless there is complete satiation of everybody's wants for all goods and services, it should always be possible to sell more of something – and these somethings will need factors of production, including labour, to produce them.[33]

Overall, therefore, increased automation need not lead to increased unemployment. On a longer perspective, in the past two centuries, despite the multifold increase in productivity due to the use of more and constantly improved machinery, employment has grown, not shrunk, in the developed world.

It is, of course, possible to imagine difficulties in the smooth achievement of full employment in the face of rapid technical change. Particular groups of employees with specific skills may find those skills no longer in demand, and, if unable to acquire new skills, they may have to take unskilled jobs at lower wages than they were accustomed to. If technical change is widespread and is strongly labour replacing, the real wages of most forms of labour may need to fall – the benefits of the change go to profits while labour as a whole would have to accept lower rewards if equilibrium is to be maintained.[34] Although possible, this extreme latter case does not seem to have happened at all widely since industrialisation began: average real wages have risen, not fallen. Even if it were to happen, the likelihood of unemployment persisting because real wages fail to fall sufficiently is subject to all the discussions of Chapter 3 above. Similarly, even if only some groups of workers have to adjust their jobs and real wages, the speed with which their real wages will adjust and so end their unemployment raises no new issue of theory.

As an explanation of the higher unemployment in the past decade, the failure of groups made redundant by technical change to adjust, does not seem compelling. Productivity growth was higher in the low unemployment 1950s and 1960s, whereas unemployment should have been higher in the earlier period if the explanations were correct.[35] In addition, in most of the countries it is not only output per person which has grown more slowly recently, but total output also. This suggests that the problem is one of a slowdown in the demand for total output rather than a speeding-up of the ease of supplying the output.

We must admit, however, that the US experience is different to the rest of the OECD countries in this respect. As a matter of accounting for the growth there, the increase in productivity has been noticeably less than in the other countries, the growth of employment noticeably higher and the growth of output not very much higher.

It is also interesting to note that during the 1970s and early 1980s many economists blamed the rise in unemployment as compared to the 1950s and 1960s on a *slowdown* in technical change and productivity growth. The view was that worker resistance to accepting that real wages now needed to rise more slowly than before raised the rate of unemployment needed to choke-off accelerating inflation, along the lines described in the previous section.

In our judgement, the conclusion remains that most economists do not think that the high unemployment of the past decade is due to the 'information technology revolution', electronically-based automation or any of the other recent forms of technical progress.

Foreign competition

The split between the views of the majority of economists and the popular perspective also applies to the possible responsibility of increased foreign competition for the rise in unemployment. As much as 'Luddism', 'mercantilism' is also a term of obloquy in the standard economics literature. If our imports increase because cheaper or better quality foreign goods have become available this is seen as a gain, not a loss.

It remains correct that, when foreign competition increases, the maintenance of full employment can require a drop in domestic real wages. This drop could occur either by a fall in the exchange rate, with money wages and the prices of domestically produced goods constant,[36] or by a fall in wages and prices with the exchange rate constant. However, once again, unemployment caused by a failure of real wages to adjust raises no new issues of theory beyond those already discussed, whether it is real wages in general which have to fall or whether those of workers in particular sectors have to fall by particularly large amounts.

There is some difficulty in assessing whether a rise in imports from Japan and the newly industrialised countries (NICs), combined with a failure of real wages to adjust appropriately, has played a major role in recent unemployment in North America and Western Europe. The analysis in the previous

143

chapter deals with the way that the exchange rate can be, and may well have been in some cases, the mechanism that *transmits* contractionary government policies – for example, in the UK in the early 1980s and the US in the mid-1980s a major part of the increase in imports and the slump in exports of manufactured goods has been attributed to domestic monetary/fiscal balance by some commentators – the resultant unemployment would therefore be an increase away from the natural rate rather than a move in the natural rate itself. It is easy to confuse the loss of competitiveness due to policies working via the exchange rate with a long-term shift in competitiveness.

It is clear that the NICs and Japan have increased their exports to the rest of the developed countries in some sectors. It is easy, however, to exaggerate the overall impact. The strategy of Japan, in particular, is often judged to be to concentrate their export effort on a narrow range of products at any one time and to take a major share of the market in those products very quickly. The results are highly visible and give rise to vocal complaints by firms faced with the upsurge of competition. However, if we take output of all manufactured goods as a whole, the balance of trade of the NICs, even plus Japan, with countries such as those in the EEC is not strongly in surplus and in many years the NICs on their own have a deficit with these countries. (As indicated in the last paragraph the US is an exception and may be a misleading one.[37])

At most, therefore, the contribution of increased foreign competition to any increase in unemployment is likely to have been a result of too slow a re-allocation of labour between those particular sectors facing decline and other sectors still competitive.[38] It is implausible to argue that a widespread, major, decline in real wages was required to meet foreign competition, and thus that the failure of real wages to decline enough was an important cause of increased unemployment across the board.

Oil prices

As shown in Table 7.1, the rises in unemployment in many countries seem to have occurred at about the same time as, or shortly after, the major increases in the price of oil in 1972–3 and 1979/80. It is an obvious question to ask whether there are causal links from oil prices to unemployment or whether these increases in both were merely coincidences.[39]

Two possible causal links have been posited. The first is that in so far as the rise in energy prices was expected to be permanent, it implied a change in the relative profitability of different industries. Intensive industries (including many of the 'heavy' or 'smokestack' industries) would need to decline relative to less energy-intensive industries (including services), unless relative wages were so flexible that workers in the energy-intensive industries were prepared to take very large real wage cuts.[40] As in so much of our earlier discussions, different economists hold strongly opposed views on how smoothly flexible labour markets are.[41] Because both the labour skills and the capital equipment

144

in the industries forced into decline are very different to those required in the now relatively more profitable industries, the structural readjustment might be prolonged and difficult – a redundant, middle-aged, shipbuilding worker might find it difficult to retrain as a hairdresser, nor does a disused steel mill make an attractive office block. Furthermore, many of the unprofitable industries tended to be geographically concentrated, so that adjustment by their ex-workers might involve a move disruptive of family ties. As long as the structural readjustment had not been completed, the natural rate of unemployment would have been higher.

The second widely posited link between oil prices and unemployment arises particularly from the fact that most developed countries are net importers of oil, and that the demand for oil is price inelastic.[42] Thus a rise in oil prices involves increased spending on imports, and implies that for a given output less is available for domestic use, as more must be devoted to exports (assuming that the whole of the extra spending in imports cannot be taken up by a fully equal increase in the current account deficit).[43] If workers resist the cut in real consumption, then the natural rate of unemployment will increase along the lines discussed at the end of the subsection covering pages 139–41.

Although both the above links seem plausible as short-run mechanisms leading from rising oil prices to rising unemployment, we find them less plausible as time goes on as explanations of a long-term rise in the natural rate of unemployment. There should be some limit to how long structural adjustment can drag on for before retirement, retraining or relocation solves the problem for most of those who used to work in intensively energy-using industries. Similarly one would have to assume extreme lack of adaptability to reality if unrealistic wage aspirations were to last for many years.[44]

At the time of writing, there has been a considerable fall in the real price of oil since 1985, yet most countries still have higher levels of unemployment than before 1979, let alone 1972. This strongly suggests that not too much weight can be placed on the role of rises in the price of oil as a cause for our current discontents,[45] within a natural rate framework.

HYSTERESIS

One objection has recurred during our discussions of suggested causes for higher unemployment: even where some cause might seem plausible as initially shifting up the natural rate in the early 1970s, it seems less plausible as an explanation of continued high unemployment. In recent years, a modification to the natural-rate approach has been advocated which can deal with this objection,[46] and which is often called 'hysteresis'.

'Hysteresis' is a term borrowed from physics (magnetism initially), denoting that the equilibrium of a system depends not only on the exogenous forces but also on its history – often as a result of inertia. As applied to the rate of unemployment, it means that the NAIRU at any one time depends on recent levels of unemployment. In particular, if an economy has recently experienced high unemployment then the NAIRU will be higher than in an economy now identical but which has a recent history of low unemployment.

Various explanations for hysteresis have been suggested. Among the earlier, informal, explanations is the view that a major part of the relevant skills required for most jobs is learned in previous on-the-job informal training, including the acquisition of 'work discipline'. If the unemployment of young entrants to the labour force rises, so that school-leavers do not get taken on in trainee and junior posts, they will not be attractive candidates for adult jobs later on. Similarly, if the initial rise in unemployment is accompanied by a fall in investment by firms (e.g. if due to a prolonged tight monetary policy), afterwards there will be a smaller capital stock than otherwise, and fewer workers will be wanted at any given real wage.[47] Both arguments imply that prolonged unemployment leads to an inward shift in the demand curve for labour.

Another argument more directly related to the concept of the NAIRU (but partly related to the first one in the previous paragraph) says that the long-term unemployed effectively exert no downward pressure on wage change.[48] This may be because they simply become discouraged from looking for jobs, or because employers do not consider them for vacancies since they assume that anybody who has been unemployed for years has either lost their work skills and motivation or must have been rejected by other employers for good reasons and is therefore not even worth the bother of interviewing. The *effective* supply curve of labour has therefore shifted inwards compared to the supply curve viewed simply as the number of people in the relevant age groups.

The final explanation that we shall outline here is a more recent formalisation, that goes under the name of the 'insider–outsider' model.[49] One version concentrates on wage bargaining between trade unions and employers about wages. The union's push for higher wages is constrained by the fear of causing unemployment for their members. However, once workers become unemployed for any reason, they drop out of the union which previously represented them, and, in the simplest version of the model, union bargainers no longer worry about their interests.[50] Thus, from now on their push for higher wages is only constrained by concern for those still employed (the 'insiders'), not by possible employment prospects for those currently unemployed and therefore outside.

To put the idea at its most basic, workers in a firm try to set their wages in the knowledge that employers have an inverse relationship between the real wage and the number of workers they employ – a downward-sloping demand curve for labour.[51] In Fig. 7.3, say, bargainers settle on a wage of W_0 in the knowledge that employment will be at L_0,[52] given the demand curve D_L. To keep the argument most transparent, we can take the most extreme assumption, which is that workers put so much weight on their continued employ-

146

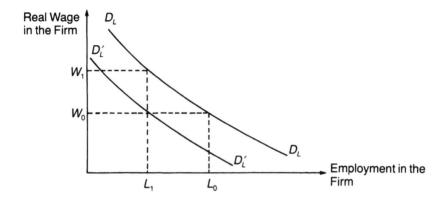

Figure 7.3 Permanently lower employment following temporary fall, with insider bargaining

ment relative to their wages, that L_0 was also the initial size of the 'insider' group in the firm.[53] Assume that, for some reason, employment in the firm falls below L_0 to L_1; e.g. for any of the reasons in the previous sections the demand for labour curve shifts to $D_L{}'$ at the firm's existing price and money wage, and the wage bargain is not renegotiated quickly enough to avoid the employer sacking $L_1 - L_0$ workers. Now only L_1 employees are represented in the bargaining groups for the next wage round, and even if after a time conditions improve, they will still only be interested in securing employment at L_1; e.g. if the demand curve shifts back to D_L they will prefer to settle for the highest wage that just guarantees their existing employment, i.e. W_1, rather than set a lower wage so that employment can increase beyond L_1 by hiring some 'outsiders'. Thus the equilibrium level of employment in the firm has fallen.[54]

Since the formal insider–outsider models are relatively recent, it is perhaps too early to say how widely acceptable they may be when analysed in more depth. It may turn out that if employers and employee representatives allow for the effects of their actions in one wage round on to what will be their options when they come to negotiate subsequent rounds, then their behaviour will be modified in ways which lead to less difference from the predictions of more traditional models of wage determination.

If any of the explanations of hysteresis are accepted, then the natural rate approach loses much of its policy implication. Reductions in unemployment below the NAIRU may lead to increased inflation and to accelerating inflation, but because the NAIRU itself shifts as a result of the period of lower unemployment, it is then possible to level off inflation at a lower rate of unemployment than before. Not only is the NAIRU at any one time not a 'natural' rate, the NAIRU is not itself invariant to *macro*economic policies.

147

Equivalently, in historical terms, while the incorporation of expectations undermined the notion and policy implications of the original Phillips Curve, acceptance of hysteresis undermines the notion and policy implications of the expectations-augmented Phillips Curve.

The welfare analysis of reductions in unemployment versus any costs in inflation becomes more difficult because of the shift in the terms of the trade-off between them. In the standard NAIRU analysis a reduction in unemployment *now* affects the *future* trade-off unfavourably because expectations change as a result of the inflation experience, and so the short-run Phillips Curve shifts up.[55] In the hysteresis analysis there is, however, also a favourable effect on the future trade-off because of the reduction in the NAIRU. The welfare analysis will depend on the speed with which the NAIRU moves compared with the rate at which prices accelerate, and this is not something which could be decided without very detailed investigation.

If hysteresis exists, it gives another argument to those who believe in incomes policy. If the economy is expanded and incomes policy simultaneously introduced, the incomes policy may only need to be temporary. Once the NAIRU has followed the fall in unemployment, the policy can then be removed without any acceleration in inflation. Hence an effective *temporary* incomes policy could allow a *permanent* reduction in unemployment without any inflation penalty.

As a concluding point to this section, it is perhaps worth noting that in the early 1980s some governments' spokesmen and other supporters of their policies made a claim which is the opposite to the standard hysteresis argument. They claimed that unemployment was high precisely because it had been low for 30 years – during the boom years the 'discipline of the market' had been lacking, workers had had too much power to impede productivity enhancing reorganisation, and firms had been able to survive without worrying too much about efficiency. A rise in unemployment was the inevitable result of the attempt to restore a more efficient economy. This approach was obviously attractive to new governments, following a change of governing party at an election, as absolving them from 'blame' for the unemployment that accompanied their new policies. Little has been heard of this claim as unemployment has continued high with the same governments in power at the end of the 1980s.[56]

DEFLATIONARY POLICIES

The ideas in the sections on pages 134–45 all concerned shifts in the natural rate, with hysteresis on pages 145–8 adding the possibility of further induced shifts in it – possibly even of such induced shifts destroying the usefulness of the natural rate concept. We now very briefly mention the alternative: which is that unemployment is high primarily because it has been driven above the natural rate, whether or not the natural rate has also shifted somewhat for any

148

of the reasons in the sections on pages 134–45, or whether an initial contraction has itself led to a worsening of the NAIRU because of hysteresis. We restrict ourselves to a brief mention of this alternative because the most likely reasons for such contractionary macroeconomic policies in the 1970s and 1980s have already been dealt with in previous chapters, as has the mechanism by which monetary/fiscal policies affect employment.

The reasons mentioned earlier include the fear that inflation was getting uncontrollable, especially as governments faced with the oil price rises of the early 1980s looked back at the inflation record of the mid-1970s; and the continued fear has meant a reluctance to reflate even when oil prices subsequently fell and even in those countries where inflation rates had fallen substantially and were back close to the levels before 1973. The other major suggested reason for deflationary policies that has been mentioned in earlier chapters was the desire to protect the balance-of-payments/exchange-rate. Again this fear may have been particularly acute in the wake of the oil price rises given (as mentioned in the section on pages 144–5) the inelastic demand for oil imports.

The plausibility of the notion that continued high unemployment is due to contractionary monetary/fiscal policies can be treated briefly, as it also depends on arguments already dealt with, viz. the acceptability of the basic natural rate analysis.[57] If the natural rate approach were correct, and yet unemployment was being kept above the natural rate by contractionary policies, we should be in the opposite situation to that discussed in Chapter 4. However, since 1982, inflation has declined, but not at an accelerating rate, while unemployment remains at its high level.[58] This suggests that if the rise in unemployment has been due to contractionary policies, the simple natural rate approach cannot be correct. Some modifications would be required: either hysteresis, so that an initial rise in unemployment due to a monetary/ fiscal squeeze is then perpetuated without accelerating deflation of prices, or the sorts of asymmetries and rigidities which Keynesians claim are wide-spread and which some Keynesians claim are long-lasting.[59] If the criticisms of the natural rate approach are correct, then the continued high levels of unemployment can be attributed to inappropriately tight macroeconomic policies, and could be cured by an expansion in aggregate demand.

CONCLUSION

In this chapter we have tried to explain some of the suggested reasons for the widespread rise in unemployment over the past two decades, and to super-ficially indicate some of the difficulties of each. Despite their variety there are some themes and common threads running through many of them.

Many of the reasons suggested in the sections on pages 134–45 for shifts in the natural rate depend on *either* (i) real wages adjusting sluggishly *or* (ii) a highly elastic labour supply curve, with movements along the labour supply schedule showing up as changes in measured unemployment, rather than just as changes in employment. In a loose sense, the first alternative is congenial to what we have described throughout this book as part of the Keynesian way of viewing the world, though with adaptations to a NAIRU. The second alternative is closer to the basic view that we have ascribed to Monetarists – particularly of the newer variety discussed in Chapter 5 – with unemployment viewed as voluntary. The ascription of high unemployment to over-tight aggregate demand policies in the section on pages 148–9 is obviously most congenial to the older type of Keynesian view of the world that rejects even the NAIRU as relevant to decisions on policy within a reasonable time period.

The other common thread is that, for many of the explanations relying on alternative (i) in the previous paragraph, the main problem is that even where they have plausibility as a description of the initial rise in unemployment they seem less plausible as explanations of its continuation. The problem for alternative (ii) is that few economists accept that the supply of labour is highly elastic in the long run.[60] The macroeconomic explanation of the section on pages 148–9 has the problems that led many economists to adopt the natural rate hypothesis in the first place.

In this book we have tried, no doubt unsuccessfully, to preserve objectivity and not to let our own views colour our presentation too much. In case any readers are still unsure, our final comments will give away our position on these issues: whenever there has been a rise in unemployment which lasts for years, there have been analysts who state that the reason is because of the high level of unemployment corresponding to 'full employment', 'equilibrium' or 'the natural rate'. This was widely true in the 1930s, in the 1950s in the US, and widely in the early 1980s. Yet when, as in the US in the mid-1980s, expansionary fiscal and monetary policies have been applied then unemployment has fallen and somehow estimates of the 'equilibrium' or 'natural' rate of unemployment fall as well. Suddenly, we hear far less, if at all, of lay statements about the need to adjust to a 'leisure society' in which most adults will either not work at all or only work a few hours a week. There is even a diminution of claims by economists that the only policies which can reduce unemployment without intolerable inflationary costs are those which alter incentives to work or break the remaining power of trade unions.

APPENDIX

BALANCE OF PAYMENTS
AND FOREIGN EXCHANGE

The purpose of this Appendix is to review some simple relationships that are often helpful in providing a way of seeing why certain propositions hold, in the context of a country's balance of payments and its exchange rate. For brevity we shall refer to the 'home' country as the UK and the 'home' currency is the £.

It is important to realise that the demand for a currency in the context of foreign exchange is not the same as the demand for money, as usually understood. The demand for money in a country is the amount of money people wish to hold. The demand for a currency on the foreign exchange markets is the total that people wish to buy per period. To demand a currency on the foreign exchange market means that one is offering another in exchange – thus, for example, if there were only two countries in the world, the demand for the £ would be the supply of $ and the supply of £ would be the demand for $. Hence, similarly, the supply of a currency on the foreign exchange market is not the same as is meant by 'the supply of money'.

The notation we shall use in this Appendix is not the same as used elsewhere in this book, instead $D_£$ and $S_£$ will denote the demand and supply for the home currency on the foreign exchange markets; X_{UK} and M_{UK} will be exports and imports of the home country; $B_{UK} \equiv X_{UK} - M_{UK}$ will be the home country balance of payments surplus. In this Appendix X, M and B refer to *total* exports, imports and balance of payments – i.e. the sum of current and capital account figures, not just the current account.

The basic insight we shall use is the relationship between exports/imports and the demand/supply for a currency on the foreign exchange markets. The relationship is that

$$D_£ = X_{UK} \tag{1}$$

and

$$S_£ = M_{UK} \tag{2}$$

One way of seeing why equations (1) and (2) hold is to consider where the $D_£$ comes from. The demand for the home currency could come from exporters who have been paid in a foreign currency and wish to switch the money into their home currency,[1] or from foreigners who wish to import from us and have to pay in our currency (which, again, are home exports). Note that the exports can be either of goods or services or of assets. Thus if foreigners wish to acquire UK bank accounts, this is part of X_{UK} on the capital account. Similarly if a UK owner of $ assets wishes to switch into £ this counts as a UK capital account export (and US capital account import).

Conversely, the supply of home currency comes from those who have exported to us (which are our imports) and either we have to acquire their currency by offering our own in exchange, or they have been paid in our currency and wish to switch back into their own.

151

By subtracting (2) from (1):

$$D_£ - S_£ = X_{UK} - M_{UK} = B_{UK} \qquad (3)$$

Equation (3) says, in words, that the excess demand for £ on the foreign exchanges is equal to the British balance of payments surplus. Obviously both sides of (3) could be negative, and then the excess supply of £ would equal the UK deficit.

The demands and supplies in (3) are *ex ante* (i.e. desired) demands by the private (i.e. non-Central Bank) sector. Two separate cases now need to be considered.

(i) Fixed Exchange Rates

The Central Bank has a commitment to stop the exchange rate changing. The only way it can ensure this is by being prepared to buy or sell the home currency at the given rate, whenever required.[2] As a result if, for example, there is a UK balance of payments surplus so that there is an excess demand for £, the Bank of England has to sell £ in order to mop up the excess demand which (like any other excess demand) would otherwise cause a rise in the foreign exchange price of the £, i.e. an appreciation. For example, in Fig. A.1, at the fixed exchange e_0, there is a balance of payments surplus equal to $X_0 - M_0$ and this is also the excess demand for £. Conversely, with a deficit the authorities have to buy the currency to meet the excess supply and prevent a depreciation.

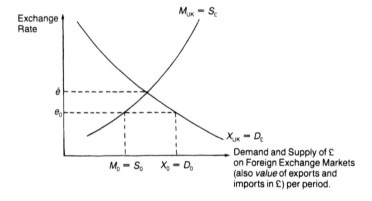

Figure A.1 Foreign exchange and balance of payments

Note: As drawn, the M_{UK} schedule assumes that demand for imports is of greater than unit elasticity (not just that the Marshall–Lerner condition holds). If it were inelastic the slope would be reversed. Marshall–Lerner would, however, ensure that $X_{UK} > M_{UK}$ for $e < \bar{e}$ and vice versa (diagrammatically even if M_{UK} were downward sloping, it would be steeper than the X_{UK} curve).

However, if the Bank of England is selling £ on the foreign exchange markets it is increasing the number of £ held in private hands, and so the UK money supply will be increasing.[3] Thus when there is a balance of payments surplus the money supply will be higher than it would otherwise have been, unless the Bank can and does sterilise the monetary effects of the balance of payments surplus by selling bonds equivalent in value to its sales of £ on the foreign exchange market, and thereby taking money out of circulation. Conversely, in the absence of sterilisation, preventing a deficit leading to a devaluation will entail a reduction in the money supply compared to what it would have been otherwise. These changes in the money supply will continue as long as the deficit or surplus continues.

Since buying/selling one currency on the foreign exchanges means selling/buying other currencies, the authorities can only continue to stop a depreciation when there is a deficit, as long as they have (or can obtain by borrowing) reserves of foreign currencies. If they run out of such reserves they can no longer mop up the excess supply of the home currency on the foreign exchange market.

(ii) Floating Exchange Rates

With (clean) floating, the authorities do not buy and sell in the foreign exchange market. As a result, once we consider *ex post* (i.e. realised) quantities, the amounts bought and sold by ordinary participants must be equal – the usual identity – since £s can only be sold if another person will buy them, and vice versa. In the fixed rate case they could be sold to the Bank of England, but not with floating rates. If, at the existing rate there is an excess demand or excess supply, then, as with any other item in any other market, we expect that the price will change. For example, in Fig. A.1 we would expect that if initially the rate were at e_0, it would be expected to rise. In this market, the terminology is that there will be an appreciation or depreciation.

Since the Bank of England does not sell £s, or buy £s in exchange for foreign currencies, there is no change in the money supply from external transactions (though the proportion held by non-residents may change).[4]

Because the amounts of £ actually bought and sold in any period must be the same, as we are simply looking at the same transactions from two points of view (that of the buyers and that of the sellers), it follows from equation (3) that $B = 0$. Therefore, if correctly measured the balance of payments should balance – the value of exports should equal that of imports.[5]

However, it is important not to misinterpret this last result, as was done by some proponents of floating rates during the 1960s. With floating rates, the fact that the balance of payments equals zero does *not* mean that floating rates ensure that the balance of payment must always be in equilibrium. $B = 0$ merely follows from identity of *realised* sales and purchases. In Fig. A.1 *realised* $B = 0$ even at e_0 – it's just that out of equilibrium *actual* transactions are not given by D_0 and S_0; some intended purchasers would not find willing sellers at e_0. For equilibrium we require that *desired* sales and purchases should be equal at the existing prices, and this is a different issue. In the diagram it occurs at $\bar{e}$. Equality of *realised* sales and purchases is compatible with a disequilibrium in which the exchange rate and the quantities of exports and imports are changing. It should be noted, however, that if desired, or planned, imports and exports are equal, then by equations (1) and (2) the desired demand and supply of the currency on the foreign exchange markets would also be equal to each other, and the foreign exchange market would be in equilibrium as normally understood.

With fixed rates, since purchases or sales of £ can be to the Bank of England, realised sales and purchases by other participants do not have to be equal. Therefore not just intended, but actual, exports and imports can differ and hence the balance of payments can be in surplus or deficit. The misinterpretation mentioned arose because with fixed exchange, since B can differ from zero, if it happens to equal zero then the balance of payments/foreign exchange markets are in true equilibrium. Incorrectly applying the same idea to floating rates led to the mistaken view that floating rates would automatically ensure that the balance of payments and exchange rate would always be in equilibrium, and therefore floating rates would enable governments to completely ignore the 'external sector' and overseas events.

APPENDIX
Stability and elasticity

We shall deal here with one of the other propositions which is illustrated by relationships (1)–(3).

With fixed rates, if a devaluation is to improve the balance of payments, this means that when the Bank of England reduces the exchange rate of the £, B should become positive if starting from $B = 0$ (or less negative if starting with a deficit). As mentioned in Chapter 6, this will not happen if the home demands for imports and the overseas demand for exports are not elastic enough. The formal, necessary, condition is that the sum of the elasticities should be greater than one (measuring elasticities in absolute (positive) numbers, and ignoring the negative signs), known as the Marshall–Lerner condition. If the condition does not hold, or even if it holds but one of the other factors which makes it not sufficient applies, then a devaluation will worsen the balance of payments.[6] This is shown in Fig. A.2 where a devaluation from e_0 to e_1 increases the balance of payments deficit from B_0 to B_1.

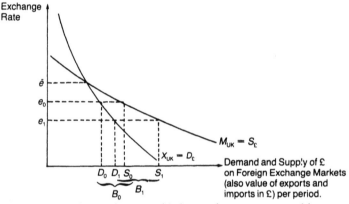

Figure A.2 Foreign exchange and balance of payments: unstable case

With floating rates, if the exchange rate is to be stable, the requirement is that if some disequilibrium develops, then forces should be set up which move the rate towards the equilibrium.[7] If the disequilibrium is that there is an excess supply of the currency on the foreign exchange market, then there will be a depreciation. Stability will require that the depreciation reduces the excess supply.

However, from equation (3), if $S_£ > D_£$ then $M_{UK} > X_{UK}$ and so $B_{UK} < 0$, i.e. there is an incipient balance of payments deficit. The foreign exchange market will be stable if the depreciation of the £ which results from $S_£ > D_£$ leads to a reduction in $S_£ - D_£$. From equations (1)–(3) this is the same as requiring that a fall in the exchange rate reduces $M_{UK} - X_{UK}$, i.e. reduces the balance of payments deficit. Therefore the exchange rate will be stable with floating exchange rates only if devaluation would improve the balance of payments with fixed rates. For example in Fig. A.2 where the Marshall–Lerner condition does not hold, at e_0 there is an excess supply of £ on the foreign exchange markets. However, a fall in e to e_1 would increase the excess supply: $S_1 - D_1$ is greater than $S_0 - D_0$.

The argument is symmetrical for an excess demand situation – since by symmetry if a devaluation leads to an improvement in the balance of payments then a revaluation would lead to a decline in B.

Since B_{UK} includes the capital account, and so $D_£$ and $S_£$ also include transactions for speculative reasons, it is possible for the Marshall–Lerner condition to hold for the current account but to be outweighed by movements on the capital account. This could occur with sufficient volumes of 'destabilising' speculation. Conversely, even if the elasticities of demands for export/imports of goods and services are low, the exchange rate could be stable or (equivalently) a devaluation could still improve the overall balance of payments, if there is sufficient movement in the 'right' direction on the capital account, perhaps because of 'stabilising speculation'.

The general consensus seems to be that the Marshall–Lerner conditions hold for the current account, even if only with a lag – otherwise domestic inflation would help the current account of the balance of payments. However, there is less agreement about the response of capital account flows (especially on the short-term, 'hot money' items), and the associated demands and supplies on the foreign exchanges. Many economists would feel that these flows may well be inherently less predictable and vary from time to time according to 'confidence' and other intangible components of expectations.

NOTES

1 WHAT NEEDS EXPLAINING?

1 In very oversimplified terms, it is tempting to say that the conclusions of those we shall describe as 'Monetarists' tend to be more palatable to those who are to the right of those who like the conclusions of those we shall often describe as 'Keynesians'. This is not always so, and also depends on what is described as the more right-wing or more left-wing view on any particular issue – the ascription is not always clear cut. Nevertheless, the general tendency may be there. It was Professor Robert Solow, himself a prominent Keynesian as well as a winner of the Nobel Prize in Economics, who once said that he knew some right-wing Keynesians but no left-wing Monetarists.
2 This will be explained much more fully in Chapters 2 and 3.
3 Governments obviously have another source of uncertainty: different economists' analyses imply different policies. For example, often the recommendations given by many Keynesians will differ from those given by many Monetarists. Yet the government must choose some policy.
4 In the one case where there might be some problems, we have provided Fig. 2.4.

2 THE KEYNESIAN VIEW OF UNEMPLOYMENT

1 Solow, quoted in Boland (1982), page 47.
2 Obviously putting the statement in terms of savings and investment alone, is only correct for a model of an economy with no government expenditure or taxation, in addition to the continuing restriction of only considering the model of a closed economy. Nevertheless, because explanations often start with such a simplified exposition, we shall continue to describe the issue as one of savings and investment, in cases where this should not lead to any confusion.
3 The same holds for the statement in the more modern terminology that is used in some introductory textbooks that 'injections' must equal 'withdrawals'.
4 The term 'multiplier' is ambiguous once we allow for a model in which interest rates and investment (and possibly prices) are endogenous. In the context of such a fuller IS–LM model (or Aggregate Demand–Aggregate Supply model) some economists, but not all, use the term 'multiplier' to refer to the change in income between the two equilibria relative to the initial change in the exogenous variable. Other economists restrict the use of the term 'multiplier' to that change in income which would occur before the repercussions from interest rates on to investment (or from the change in the level of prices). In the latter usage the multiplier

therefore predicts the horizontal shift in the IS curve, rather than the full change in income once we allow for the interaction with the LM curve. Equivalently, it is also the change in income that would occur in a 45-degree diagram. We shall follow this second usage for the 'multiplier'.

5 These statements about the value of the multiplier are, of course, dependent upon the second usage referred to in the previous note.

6 The expressions 'relatively acceptable' and 'powerful' are purposely imprecise – we are dealing with political appeal rather than economic predictions at this point.

7 The 'Robinson Crusoe' example is that of a one-man economy, with Robinson Crusoe having to decide how much of this year's harvest to consume and how much to save and use as the seed for next year's crops.

8 In terms of the preceding note, planting grain as seed instead of consuming it this year is simultaneously an act of investment and of saving.

9 It is important to remember that economists use the term 'investment' in a specialised sense – it refers only to *additions* to real capital or to the stock of inventories. It excludes much of what is called investment in everyday usage, including the acquisition of financial assets.

10 The issue of whether the government can control its own expenditure will not be dealt with in this book. However, it is important to remember that the government expenditure summarised by G in equations (2.1) and (2.2) refers to that part of government expenditure which uses up resources – either directly by the government employment of labour and use of capital, or indirectly via the government purchase of goods. It excludes transfer payments, such as unemployment benefits. Any such transfer payments are to be considered as netted out of the taxation which makes up the difference between income and disposable income within the consumption function.

11 Unfortunately the common terminology used in textbooks and elsewhere can be somewhat confusing on this point. The expression 'aggregate demand' is often used to denote what we have tried to call 'desired expenditure', i.e. the sum of the variables on the right-hand side of equation (2.1). Although closely related, it is not quite the same as the aggregate demand *schedule* or curve, which shows the relationship between aggregate demand and the price level. Even more confusion can be caused by economists who use the terminology of excess demand, or demand exceeding supply, in a context in which prices are not considered variable.

12 In other words, for a given IS curve an increase in the supply of money will shift the LM curve rightwards and it will therefore intersect the IS curve at a lower rate of interest; while equivalently to achieve a lower rate of interest with a given IS curve it is necessary to shift the LM curve rightwards. One could think of the monetary policy either as an increase in the money supply with interest rates adjusting, or as achieving a lower interest rate and supplying the amount of money necessary to shift the LM curve to the required position.

13 Later on, Poole (1970) showed that in an uncertain world it may or may not be preferable to hold constant the interest rate rather than the money supply. The choice depends in a complicated way on the relative variability of the behavioural functions (consumption function, investment function and demand for money function) as well as on their responsiveness to income and interest rates.

14 In some countries this is referred to as 'high powered money'.

15 Remember that the money supply is defined as the sum of cash plus deposits with the commercial banks.

16 For diagrammatic simplicity we take the case where the level of income is held constant while we move up and down the demand curve for money, but this is not essential for the argument.

17 If the Central Bank does not have an exact knowledge of the parameters in the money demand function, it may have to change interest rates iteratively as it experiments to find the correct rate to achieve its target. For example, this seems to have been the position in the United Kingdom in 1979–81, as interest rates went higher and higher without the government managing to achieve its monetary target.

18 Understanding is not helped by the common practice of calling the desired quantity of money which the Central Bank hopes to reach in this sort of system by the name 'money supply' target.

19 This term was used by the Bank of England in particular. The reference was to the situation (see a large number of Victorian or Edwardian novels for examples) where a man died leaving behind a widow and/or orphans, who were advised by the reliable family solicitor not to gamble with their bequest but to place it in a completely safe asset, particularly government bonds. Allowing the price of government bonds to fluctuate because of changes in interest rates, given the inverse relationship between the two, might involve these unsophisticated investors having to sell at a loss, which would be a betrayal of their trust.

20 It should be noted that in the basic Keynesian model the feedback from changes in wealth on to changes in consumption is ignored. Furthermore, even in a more sophisticated model, Keynesians stress that in a pure monetary policy (that is when the increase in money is not to finance a fiscal deficit) the increase in money occurs, in reality, by open market operations. Since the value of bonds bought back by the Central Bank equals the value of the increase in the money supply that the sellers of the bonds receive in exchange for their bonds, there is anyway no immediate increase in wealth. There would only be a wealth effect if the increase in money is what Friedman describes as 'helicopter money', that is, we ignore how the money gets into circulation and treat it as if it were simply dropped from a helicopter. Keynesians say this is unrealistic, and that Friedman's use of the device of helicopter money is not a harmless simplifying assumption, but seriously distorts the issue. Also see note 4, Chapter 5

21 Similarly the LM curve would become horizontal.

22 It should be noted, however, that the same effects as a liquidity trap occur if the Central Bank tries to keep interest rates constant at *too high* a level for some reason. For example, Keynes had been one of those opposed to the attempt by the Bank of England during the second half of the 1920s to peg the sterling exchange rate at an unrealistically high level, necessitating a high level of interest rates to protect the exchange rate.

23 That is, in terms of the standard IS–LM model, provided that neither the LM curve was flat nor was the IS curve vertical, a rightward shift in the LM curve would lead to the two intersecting at a higher level of income.

24 The quotation marks are because one can find some writing before Keynes that recognised that the demand for money may depend on interest rates. See note 28.

25 In the IS–LM framework, it is equivalent to saying that the LM curve is vertical.

26 The quantity theory is sometimes put in terms of $MV = PT$, where T stands for the volume of transactions. In this version V stands for the velocity of circulation of money in all transactions, not just those giving rise to national income. If, as it is reasonable to assume, the relationship between the volume of transactions and national income only changes exogenously over time, then the two versions are equivalent. The T version is the original Fisher equation, the Y one is the more modern approach both because it fits in better with our general concentration on real income, and also because we actually have data on real income and not on total transactions.

27 Note that the use of the constant velocity assumption in this context, is exactly the opposite to its more traditional use as an explanation of why inflation must be due to monetary forces alone – in the latter use, it is real income and output which is assumed exogenously constant, and therefore it is the price level which varies if, and only if, the supply of money changes. This will be discussed further in the section entitled 'Money and inflation' in Chapter 4.

28 Equation (2.4) is often called the 'Cambridge' version of the Quantity Theory. Although, formally, equations (2.3) and (2.5) are the same, the Fisher and the Cambridge discussions why the variables should be constant tended to focus on different factors. It has been suggested that the Keynesian approach to the demand for money stems more naturally from his Cambridge background, as it can be seen as a generalisation of equation (2.4). In fact, Pigou (1917) partially foreshadowed Keynes' demand for money function by already allowing for the demand for money to depend on the interest rate. But this was not incorporated into a general macroeconomic theory.

29 The full crowding out is even clearer in the IS–LM framework, where if the LM curve is vertical, a rightward shift of the IS curve has no effect on income, but does raise interest rates. It might also be easily noted in that framework, that if we were to believe in both the special Monetarist case of a vertical LM curve and the special Keynesian case of a vertical IS curve, the model generally becomes inconsistent and there is simply no equilibrium available.

30 Friedman (1959).

31 We shall deal in the next chapter with the reason why Monetarists were not happy about using even monetary policy to try to stabilise the level of income.

32 Even Friedman himself, in a letter he wrote to a British Parliamentary Committee in 1980, made statements that could be interpreted as saying that although the budget deficit might affect interest rates, this was completely unimportant compared to the importance of controlling the money supply. As explained in Chapter 5, some 'New Classical' economists would not even accept that a bond-financed deficit will affect interest rates.

33 One might consider it relevant that those who are against large government spending and/or high taxation on other grounds would be tempted by a version of Monetarism which said that fiscal policy is irrelevant as a macroeconomic policy – if the budget has zero effect on output once we allow for feedbacks, then cuts in government expenditure and/or taxes have no effect on employment. Conversely, if one wishes to manipulate government spending for macroeconomic reasons, it is useful to have large government programmes to start with, as this gives room for alterations. Compare note 1 in Chapter 1.

34 In their theoretical work, economists may also sometimes simplify in order to be able to focus attention on a particular point that interests them. There may be a somewhat similar tendency for different economists to fall back on a particular simplification. This was noticeably the case for a lot of the Keynesian work in the early years after the appearance of the Keynesian model, and is still the case for some Monetarist work as well.

35 We leave until Chapter 3 issues involving the relative speeds of implementation and of effects of the policies.

36 For example, many commentators viewed the obvious overvaluation of the US dollar in the early 1980s as largely due to the combination of a lax fiscal policy and a tight monetary policy – resulting in high US interest rates.

3 DEFICIENCIES IN THE KEYNESIAN EXPLANATION AND POLICY PROPOSALS

1 After 1980 President Reagan officially concentrated on viewing fiscal policy primarily for its 'supply-side' effects, and also *officially* believed in a balanced budget. However, a very large budget deficit actually ensued and, it has been argued, that the greater United States success in reducing unemployment (at least as compared to most other developed countries) is due to the unwitting adoption of 'Keynesian' deficit spending.

This is a convenient point at which to note that the phrase 'supply side' is *not* simply the same as the aggregate supply curve (although it may involve shifts in it). The phrase refers to *micro*economic measures to increase economic output and growth, primarily via the supposed incentive effects of tax cuts and deregulation.

2 The expressions 'money wages' and 'nominal wages' are treated as interchangeable. They are simply the wage measured in monetary units. Furthermore, except when we are dealing with the relative wages in different jobs, the terms 'money wages' and 'the money wage' will also be treated as equivalent. The term 'real wages' refers to what can be bought with the money wage. It is conventionally measured by dividing the money wage by some index of the price level.

3 We shall return to this question when we discuss inflation in the next chapter, especially 'cost-push' inflation.

4 The Retail Price Index goes under different names in different countries. Very common alternative names are 'cost-of-living' index, or the Consumer Price Index.

5 See, for example, Solow (1980), (1990) or Akerloff (1980).

6 Depending on the exact formulation of the assumptions, it may or may not be the case in such theories that employers would feel that they have to raise money wages if there is a rise in the price level. One problem with the fairness versions is that they often rely more on plausible assertions about what people will consider fair, and have not yet been tested in a form which is precise enough to give quantitative answers to the importance of different notions of fairness under different circumstances.

7 See, for example, Lucas (1978) or Barro (1979). The former is also relevant for the next section.

8 It is also related to the issue to be discussed in Chapter 7 of whether too high a level of unemployment benefit, or minimum wages in some countries, is responsible for unemployment. Obviously, it can be argued with some plausibility, that one factor helping to determine whether people will seek a job at a very low wage is whether they can get more money in benefits while remaining unemployed.

9 On pages 36–71 we consider whether a cut in the wage demands of workers would itself lead to an increase in aggregate demand. Even if the view is taken that a fall in all money wages could increase aggregate demand, it is still possible to argue that where the cut in money wages occurs only in a very small number of unimportant sectors of the economy, that the effect on aggregate demand will be negligible. Hence Keynesians could argue that provided that money wages are rigid in the major sectors of the economy, there will be no increase in aggregate employment, and that unemployment can be treated as involuntary.

Note that the whole issue of workers switching to different sorts of jobs cannot be analysed formally within the standard macro models, because they are macro models which treat the production side of the economy as a single sector.

10 This view was, perhaps, more plausible before the large increase in the participation of married women in the labour force. Even now, it is probably not too unfair

to say that some Keynesian discussions of unemployment still treat the typical worker as an adult male head of household. If nothing else, approaches which consider unemployment to be the main economic problem, sound more compelling when the unemployed is treated as the major wage earner for a family. Similarly, statements about the *social* cost and stigma of unemployment seem more compelling if the image is of this group.

11 It is also involuntary in the 'special' Keynesian cases in which a cut in money wage would lead to an equi-proportional fall in prices. See next section.

12 The references to 'ordinary' jobs, in our exposition of the more general Keynesian reason why they do not consider that unemployment is necessarily voluntary, may be linked to the issue discussed in note 10. It can also be linked, perhaps, to the distinction between 'primary' and 'secondary' labour markets, as developed by Doeringer and Piore (1971).

13 In microeconomic terminology the change is an unambiguous Pareto-approved improvement (except for the effects on the real income of those who were already employed, if they are not compensated for their loss).

14 This is even more true of the alternative terminology that refers to 'pure' competition.

15 Those who advocate tariffs typically talk about 'protection', rather than 'unfree' trade.

16 An interesting discussion of the modes of discourse of economists, which goes very much further than our particular concern in this paragraph, can be found in McCloskey (1983) and (1988). The book containing the latter reference includes other viewpoints.

17 This is seen very clearly in the aggregate demand–aggregate supply analysis, where a rightward shift in the aggregate demand curve leads to both higher output and higher prices, since the aggregate supply curve is upward sloping as long as money wages remain constant.

18 Some Keynesian discussions incorporate the notion that because a cut in the money wage means a cut in the purchasing power of workers, as long as prices have not fallen by the same amount, there will therefore be a reduction in desired expenditure, which will itself trigger the fall in prices. However, a cut in wages with constant prices means an increase in profits. As long as we stick to models (possibly unrealistic ones) in which we do not distinguish between the propensity to consume out of wages and that to consume out of profits, but simply consider a marginal propensity to consume out of total income, this problem may be ignored – particularly if the formal models considered remain static rather than dynamic. If workers react more quickly to changes in their real income then so do shareholders to changes in profits, then in the short run there could be a fall in expenditure (and output) causing a short-run increase in unemployment. Thus concentration on short-run effects could reinforce opposition to wage cuts, while concentration on longer-run effects would support wage cuts.

19 The possibility that even if workers were to take cuts in money wages, nevertheless unemployment would still not fall, could be seen as helping Keynes' definition of 'involuntary' unemployment.
   Although at the level of theory, Keynes' argument fails if consumption/savings decisions depend upon wealth and some wealth is fixed in nominal terms, so that its real value increases as prices fall (the 'Pigou effect'), Keynesians deny that the Pigou effect is strong enough to alter their policy conclusions.

20 For example, Irving Fisher. These arguments also reinforce the view that the Pigou effect (note 19) is irrelevant for policy.

21 Also, during the period while prices are falling, if interest rates do not fall by the

same amount, then *real* interest rates will rise. This will be a disincentive to investment.

22 A thorough discussion of the evidence on real wages and business cycles is in Michie (1987).

Recently some 'New Classical' (see Chapter 5) explanations of business cycles, known as 'real business cycle theories' have viewed cycles as due to shifts in demand curves for labour. As a result the equilibrium real wage (w_F in Fig. 3.1) alters. Thus the intersections of the demand and supply for labour curves are movements *along* the supply curve over the course of business cycles. Hence higher employment should be associated with higher real wages and vice versa. The detailed accounts of such theories are usually highly technical, an early example was Long and Plosser (1983).

23 We return to this point in Chapter 7, when we discuss some of the explanations provided for high levels of unemployment in Western Europe in the 1980s.

24 See, for example, the discussion in Okun (1981).

25 Most of these articles are much more technically demanding than the book referred to in the previous note, for example Mankiw and Romer (1991). Unlike the original mark-up pricing model, some of these newer Keynesian models imply that prices may remain unchanged even if money wages do change, provided they don't change by too much.

26 If there were perfect competition, then individual firms could not *choose* whether to cut prices or keep them unchanged – they would have to follow the market price immediately – or lose all of their customers.

27 'Clearing' means that the demand equals the supply. It is assumed that if prices are fully flexible in any market, then that market will be in a position where planned demand equals planned supply, i.e. where the demand curve intersects the supply curve. In normal microeconomics this is the condition for equilibrium, but (as we have seen in Fig. 3.1) in Keynesian analyses it is possible to have equilibria even with excess supply.

28 For example, the aggregate demand/aggregate supply analysis of some textbooks.

29 For example, the use of the IS–LM diagram to analyse changes in policies without any endogenous shift in the LM curve to reflect induced changes in the price level is only correct if prices are not flexible.

30 We return in the next chapter to whether *measured* unemployment will also fall if real wages fall. As stated earlier, for such theories there is no 'unemployment problem', since measured unemployment reflects a level of employment given by the intersection of the demand and supply curves of labour. The non-Keynesian 'real business cycles' of note 22 do not require a fall in the real wages for an increase in employment, but they are embedded in models where systematic government actions cannot affect employment anyway.

31 For example, those textbooks providing an explicit modelling of the labour market usually, but not always, have some variant of our Fig. 3.1.

32 Here, as in the rest of this chapter, we follow most treatments of these issues by ignoring technological change or capital accumulation that would allow a rise in the real wage at each level of employment. That is, we ignore the possibility of upward shifts in the demand curve for labour. For the possibility of random shocks to the demand curve, see note 22.

33 After many years in which Keynesians who assumed price rigidity as well as nominal wage rigidity did not bother to explicitly model the labour market, there were attempts to look explicitly at the consequences of assuming that it is possible for real wages and employment levels to be such that not only are workers off their supply curves of labour, but firms are off their demand curves for labour because

they cannot sell as much as they would like to at the going price level. One of the earliest such analyses was that of Barro and Grossman (1971), though the idea is often traced back to Patinkin (1965).

34 For example, in the UK in the mid-1980s, once the idea had dwindled that monetary targets would *automatically* solve inflation, whatever happened to wages. See pages 55–6. The actual UK context of the time made it clear that behind the first reason was the notion that unemployment was caused by real wages which had risen too high. (After autumn 1990 when the UK fixed its exchange rate within the EEC, the reasoning changed to include the loss of sales caused by international uncompetitiveness should prices rise too much.)

35 In this chapter, and particularly in this section, we are concerned with levels of unemployment corresponding to aggregate excess supply of labour. Hence we ignore frictional and structural unemployment, and are only concerned with unemployment above these levels, i.e. above that corresponding to 'full employment'.

36 Note that this and the previous argument may not be mutually consistent. They are probably best seen as alternatives.

37 For example, Tobin (1975).

38 The 'accelerator' theory of investment. Influential examples of cycle theories, incorporating the accelerator, included Samuelson (1939) and Hicks (1950).

39 Without some further lags in adjustment, swings in entrepreneurial expectations would be unlikely to provide any sort of regular business cycle.

40 The relationship between high levels of economic activity and inflation will be treated in detail in the next chapter.

41 See Friedman (1948). For an interesting discussion by another prominent Monetarist, which stresses uncertainty, see Brunner (1981).

42 The type of diagram used here is often attributed to Phillips, but is *not* the 'Phillips Curve' which will be discussed in the next chapter. Attempted stabilisation might have perverse effects even in the absence of lags (as in Baumol (1961)),but lags will exacerbate the problem, and are the most commonly discussed reason for suspecting perverse results from stabilisation policies.

43 The original Friedman (1948) article already mentioned some of the types of lags. They are discussed more fully in textbooks on Fiscal Policy or Public Finance.

44 For example, in the UK in 1988/9 the Chancellor insisted that there was no alternative to relying on interest rates to cool a consumer boom. The 'reason' why there was no alternative was that he had claimed much credit the previous spring for a major reduction in taxation, justified by a 'supply-side' rhetoric, and to have raised taxes in 1988 would have exposed him to ridicule by political opponents.

45 Another way that would shorten or by-pass the recognition lags was based on techniques similar to those used by engineers. See, for example, Phillips (1962), who was initially trained as an engineer. This involved looking not just at the *level* of some economic variable such as output, but also at other aspects of its recent past – such as the rate of change. Provided that the cycles were reasonably regular, this could help avoid mistakenly taking destabilising action.

46 This was a common theme, for example, of the Conservative government that came to power in the United Kingdom in 1979.

47 In this paragraph, we have used the term 'equilibrium' of the macroeconomy to be equivalent to 'full-employment equilibrium'. Obviously, the Keynesian view is compatible with a belief that there can be 'unemployment equilibrium', and that such an unemployment equilibrium could be stable.

48 For an example of a strong defence of the Keynesian approach see Modigliani (1977).

49 The terminology of rules vs. discretion is misleading. The Monetarist position was

not just in favour of rules, but for rules of a particularly simple kind, i.e. where the rule was independent of the state of the economy. Keynesian approaches did not just depend on discretion being given to the authorities, since stabilisation could be attempted via rules which allowed for feedback from the state of the economy, e.g. for every 1% increase in output above its long-run trend level, reduce government expenditure by x%, where x would be fixed in advance (possibly based on estimates of the multiplier in a complete model of the economy). The use of the rules vs. discretion terminology may be linked to the points in the next paragraph of the text.

50 The fear of electoral business cycles is also inconsistent with a belief in Rational Expectations (to be discussed in Chapter 5). The argument assumes that voters can be fooled and not realise that the expansion has been engineered, is unsustainable, and will itself require inducing a subsequent recession.

51 Discretion also becomes inevitable if there is a breakdown of belief that there exists a single measure of 'the' money supply to be achieved. As soon as various measures of money are used, choices have to be made if they diverge. In the US and the UK in the mid-1980s the view that the existing single monetary aggregates used as the targets were no longer reliably linked to expenditure, because of changes in banking structures, was part of the reason for the dropping of simple targets.

4 DEMAND MANAGEMENT AND INFLATION

1 See note 4 in Chapter 3. Some economists prefer to use the index provided by the 'implicit price deflator' of the GNP – this often gives a clearer guide to the domestic causes of inflation, but is not as meaningful to the general public.

2 The reference is particularly to the IS–LM model and its aggregate-demand/supply extensions.

3 That is not to say that it is impossible for what would otherwise be a once-and-for-all increase in the price level to feed into an inflationary process and make it worse. This point should be obvious once we deal with expectations in the inflationary process.

4 As with the discussion of the first half of the definition, it is necessary to enter a proviso: it is possible to conceive of circumstances where a rise in the price of one product may contribute towards a more general inflationary process. For example, see the later discussions on shifts in the NAIRU – a rise in the price of a product as important as oil could lead to a shift in the NAIRU according to some cost-push theories.

5 See Chapter 3, pages 27–31, for a more detailed discussion. At that point the discussion was in terms of resistance to wage cuts, but the approach generalises.

6 Though the habit goes back further. Joan Robinson once said that the Classical (by which she meant pre-Keynesian) economists tended to write as though £-notes had legs and walked into shops and bought things.

7 See, for example, Parkin (1975).

8 Letter from F. Capie and G. Wood in the *Financial Times*, 17 January 1989.

9 In a barter economy, it is impossible for *all* prices to rise, since prices in such an economy are the rates at which goods are exchanged for each other.

10 The argument (e.g. as in note 9) confuses the unit of account function of money with its other functions. In addition consider the analogy that since food poisoning could not occur if there were no such thing as food, the way to eradicate food poisoning is for people to stop eating. The letter referred to in note 8 also included the argument that, as with any other good, a cut in the supply of money

or an increase in demand for it, is the only way to avoid a fall in its value. Readers should be able to assess this argument better by the end of this chapter.

11 For the purposes of this book the proof is unimportant. For those readers who know calculus it might be noted that, strictly speaking, the properties only apply if the variables are measured in continuous time, so that $\dot{x} \equiv 1/x.dx/dt$. The properties follow from the result that if x is a function of time, $x(t)$, then

$$\frac{d \log[x(t)]}{dt} = \frac{1}{x(t)} \cdot \frac{dx(t)}{dt} = \dot{x}$$

12 Most policy-makers simply took it for granted that even moderate inflation was undesirable, and not just hyper-inflation. See note 48. In economies where international trade is important and while exchange rates were fixed, there were particular worries about loss of competitiveness.

13 See Chapter 3, pages 27–31, for the unemployment case. Even in those models which explicitly had a labour market and endogenous price level, the level of money wages was unexplained except at full employment. In the pre-Keynesian and Monetarist approaches, money wages were endogenously determined by the assumptions that they were flexible and quickly reached the level required for full employment.

14 In this case, the most common predecessor mentioned was Irving Fisher.

15 Lipsey (1960). The article contained other important insights, besides those we concentrate on here. Although we have described the Phillips/Lipsey approach as demand-pull, this is on what we consider the most common definitions. Others, using other definitions, might not agree.

16 In the standard calculus notation $g' > 0$.

17 In terms of equation (4.1), $g(0) = 0$. See also note 19. This assumption is not made in some of the cost-push theories we shall consider in the section on pages 72–8.

18 In the standard calculus notation $h' < 0$. Similarly, in equation (4.3) summarising the Phillips Curve $f < 0$.

19 Although a common approach is to identify the natural rate of unemployment with $\dot{W} = 0$ as well $D_L = S_L$, this is not necessarily sensible if there is ongoing growth in labour productivity due to technical change/capital accumulation. With such growth (at least if it is 'neutral' so that marginal and average productivity grow at the same rate) one might expect that if $D_L = S_L$ then $\dot{W}$ will equal productivity growth. The natural rate would then be where $\dot{P} = 0$ – see note 24 for the algebra.

20 It might be noted that so far we have avoided specifying time periods, so that there is no implication that unemployment affects wage change immediately rather than after a lag, and similarly for the effects of price inflation on wages.

21 In addition, as mentioned in Chapter 2, the Keynesian models of the time usually had very weak links between interest rates and spending. Thus there was little feedback between price changes and expenditure (especially since the monetary authorities were primarily concerned with controlling interest rates rather than the money supply). The only important feedback from prices on to expenditure was in econometric models of countries where international trade was important. Even there, the lags meant that Keynesian notions of causation were not disturbed.

22 See especially the next chapter on policy ineffectiveness, and the section in this chapter (pp. 67–9) on the possible meanings of Friedman's revision to the Phillips Curve.

23 One could speculate on why the distinction as a source of disagreements remained

unremarked on during much of the heyday of Keynesianism. Partly it is because it is not as important for the monetary versus fiscal debate as for the earlier or later debates which are now viewed as more fundamental. It may also be related to the mainstream Keynesian approach, during the 1940s–1960s, of ignoring the labour market side of Keynes' theories.

24 The assumption usually made was that price inflation equalled wage inflation minus the change in average labour productivity. At the time, the possible contradiction between this assumption and the common rationale for the Phillips Curve was not generally realised. The assumption followed from the assumption of prices as a constant mark-up over average labour costs (see Chapter 3, pages 39–40). Using the rules given earlier in this chapter, if k is the mark-up, W the wage rate per worker, L is labour employed and Q is output, then

$$P = (1+k) \ \frac{W.L}{Q} = (1+k) \ \frac{W}{Q/L}$$

Since k is constant, the rate of change of $(1 + k) = 0$ and therefore

$\dot{P} = \dot{W} - (\dot{Q}/L)$ but $\dot{Q}/L$ is productivity

The possible contradiction will be explained later.

25 Friedman (1968) and Phelps (1968) are the most commonly quoted sources.

26 Similarly there are important differences between Phelps' own paper and the others published in the book he edited in 1970, which focus more directly on 'search theories' of unemployment, even though they have similar implications about the stability of the Phillips Curve.

27 For example, Friedman (1976), Chapter 12. An example of the majority interpretation was Marin (1972).

28 Later in this chapter and in Chapters 6 and 7 it will be necessary to distinguish real wages as they affect employers from those affecting employees. For now we can ignore the distinction.

29 See Chapter 3, pages 27–31. 'Rationality' in this context simply means a lack of money illusion. It is not the same as 'rational expectations', which will be discussed in the next chapter.

30 It is much more difficult to formalise models explaining the *regularity* and conventional nature (e.g. one calendar year rather than 57 weeks or whatever) of the time lags. It is also difficult to formalise why wage agreements are usually fixed in money terms, with either no link at all to prices or at most a partial indexing to changes in the cost of living between settlements. As a result both the Friedman type of models and some newer Keynesian wage models (e.g. the type referred to in Chapter 5 note 18) tend to just assume, rather than explain, the infrequent revision of money wages. Attempts at formalisation have been made, but these usually explain only some of the features of typical wage contracts.

31 At this point it is necessary to add the time-subscript to the wage and expected inflation variables. This has been done in the simplest way, so that $\dot{P}^e_t$ refers to the beliefs held at the time money wages were set for period t about the price changes that would occur during period t. Other notation is often used but is unnecessary here.

32 As will be discussed later, unlike many Keynesian models, the argument here breaks down if the supply of labour is insensitive to the real wage – i.e. vertical in Fig. 4.7. Furthermore, like many Keynesian models, the policy implications depend on labour demand and supply variations translating into variations in employment and not just into hours per employee. (See Fig. 3.1 and the subsequent discussion for the labour demand side of some Keynesian models.)

33 Because, on the standard definitions, $\dot{P}_t \equiv (P_t - P_{t-1})/P_{t-1} = (P_t/P_{t-1}) - 1$ and $\dot{P}_t^e = (P_t^e - P_{t-1})/P_{t-1} = (P_t^e/P_{t-1}) - 1$, it is possible to switch between models expressed in terms of unexpected inflation (or, more precisely, incorrectly expected amount of inflation) and those expressed in terms of mistakes in the expected level of prices.

34 As well as the references in notes 25 and 26 other versions can be found in various sources, including intermediate macroeconomics textbooks which differ as to which explanation they present as standard.

35 The second explanation is similar to the theories of some of the proponents of the rational expectations approach in the next chapter, e.g. Lucas, and it will also be relevant in Chapter 7.

36 See note 10 in Chapter 3.

37 For example, because the perceived real wage change is thought to be temporary and hence will affect the timing of those periods when employees do not wish to work, as in the model of Lucas and Rapping (1969).

38 For this chapter we shall follow the assumption that people's expectations of future price changes adapt to what has actually happened in the recent past.

39 Economists (including this book) often refer to this as 'accelerating' inflation. Strictly speaking this is incorrect – the theory predicts increasing inflation but it may increase at a steady state. What accelerates is the price level, not the change of prices.

40 If there is productivity change, then the natural rate is where $f(U) = (Q/L)$, as in note 19.

41 It is because the Great Depression seems to be a period when most people would accept that there was excess supply of labour, and yet there was only a limited fall of wages, that there was a revival of interest about the 1930s among economists. Some authors (e.g. Benjamin and Kochin (1979)) tried to show that there were special factors which meant that the 1930s were not simply a long period of excess supply. In Europe there has been a similar reaction to the 1980s experience.

42 Some think that (at least in some countries or periods) inflation depends only on the *change* in unemployment, and not on the level, e.g. Gordon (1988). This has very different policy implications, as do the 'hysteresis' theories discussed in Chapter 7, which make the natural rate shift endogenously as a result of *macroeconomic* policies.

43 Typically the natural rate is estimated to have increased since the 1960s. Some of the explanations offered are covered in Chapter 7. The procedure for estimating the natural rate, and its shifts, can be more sophisticated, especially with the theories which go beyond the simple competitive market-based explanations of the Phillips Curve, for example, Layard and Nickell (1987a).

44 If the initial impetus was a fiscal expansion. If the initial impetus was a monetary expansion, it is to stop real interest rates returning to their initial level.

45 See note 17. The theories considered here have $g(0) > 0$.

46 See, for example, Layard (1986). The notion is often traced back to Sargan (1964). The Layard and Nickell (1987b) approach is more explicitly grounded in a trade union bargaining approach, as are various other modern theories in which unemployment affects either union bargaining power or the extent to which they are prepared to see some members lose their jobs so that the remaining ones can achieve higher real wages.

   With theories involving target wages, failure to adjust the aspirations to changes in what is 'objectively feasible' may lead to changes in the NAIRU, as will be discussed in Chapter 7.

47 The same argument should also imply that if we started near the natural rate then

attempts to reduce inflation by using deflationary policies are wrong. Deflation will lead to a period during which unemployment is above the natural rate and during this period people will be fooled into thinking that prices are higher than they actually are. For some reason, this argument against trying to reduce inflation is rarely proposed by those who oppose expansionary policies on the grounds that they are inefficient.

48 In this book we do not deal with the issue of whether inflation is particularly harmful, at least once it is correctly anticipated (i.e. when everybody has $\dot{P}^e = \dot{P}$). The issue is not as obvious as it might seem – for a relatively simple account see Bootle (1981); and for some empirical studies see Hibbs (1987).

It is sometimes asserted that inflation itself is harmful for growth. The evidence does not support this assertion, at least for developed economies without hyper-inflation.

49 A fairly recent account is Chater et al. (1981), or, slightly more technical, Holden et al. (1987).

When examined closely, some modern proposals for incomes policy are best thought of as ways of altering the NAIRU. These include some of the TIP (tax-based incomes policies). These are advocated as attempts to avoid the complete freezing of wage differentials without a cumbersome vetting procedure to examine when extra wage increases are justified by economic circumstances. See, for example, the advocacy in Layard (1986). The advocacy in other countries of the sort of 'wage consensus' that some see in Germany, Austria and the Scandinavian countries can also be seen as a way of avoiding the rigidities of a government-imposed wages policy.

50 See Chapter 2, which also explained the link between Chapter 5 and the interest-elasticity of the demand for money.

51 It is particularly necessary on these comments to note again that in this book we are taking what we see as the main points of the development of the policy debates, not necessarily examining the exact (often much more subtle) views of all of the best writings of the 'classical' (in the Keynesian sense) economists. The simplified account here is relevant because many modern discussions have a carry-over from the general impressions of the conclusions of the traditional quantity theory approach.

52 The argument in this paragraph of the text would only fail to apply in the two 'extreme Keynesian' cases of Chapter 2, when $\dot{V} = -\dot{M}$. (Even in the second case, i.e. investment completely insensitive to interest rates, interest rates would always change by the amount necessary to achieve this full offsetting of velocity.)

53 As stated on page 58, Y and U are inversely related. Using more complicated diagrams than we have used in this book, some intermediate macro texts show jointly the Phillips Curve and a schedule corresponding to equation (4.7). The intersection will give the value of $\dot{P}$ and $\dot{Y}$ in each period. For example, Gordon (1987), Appendix to Chapter 10.

54 In fact, if velocity is constant, so that the LM curve is vertical, then an expansionary fiscal policy will not affect output, or the price level, at all. There will merely be a rise in interest rates leading to full crowding out of investment. However, autonomous 'cost-push' changes could still lead to a fall in output and rise in the price *level* – in an AD–AS diagram with the price level on the vertical axis, the AS curve will have shifted up. However, if one then adds in a Phillips Curve, the NAIRU must also have shifted, as otherwise the fall in output would lead to negative inflation until output rose back to its previous level. Hence the reference in the next sentence of the text to 'halted or reversed'.

55 Even those which can be thought of as shifting the NAIRU.

5 FORESIGHT, RATIONALITY AND THE EFFECTIVENESS OF POLICY

1 Advanced treatments do deal with the implication of the fact that the financing requirement continues for as long as there is a non-zero deficit/surplus, and therefore eventually there may be a non-negligible change in the outstanding stocks of bonds and money, which will alter various expenditures. In the standard short-run analyses these bond stock changes are treated as negligible, just as Keynesian short-run analyses ignore any feedback from investment via the growth in the capital stock. For a not too technical discussion of these issues from a Keynesian viewpoint see the article by A. S. Blinder and R.M. Solow in Blinder *et al.* (1974), which includes comments on the Monetarist viewpoint of Friedman (1972) on this issue.

2 Although the reasoning was suggested by Ricardo, he did not accept the conclusion as he felt that the assumptions needed were unrealistic – see G.P. O'Driscoll (1977).

3 Known as the 'permanent-income' hypothesis. Introduced by Friedman (1957). Barro's version of the theorem, mentioned in the next paragraph, is also compatible with modified versions of the 'life-cycle' hypothesis of Modigliani and his collaborators, e.g. in Modigliani and Brumberg (1954).

4 Ricardo also dealt with the case of bequests. See the references in the preceding footnotes.

5 This explanation was suggested by our colleague Morris Perlman.

6 In a sense, over the economy as a whole, if we think of each individual as buying a government bond the future tax payments are paid to themselves. Thus the lending to offset future taxes is made to the government. This way of seeing the mechanism will be explored later. If people are super-rational it will not matter whether they buy the bonds directly, or they are bought by pension funds or other financial institutions in which they have a stake.

7 Note that for the 'representative' household owning a bond and paying taxes, the interest receipts in each future year will be exactly offset by the tax needed to finance the interest payments. Therefore in future years the net disposable income of the representative household will be unaffected by the existence of the bond, and there will be no difference in future disposable income to affect current consumption via the permanent income hypothesis.

8 For example, the articles by Barro and others in the *Journal of Economic Perspectives*, Spring 1989 (though there is some casual empiricism in a few paragraphs).

9 In this case one could formally repeat the analysis of the preceding paragraphs but treat these individuals as able to borrow only at an infinite rate of interest – which is obviously greater than that at which the government can borrow.

10 A point not dealt with in this chapter is that the non-wealth of bonds also strengthens open-market operation-based monetary policy – if bonds are wealth, then an open-market operation increase in money has a weaker effect because of the concomitant fall in the supply of bonds, and vice versa for a decrease in money supply. In terms of note 25, Chapter 2, if bonds are not wealth at all, then there is no difference between open-market operations and 'helicopter money'.

11 The theorem also complicates the analysis mentioned in note 1. This is related to the argument in the next paragraphs.

12 See note 32, Chapter 2. However, Friedman's acceptance that there will be interest-rate effects from bond-financed deficits differs (as will be shown) from the Ricardo–Barro theorem. The oft-cited article by Sargent and Wallace (1981) places

arbitrary limits on bond-holding and seems motivated by an attempt to avoid the conclusion of the equivalence theorem that deficits are irrelevant.

13 As stated earlier, the bond sales resulting from a deficit are usually ignored in short-run Keynesian analyses. The lack of effect in the long run is relevant for the analyses mentioned in note 1 – if bonds are not wealth, then there is no difference between the short- and long-run effects of bond-financed deficits since there are no effects from the cumulative bond issues.

14 We shall not deal with the so-called 'Lucas critique' of econometric modelling (Lucas (1976)), details of which can be found in more advanced books concentrating on rational expectations, e.g. Begg (1982), Sheffrin (1983). Such books also provide an account of Lucas' own microeconomic model used for developing the proposition, rather than the approach used here which is more convenient for this book.

15 The independence of the 'real economy' from money, even in the short run, is possibly the reason for the description 'New Classical macroeconomics'.

16 There may also be side-effects from the monetary/fiscal balance upon the composition of output between investment, consumption and government expenditure which could affect output in the long run via changes in the rate of capital accumulation.

17 See note 22, Chapter 3, for the 'real business cycle' theories, which are one set of extensions to the original model.

18 This argument is due to Fischer (1977), Phelps and Taylor (1977).

19 The argument assumes, realistically for most developed countries nowadays, that money wages are not fully indexed to changes in price levels that occur during the average contract period.

20 Barro is often mentioned in this context. His 1977 and, less technically, 1979 articles come close to such a statement but do not quite state it explicitly in this form.

21 For a full account, involving some technically advanced material which will not be dealt with here, see Buiter (1980) as well as the texts in note 14.

22 This example is due to Baily (1978).

23 The most commonly quoted is Lucas (1972). The resulting equations (like our (5.5) but with $Y-Y^*$ on the left-hand side) are often called 'surprise supply functions' because the divergence of output from the natural rate occurs only when there is a price 'surprise' – i.e. $\dot{P} \neq \dot{P}^e$.

24 See the texts in note 14 for references to the testing, some of which are not unproblematic. In asset markets, rational expectations are part of the 'efficient markets' hypothesis, that rules out systematic, anticipatable, movements in asset prices – which would allow unlimited capital gains.

25 For a discussion of the minor costs of anticipated inflation see Bootle (1981). Note the costs are particularly low when there are bank accounts available which pay interest.

In the context of this section, if systematic policy cannot affect aggregate real variables, such as output, obviously the inflation changes it also entails cannot affect these real variables. The flexibility assumptions mean that rigidities which might lead to distributional effects will not be very important either.

26 Obviously, as already mentioned, the older Monetarist criticism in Chapter 3 is wrong if the policy ineffectiveness proposition is correct.

27 The Lucas econometric critique mentioned in note 14 could be viewed within such a perspective as discrediting the simulation studies which Keynesians were using to bolster their policy recommendations.

28 See, for example, Okun (1981) or the discussion by Fellner (1982) and others. Kydland and Prescott (1977) is a commonly cited source, though in some ways this

article is more closely related to the Lucas critique of note 14 than it is to the analysis we shall consider.

29 Our example here is not that in the article by Kydland and Prescott (1977) which includes the term in its title.

30 We are ignoring some complications in the very short-run dynamics which may result from the exact timing and duration of wage settlements and price changes as compared to changes in the money supply.

31 If actual deflationary policy is correctly anticipated, the other assumptions behind the policy ineffectiveness proposition would imply that inflation can be reduced with no increase in unemployment – since no correctly anticipated policy can affect output and employment in either direction. In this sense the policy ineffectiveness proposition has the same political appeal as a black-box monetarism. In both cases governments can reduce inflation by a simple tool without having to worry about unemployment. Conversely since they cannot affect unemployment they have no responsibility for it (at least by their macro policies).

32 This would not be strictly correct if wage contracts overlapped at all, as in the Taylor (1979) model, since the overlapping 'spreads' the effect of expectations into other periods. However, as Taylor showed, overlapping contracts destroy the 'New Classical' conclusions anyway.

33 This particular criticism does not apply to the specific example in the cited article by Kydland and Prescott.

34 See note 25.

6 INTERNATIONAL LINKS

1 In talking about international economics the terms 'capital' and 'investment' are used by economists to include financial assets, such as money or bonds, and their purchase. Economists do not restrict the meaning of these terms in the way that they usually do, e.g. in discussions of national income where 'investment' is limited to the formation of new real assets, as was mentioned in note 9, Chapter 2.

2 The slowing down of exchange rates movements is more likely to influence the speed with which policies affect the economy. Most formal analysis concentrates on initial and final equilibrium points. The path between equilibria, and the speed of movement along it, generally received a less formal and more impressionistic treatment. Thus, attempts by the authorities at slowing down exchange rate swings are less likely to materially alter the conclusion. We shall indicate when speed of adjustment matters.

3 The exception of 'perfect capital mobility' will be dealt with later.

4 Known as the Marshall–Lerner condition. It is a necessary, not a sufficient, condition. This condition may be more familiar as a necessary condition for a devaluation to lead to a balance of payments surplus.

5 Some of the original contributions to this approach are collected in Frenkel and Johnson (eds) (1976). There seems to be little necessary logical connection between this 'international monetarism' and the domestic 'monetarism' as discussed in the previous chapters. In addition to the name, all they necessarily share is a view that focuses primarily on quantities of money to a somewhat greater extent than alternative theories.

6 Much of the earlier work on the monetary theory of the balance of payments concentrated on fixed exchange rate systems. Despite the lack of logically necessary links to other forms of monetarism (see previous note), in practice

most of the articles made similar assumptions about domestic wage flexibility and automatic full employment. The difference was that by assuming completely open economies, and therefore prices fixed by world trade, attempts at expansionary monetary policies led not to inflation but to deficits and hence loss of reserves until the money supply was back in line. As will be seen later in this chapter, the full approach also has implications about the impotence, as well as the lack of need, of devaluation as a way of increasing employment.

More recently, a somewhat similar approach involving more assets has been developed called the 'Portfolio Balance' approach. Accounts of this, and the monetary approach, can be found in more advanced textbooks, such as Macdonald (1988).

7 The terms 'improvement' and 'deterioration' are standard in describing directions of movement in the balance of payments. The air of commendation and disapproval respectively may not be justified. Whether an increase in a surplus or decline in a deficit are desirable or not depends on circumstances and on bases of welfare judgements.

8 This is part of the similarity noted in note 5.

9 Sometimes called speculative 'bubbles'.

10 As shown in the Appendix, instability of floating rates can be related to the Marshall–Lerner condition of note 4. Stability of floating rates would require applying the condition to all the components of the balance of payments, not just those of the current account.

11 See, for example, Friedman and Roosa (1967).

12 In almost standard notation $Y = C + I + G + X - Z$, where $(X - Z)$ is the current account. We have used Z rather than the slightly more common M for imports, to avoid confusion with M for money.

13 Such cuts are not unknown, especially with floating rates and when suppliers think that a depreciation may soon be reversed. This behaviour makes sense with the 'customer relationships' described by Okun (1981), and discussed in Chapter 3, in the section on pages 35–40. See Krugman (1989) for an account that stresses that exporters are sluggish about changing their prices in overseas markets.

14 The latter rise will tend to negate the effects of the exchange rate on the balance of payments, and is one of the ways in which even the Marshall–Lerner conditions of notes 4 and 10 may not be sufficient to ensure that exchange rate changes have their desired effects. If the rise in the cost of living also affects expectations of future inflation (when expectations are not 'rational') then the eventual percentage rise in domestic wages and prices could be even greater than 10%.

15 The effects on output and employment depend on an assumption that domestic money wages and home production costs do not immediately change by the same proportion as the exchange rate (but in the opposite direction, if we stick to the UK convention on 'rises' and 'falls' in exchange rates).

16 These living-standard changes are part of the 'terms-of-trade' effect of the 'real exchange rate' alterations.

17 See Appendix for an explanation.

18 Though there is the difference (which may sometimes be important) that the monetary effects stem from the overall balance of payments including the capital account, whereas the direct income effects, and any multiplier, depend only on the current account.

19 See note 14 in Chapter 2.

20 If there is 'perfect' capital mobility, then attempts at sterilisation will always be swamped. Thus, for example, the monetary theory of the balance of payments referred to in notes 5 and 6 tended to assume perfect capital mobility and

hence domestic authorities could not control the money stock. They could only alter the proportion based on exchange reserves and that on domestic money base.

21 This view is based both on *a priori* reasoning and on looking at particular episodes, as well as on some unpublished and published empirical studies, e.g. Mastropasqua *et al.* (1988).

22 Textbooks on international economics do work through many of the cases and can even run into several volumes. A relatively early example is Meade (1951, 1955). A more modern example might be Kenen and Allen (1980).

23 See Mundell (1963) and Fleming (1962). Note that the reference is not to the other famous Mundell analysis, which is of the assignment of monetary and fiscal policies to internal and external targets.

24 Most 'intermediate' macro-textbooks have chapters on the open-economy IS–LM model. As in the first paragraph of this section, different texts may arrive at different conclusions according to the precise assumptions they make even within the Mundell–Fleming approach.

25 Though of course real wages will be different. As in Chapters 3 and 4, if money wages are assumed to be very flexible in response to excess demand/supply for labour and the economy is stable, then anyway there is no unemployment problem requiring macroeconomic solutions.

Mundell–Fleming is also usually used in analyses which are short run, ignore wealth effects and also the profit/interest remission account of the balance of payments.

26 As stated above, standard Mundell–Fleming analysis also treats as negligible any change in the overall home price level resulting from changes in the domestic price of imported goods, due to exchange rate changes.

27 Diagrammatically, in income/interest-rate space, there will be a surplus if the LM curve is steeper than the balance of payments/exchange rate equilibrium curve, and vice versa.

28 See Appendix or a standard textbook.

29 As before, we shall assume Marshall–Lerner conditions to hold throughout.

30 As long as the conditions of the second part of note 25 remain reasonable approximations.

31 In the UK case it was not that fiscal policy was expansionary, but that it was not restrictive enough to avoid the large rise in interest rates imposed to try to reduce monetary growth.

32 Government politicians in both countries, and some of their supporters, at times initially took the line that the 'strong' exchange rate reflected world confidence in the correctness of their policies – somehow the same people did not publicly state that the subsequent falls in exchange rate reflected world condemnation of the government policies.

33 Unless the initial position was one of balance of payments surplus, and the policy merely reduces the surplus without producing an actual deficit.

34 It can be shown in formal treatments that floating rate open-economy monetary policy has a greater effect the more mobile is international capital.

35 Only if the balance of payments is completely insensitive to interest rates and the government also sticks to a fixed exchange rate will neither monetary nor fiscal policy be able to expand income, i.e. if the balance of payments is limited to the current account and prices are rigid then there is only one level of income at which imports will equal exports. As stated in the text, we regard this case as unrealistic for modern developed economies.

36 Formerly many economists used to assume that PPP holds all the time. Some models still make this assumption, e.g. the simplest version of the monetary theory

mentioned in note 6. Most economists accept that PPP does not now correctly describe short-run movements in relative prices/exchange rates. For example, Frenkel (1981). Evidence on PPP in the long run is less conclusive, e.g. Frankel and Meese (1987).

37 From the strict viewpoint the formula is only an approximation if discrete time periods are used.

38 No causation is determined within equation (6.1) and it could just as well be written:

$$\dot{e} = \dot{P}_w - \dot{P} \qquad (6.2)$$

This is more usually the form with floating rates.

39 Compare the discussions in Chapter 5.

40 Or inflation will increase, if it is expected that the money supply will continue to grow faster.

41 Results would differ in the case of an expansionary fiscal policy financed wholly by borrowing, however. Using the PPP argument the exchange rate would drop. Using the simpler 'monetary theory' approach it would not drop. Also see the next note.

42 For the moment we are ignoring any interest rate effects in the presence of capital mobility, or at least assuming that they are outweighed by the price (inflation) expectation effect.

43 See Chapter 2 for a discussion of the implications of the inability of many Central Banks to control the money supply directly.

44 Sometimes called 'destabilising speculation' in this context.

45 In this, and in the case of the next paragraph, we leave aside the role played by the IMF, or by other countries, if they are called in to help stabilise the situation. The scenario of this paragraph fits several cases, e.g. with the inclusion of the IMF it would be part of UK experience in 1975/6 – though this was complicated by the oil price rise of 1973. (This is our view; at least one reader of the draft of this work was dubious.)

46 Sometimes called a 'hot money exodus'.

47 A full account would involve the reactions of France's partners in the European Monetary System, and thus also involve the considerations in the sections on pages 121–8.

48 The idea of combining quickly clearing asset markets with labour and goods markets which do not clear in the short run is usually attributed to Dornbusch (1976).

49 As with the natural rate models of Chapter 4, by 'equilibrium' here is meant a situation where people's expectations are satisfied and where demand equals supply. It does not mean here that exchange rates are constant, just as with the natural rate it did not mean that the price level is constant.

50 As we have expressed it here, with e as standard 'nominal' exchange rate i and i_w are nominal interest rates. In some articles, the right-hand side has real interest rates, which are approximately $r = i - \dot{p}$; $r_w = i_w - \dot{p}_w$. The left-hand side is then meant to be a 'real' exchange rate, which is a measure of competitiveness. But the change in competitiveness is $\dot{p} + \dot{e} - \dot{p}_w$. The other version is therefore:

$$\dot{e} + \dot{p} - \dot{p}_w = r_w - r$$

Therefore

$$\dot{e} + \dot{p} - \dot{p}_w = (i_w - \dot{p}_w) - (i - \dot{p}) \qquad (6.4)$$

Which is the same as equation (6.3).

51 In the case of an expansionary fiscal policy with no accompanying monetary increase, the combination of rational expectations with quickly moving exchange markets speeds up the crowding out via appreciation that occurs when there is high capital mobility (the discussion of the Mundell–Fleming model earlier gives the essential components of the mechanism for appreciation and crowding out). If there is perfect capital mobility, then rational expectations and instantaneously adjusting exchange markets assumptions imply immediate full crowding-out of fiscal policy, since the exchange rate jumps up to its new fully appreciated level. If the fiscal policy is announced prior to its implementation there will even be a temporary fall in income, as the appreciation and loss of competitiveness start as soon as people expect that the rate will have to be higher in the future. This reduces income immediately, whereas the increase from the fiscal policy will only come with its implementation.

52 For example, Dornbusch-type models, which allow for inflation rather than price levels, often incorporate a Phillips Curve which is not vertical in the short run.

53 There are various sources. One of the most thorough is Bruno and Sachs (1985).

54 Although growth is often ignored, in the theory of the open economy version, growth is often ignored, the empirical applications do allow for growth. Many of the models of 'real wage targets' behaviour in open economy contexts ignore any modifications of the real wage aspiration due to the state of the labour market, and to this extent differ from those discussed in Chapter 4.

55 Formal analyses often use a variant of the 'production real wage' by using a 'value-added' price index. This is to deal with the use of imported inputs of raw materials. For simplicity we shall write as if imports were all of consumer goods, but this will not alter the conclusions.

56 Compare Chapter 3, pages 35–40, where it is pointed out that Keynesian models which include a labour market such that prices are flexible but money wages are not (often referred to as the aggregate-demand/aggregate-supply model) can achieve an increase in employment using monetary/fiscal policies but that real wages have to fall as demand is increased. If money wages increase with prices, so that real wages do not fall, then employment cannot be increased.

57 See the discussion of the 'J'-curve, above. With flexible rates, if the Marshall–Lerner conditions do not hold in the short run, then there are likely to be swings and overshooting of exchange rates in the absence of 'stabilising speculators' who take a long view.

58 The lags may also raise the problem of unintentionally destabilising effects of stabilisation policies, dealt with in Chapter 3. In the 'overshooting' model of this section, this problem is mitigated by the greater strength of the short-run, as compared to long-run, effects on employment.

59 Diagrammatically, only if the LM curve is flatter than the balance of payments equilibrium locus will there be a deficit if the money supply effects are sterilised (thus preventing any induced shift in the LM curve).

60 Note note 25 above, second part.

61 Once we start to consider long-run effects of the balance of payments, the static assumptions implicit until now became less and less convincing. For example, the sacrifice of consumption (or other components of what is called 'domestic absorption') needed to reverse the capital account deficit becomes easier as output grows.

62 See Chapter 1. Some examples are the discussion in Chapter 3 over the desirability of waiting for wages to fall enough to restore full employment, or that in Chapter 4 over the relevance of the vertical Phillips Curve. It is logically tenable, though perhaps psychologically less common, to come down on different sides of the divide according to the precise application under debate.

63 Again, the quotation marks indicate that these are issues of feelings and judgement rather than precisely quantifiable amounts.

64 As already noted, the crowding out of investment will be less than in a closed economy if, as we have tended to assume, the balance of payments is more interest responsive than the domestic monetary equilibrium relation.

65 In the French case cited, these last two possible alleviations of the constraint were lacking from their EMS partners.

66 Even in the case of zero capital flows – when neither monetary nor fiscal policies would work under fixed rates.

67 And the whole 'value-added' price index also remaining unaltered.

68 A reluctance to use a stronger fiscal policy may be because of worries about budget deficits effectively financed by borrowing from abroad, in line with the previous sentence in the text.

69 If a feared amount of depreciation is greater than the interest rate differential, people will want to move out of domestic currency denominated assets into overseas assets.

70 It is also import-substitution led.

71 See Chapter 3, pages 35–40. At this point we are not considering whether higher-than-expected inflation can increase employment, as discussed in Chapters 4 and 5.

72 A related way of putting the same point is that it is impossible for all countries to simultaneously 'improve' the current account of their balance of payments, just as it is impossible for all countries to have a surplus on the current account (assuming they use the same definitions and measure accurately), since Country A's exports to Country B are Country B's imports from Country A.

73 Note that since domestic inflation has fallen together with the reduction in money supply growth, there need be no contraction in real domestic demand, and hence no unemployment.

In the UK this argument was advocated by some economists who were closely associated with the Thatcher government, under whose auspices no actions were taken to alleviate a large appreciation of the £ during its initial macroeconomic policies. Our own view at the time was sceptical of this argument and remains so in the light of UK experience.

74 The announcement (if believed) of a long-run monetary target would have a strong effect on the exchange rate due to its effects on expectations. Note, however, that the overshooting model of the section on pages 114–15, which would imply a further amplification of the appreciation, relies on sluggish wage and price behaviour and hence is not relevant for the argument of this paragraph.

75 Given the existence of a short-run Phillips Curve, it may also not want the increased demand for output and employment that would follow from an improvement in its competitiveness as a result of a fall in its exchange rate.

76 If there are floating rates, the lack of ability to determine unilaterally the balance of payments applies to the components (such as the current account) rather than to the total realised balance of payments. See Appendix.

77 Remember (see Appendix) that the excess supply of one currency on the foreign exchange market is equal to the excess demand for other currencies in return. It is this excess demand for other currencies which has to be met out of foreign exchange reserves.

78 Provided that it is prepared to allow its own money supply to increase, or can sterilise such an increase. See Appendix.

79 In Chapter 5 we mentioned the contractionary aspects of such shocks, here we mention their inflationary aspects. However, both hold; such shocks will tend to raise prices and to reduce output, if nominal aggregate demand is unchanged.

80 It also has some, but not complete, similarities to the rule which some economists have favoured, of keeping the growth rate of *nominal* income constant.

81 West Germany had this freedom partly because it was the largest economy in the EMS, but also because it was the natural balance of payments surplus country in the group because of its low inflation rate. As mentioned in the Appendix, there is an asymmetry in that surplus countries can always acquire reserves, but deficit countries will be run out of them. The EMS was supposed to avoid this asymmetry but did not.

82 In the late 1980s, part of the motivation of the French and Italian governments in pushing for further EEC monetary and political unification, was because they resented having to subordinate their policies to that of West Germany. In the mid-1980s they had been happy to use the link to the Deutschmark as a way of enforcing tough domestic policies to reduce inflation. By the end of the 1980s they felt that the unemployment cost had risen too high, inflation was low enough and therefore they would have preferred more expansionary policies. But they were inhibited by the commitment to keep their currencies fixed against the Deutschmark.

83 Co-operation is therefore easier when the countries have other, possibly non-economic, ongoing relationships that encourage a spirit of working together. This is one factor in the success of the European Monetary System, as well as the greater advantages because of close trading links between members.

84 It is also unpopular with others who believe that markets virtually always work smoothly, even if they do not take the whole rational expectations approach. See note 12, for the opposition of Friedman to the notion of 'destabilising' speculation, and in more detail his 1953 chapter.

85 Part of the French case discussed on pages 113–14.

86 The foundation of the European Monetary System, and its predecessor the 'Snake' involved much discussion of these issues. At the time of writing (early 1991) the experience of the European Monetary System has added impetus to EEC discussions of political, as well as formal, monetary unification.

87 'Accidents' in inverted commas, as we do not want to get involved in arguments over whether or not national states correspond to deep determinants of national identification.

88 This is possible if e responds on a one-to-one basis to changes in P_W, and does not change for any other reason as long as the rate of change of prices of domestically produced goods remain constant.

7 WHY UNEMPLOYMENT HAS INCREASED

1 In the UK in the early 1980s the reiterated claim by the government that its policies had nothing to do with unemployment were part of the reason why it was summed up by its opponents by the acronym Tina – which, as mentioned in Chapter 1, stood for the government's statement 'there is no alternative'.

2 We use 'other causes' rather than the term 'supply' changes, in case the latter is limited to an aggregate supply curve.

3 Lipsey's (1960) original explanation of the Phillips Curve had already made a somewhat similar point in his discussion of the relationship between measured unemployment and the excess demand/supply of labour.

Many of the early discussions of the existence of a short-run Phillips Curve and the longer-run natural rate were based on variants of search theory, e.g. the articles in Phelps *et al.* (1970).

4 In those countries where unions have political influence, the government attempts to help workers may themselves have been influenced by trade union pressure.

5 These are sometimes called 'severance payments'. It seems to have been forgotten that (at least in some cases, such as the UK) redundancy payments were actually introduced in order to improve labour market flexibility. The idea was that unions, and the workforces they represented, would be less resistant to structural changes involving lower employment in particular firms if workers received payments that would help them over temporary unemployment and retraining/relocation costs.

6 For our purposes it does not matter whether these contributions are strictly linked to health etc. (as in some countries, e.g. France) or are really a disguised form of general taxation (e.g. in the UK).

7 E.g. Giersch (1985). The contrast drawn between the US and Western Europe is usually in employee job security provisions.

8 Redundancy payments can also have effects on those who become unemployed that could act somewhat similarly to those of unemployment benefits, which are discussed later, although the evidence suggests that the 'lump-sum' payments and continuing benefits do differ in their effects.

9 The argument as just presented applies to a heterogeneous economy in which there are always some firms with increases in demand and others with declines. If there is a business cycle such that during some periods there is an increase in the demand for most products, then during such periods employment protection measures will mean lower employment. However, during the contractionary phase of the cycle when most firms face falling demand, employment will decline less rapidly than without the measures. Much more careful specification is required to be able to predict what will happen to the average level of unemployment over the cycle as a whole. This is another example of the point mentioned above that policies usually analysed in terms of their effect on the natural rate of unemployment may also have some implications for moves around the natural rate.

10 There might be some effect on unemployment if the labour supply and job search behaviour of the unemployed is sensitive to the level of real wages – this, as usual, relates to the whole question of the 'voluntariness' of unemployment and its measurement. See the discussion following Fig. 7.1, which recapitulates that in Chapter 4.

11 The inability of firms to recoup training costs is part of some theories of efficiency wages. See Chapter 3. A non-technical, Keynesian treatment stressing the role of hiring costs and the inability of firms to cut wages for new entrants is Okun (1981).

12 In terms of the distinction in the previous chapter, a wedge is driven between the producer and employee real wage.

13 Those who have studied microeconomics will recognise all this as an example of the incidence of taxation.

14 The same feeling, in our opinion, lies behind taxes labelled 'employee contributions to social insurance'. Ironically, supposed ignorance of what these contributions really are has prompted their increase, while the justification for cutting income taxes has been that people are rational and know better than governments how to achieve their own desires. Another factor may be that the taxes called social security contributions are often less progressive than ordinary income tax.

15 For example, some of the studies in Bean, Layard and Nickell (1987).

16 Another common fallacy exploited by government spokesmen in the 1980s is the claim that increases in income taxes would adversely affect incentives (assuming, implicitly, that supply of labour curves are upward sloping) and yet ignoring the implication that increases in sales taxes will have the same effect since they similarly reduce the consumption of goods that can be obtained by an extra hour's work.

17 See note 13.

18 Therefore if $w_6 - w_0$ in Fig. 7.2 equals $w_1 - w_0$ in Fig. 7.1, then L_3 represents the same demand for labour as L_1. This will occur if the taxation is a constant per period worked, unlike the next stage of the argument which will hold even with proportional taxation, provided only that the tax rate at the final equilibrium raises the same amount whoever it is levied on (for simplicity the effects of tax thresholds are ignored here).

19 Even those authors who have discussed income tax as a cause of a rise in unemployment have done so primarily in terms of the sort of real wage aspiration models mentioned in Chapter 4, e.g. Bacon and Eltis (1978).

20 Whether they will continue to be measured as unemployed depends on the measurement procedure used. In countries, such as the US, where unemployment is measured by questionnaire rather than by registering for benefits, the inclusion of such people in measured unemployment will depend on the honesty of response to questions and on self-knowledge of one's own motivation.

21 In this sort of model, it is the level of unemployment benefit which is exogenous, not the replacement ratio. The denominator of the ratio, the wage, is endogenous and itself depends on the numerator. The ratio could increase or decrease when benefits are raised.

22 For example, see the studies in note 15 or Minford et al. (1985) and Nickell (1984). The measurement of the replacement ratio is itself controversial. A useful summary of many studies is given in Table 5.2 of Atkinson (1987).

23 A few authors, e.g. Layard (1986), have claimed that there has been a steady decline in the opprobrium attached to accepting benefits, and therefore benefits are partly to blame for the rise in the natural rate. However, they have provided no evidence for this claim – it is simply an assertion to explain the unexplained part of the rise in their estimates of the natural rate.

24 The idea, discussed in Chapter 3, of 'efficiency wages' could be used to imply that employers worry about their wages compared with those in other firms, even when excess labour is available – this, however, might not be relevant for firms employing 'secondary' labour. The question then becomes why displaced union sector workers do not become 'secondary', and the reluctance to give-up 'primary' status may be an explanation, as in McDonald and Solow (1985).

25 Another way of putting the same point is that until money wage change is linked to the level of unemployment, the notion of the natural rate is otiose.

26 The plausibility of such a process is increased by the incorporation of the earlier distinction between the 'product real wage' of relevance to the firm (i.e. money wage relative to its own price) and the consumption real wage of concern to the union (i.e. money wage relative to prices of all consumer goods). This distinction enables one to avoid the requirement that unions are irrational in not foreseeing that increased money wages will lead to increased prices.

27 The likeliness of this last assumption may depend on the sensitivity of the demand for labour to real wages – so that unions expect some of their members to lose their jobs if they push for higher wages. The crucial difference between the two routes is that the first requires that real wages actually rise, the second only that unions try to obtain a rise, even if unsuccessfully ex post.

28 The mechanism of this paragraph applies to any other changes which shift firms' demand for labour schedule or the union-wage functions, as well as to changes in sheer union militancy. It is thus relevant to explaining the transition process to higher unemployment for any of the other causes suggested for shifts in the natural rate, as discussed in the last two paragraphs of this section. See Layard (1986) for a full account.

29 See note 22.

30 E.g. compare Gordon (1988) or Schultze (1987) with Schultze (1984).

31 M. Bruno was one of the economists who stressed the role of real wage rigidity in the face of supply shocks, but he says that in the early 1980s the real wage rigidity of the previous decade has moderated in most of the EEC. E.g. Bruno in Bean et al. (1987).

32 See, for example, Leech and Wagstaff (1986) on technological change and Beenstock (1984) on imports from the newly industrialised countries.

33 In so far as people wish to save some of their extra income, some increase in Keynesian-style budget deficits might be required, though, in general, over longer periods of time, interest rate changes should allow private investment to reach levels consistent with full employment. All this is no different to the general discussion of aggregate demand in Chapters 2 and 3.

34 For an older, but exceptionally lucid, description of the possibility of a clash between average prosperity and an acceptable income distribution see Meade(1964).

35 One cannot rule out a priori the possibility that technical change has been more biased to capital recently. One exception to the slower productivity growth has been the UK since 1981 – even here, however, total output over the whole of the period 1979–88 did not grow in the way one might have expected.

36 See Chapter 6, in the section on pages 108–117.

37 The figures in the OECD report (1988) show that for the main West European countries, imports of manufactures from NICs were still less than 1.5% of domestic output by 1985.

38 Similarly to the argument on pages 141–3, the increased exports of some goods by the NICs requires increased capital equipment which they import from more developed countries.

39 One could also try to see if there are links from unemployment to oil prices. Most commentators have ignored such possibilities, preferring to concentrate on the more colourful political events accompanying the rise and later decline of the OPEC cartel.

40 Depending on the complementary/substitutability relationship between labour, capital and energy in the different sectors, it might also be necessary to have a general decline in wages. This fits in with the discussion in the next paragraph. If one also allows for some industries to trade externally and others not, and also for degrees of mobility of different factors of production between industries, the possible patterns of real wages/profits rapidly becomes very complex. Similarly if one allows for different propensities to consume between owners of different factors of production.

41 Countries with high enough inflation during the years soon after the oil price rises could achieve the required changes in relative real wages simply by having zero or low increases in money wages in the energy-using industries. As discussed in Chapter 2, Keynes and his followers believed that it is easier to cut real wages by holding money wages steady in the face of rising prices than to cut money wages themselves. From this point of view, the stronger anti-inflation stance after the second oil price shock might have been a mistake.

42 As noted in note 40 above, a general decline in real wages might be required even if all oil was produced at home. An interesting case is the UK, which had discovered major oil fields between the two oil price rises. In the UK the rise in oil prices was blamed by some for exacerbating unemployment via the increased need to switch between manufacturing and other sectors. Others claimed that the rise in the exchange rate was far greater than could be attributed to the UK becoming an oil exporter while prices rose, and was due to what they saw as perverse

government policy at such a time. See notes 31 and 73 in Chapter 6.

43 To the extent that the current account deficit increases, this has the familiar contractionary effect on the economy, as shown via the standard national income equation in note 13 of Chapter 6. However, this involves a movement above the natural rate of unemployment, not a shift in the natural rate itself.

44 Also see the Bruno reference in note 31 above, as to the difference between the first and second oil price rises. Thus at least one prominent economist whose work helped to ensure the widespread acceptance of the role of oil prices in unemployment in the 1970s, does not accept that continuing high unemployment is still due to this cause.

45 Strong believers in the role of oil price rises could claim the results are asymmetrical, but this would seem a rather unconvincing excuse without further explanations. The link from oil price to unemployment via structural adjustment could plausibly be claimed to suggest that unemployment will rise as a result of any sharp change in raw material prices, whether up or down. However, given the high unemployment in 1985, on this approach, the adjustment to the previous price rise could not have been complete and therefore adjustment to the price fall should have been relatively easy. We ignore the possibility that the adjustment to the previous price rise had been very slow and prolonged and that it suddenly completed itself just on the day that it became obvious that oil prices were going to remain lower. An econometric test claiming symmetry is Tatom (1988).

46 E.g. Blanchard and Summers (1986). Although the formalisation of hysteresis may be recent, the idea has long been mooted in informal discussions. For example, hysteresis is implicit in the widely held view that World War Two allowed higher employment afterwards because the previously 'unemployables' of the 1930s acquired experience in munitions factories, or even in the armed forces, which fitted them for subsequently holding jobs.

47 This depends on the (reasonable) assumption that a lower capital stock reduces the marginal productivity of labour.

48 See Layard (1986) for an espousal of this view, based on empirical studies such as Layard and Nickell (1987a).

49 Several other economists published articles with somewhat similar ideas at about the same time, but we follow the type of argument in Blanchard and Summers (1986).

50 In those countries, primarily the US, where unemployment often takes the form of explicitly temporary lay-offs, the group of unemployed whose interests may be ignored exclude the temporarily laid-off.

51 As we are sticking to the version of the insider–outsider model in which bargaining takes place at the level of the individual firm, we are here assuming that each firm/union bargain covers few enough workers for the bargainers to ignore any effects of their own bargain on aggregate wage, price or employment levels.

52 L_0 can be expected employment if aggregate wages, price or demand are known to be subject to fluctuations.

53 This extreme assumption also ignores voluntary quits from the firm and retirement.

54 If there are some firms which are not unionised (nor subject to the other 'inside' consideration in the non-union versions of the model) or if new firms can easily start up, an extra analysis is required of why the 'outsiders' do not find jobs in the other sectors. The suggestions in the subsection on pages 139–41 could be relevant to an explanation.

55 We ignore the rational expectations of Chapter 5 here.

56 It is also ironic that the claim was typically made in support of new governments, such as in the UK, which were avowedly to the right politically of their

predecessors. Previously Marxists had said, as part of their critique of capitalism, that the need for high unemployment to discipline workers and to remove their ability to raise wages was a drawback of capitalism. See Kalecki (1943). An opposite view had been taken by left-wing parties which supported the feasibility of a low-unemployment mixed economy: workers who had lived through prolonged high unemployment would be suspicious of new technology which displaced workers and they would impede its adoption. Workers who had had the security of always being able to find new jobs easily, would not worry about the prospect of redundancy because of their confidence that any unemployment would be transitory.

57 Unmodified by hysteresis.
58 As mentioned in the section on pages 134–41, the US is an exception. In the UK, a fall in unemployment which still left the rate well above 1979 levels was accompanied by a reversal of the fall in inflation. Note, however, that the frequent criticism in the UK that high unemployment has been accompanied by rising *real* wages, is not itself really a criticism of the natural rate approach, because productivity has been increasing faster than real wages – as shown by the rise in real profits.
59 See Chapter 3.
60 The short-run elasticity of Lucas and Rapping (1969) types of theory of the *cycle* do not seem plausible to explain fifteen years of high unemployment.

APPENDIX   BALANCE OF PAYMENTS AND FOREIGN EXCHANGE

1 If exports are paid for in foreign currency, and the exporter wishes to hold on to foreign currency, this should be considered as two transactions: (i) a current account export and (ii) a capital account import.
2 It simplifies the exposition here, but makes no essential difference to it, if we ignore the fact that fixed exchange rates usually incorporate a small margin within which the rate can vary. All this means is that the rates at which the authorities buy and sell are slightly different.
3 This is an increase in the 'monetary base' and may lead to further expansion of the total money supply.
4 Thus the independence of the money supply from the balance of payments with floating rates only strictly holds for definitions of the money supply which include non-residents' holdings. For some purposes of macroeconomic policy, it can be argued that only the monetary holdings of residents' are relevant, and that measures of the money supply excluding non-residents are the ones to be stressed.
5 In practice, difficulties in collection data mean that there can be 'measurement' errors leading to discrepancies. Similarly, with fixed rates, from equation (3) it follows that B_{UK} should equal the value of the foreign reserves acquired by the Bank (the value of £ sold by the Bank in meeting $D_\pounds - S_\pounds$), but in practice they may differ because of 'errors and omissions'.
6 The early discussion of the Marshall–Lerner conditions were in the context of the current account only, where conditions expressed in terms of elasticities of demand are, perhaps, more natural. Formally, however, as in this Appendix, they can also be applied to the overall balance of payments.
7 For the purpose of the outline in this Appendix we ignore the possibility that the rate will initially move towards the equilibrium but then overshoot further away in the other direction.

BIBLIOGRAPHY

Akerloff, G.A. (1980) 'A Theory of Social Custom, of which Unemployment May be One Consequence' *Quarterly Journal of Economics*, 95, pp. 749–75.

Atkinson, A.B. (1987) 'Income Maintenance and Social Insurance' in Vol. 2 of A.J. Auerbach and M. Feldstein (eds) *Handbook of Public Economics* (North-Holland, Amsterdam)

Bacon, R. and W. Eltis (1978) *Britain's Economic Problem: Too Few Producers* 2nd ed. (Macmillan, London).

Baily, M.N. (1978) 'Stabilisation Policy and Private Economic Behaviour' *Brookings Papers on Economic Activity*, pp. 11–50.

Barro, R.J. (1974) 'Are Government Bonds Net Wealth?' *Journal of Political Economy*, 82, pp. 1095–117

Barro, R.J. (1977) 'Long-term Contracting, Sticky Prices and Monetary Policy' *Journal of Monetary Economics*, 3, pp. 305–16.

Barro, R.J. (1979) 'Second Thoughts on Keynesian Economics' *American Economic Review*, 69(2), pp. 54–9.

Barro, R.J. and H.I. Grossman (1971) 'A General Disequilibrium Model of Income and Employment' *American Economic Review*, 61, pp. 82–93.

Baumol, W.J. (1961) 'Pitfalls of Contracyclical Policies: Some Tools and Results' *Review of Economics and Statistics*, 43, pp. 21–6.

Bean, C.R., P.R.G. Layard and S.J. Nickell (eds) (1987) *The Rise in Unemployment* (Blackwell, Oxford).

Beenstock, M. (1984) *The World Economy in Transition* 2nd ed. (Allen & Unwin, London).

Begg, D.K.H. (1982) *The Rational Expectations Revolution in Economics* (Philip Allan, Oxford).

Benjamin, D.K. and L.A. Kochin (1979) 'Searching for an Explanantion of Unemployment in Interwar Britain' *Journal of Political Economy*, 87, pp. 441–78, discussed (in same journal), 1982, Vol. 90, pp. 369–436.

Blanchard, O.J. and L.H. Summers (1986) 'Hysteresis and the European Unemployment Problem 'in *NBER Macroeconomics Annual 1986* (MIT Press, Cambridge, Mass.), pp. 15–89.

Blinder, A.S., R.M. Solow, G.F. Break, P.O. Steiner and D. Netzer (1974) *The Economics of Public Finance* (Brookings Washington D.C.).

Boland, L.A. (1982) *The Foundations of Economic Method* (Allen & Unwin, London).

Bootle, R. (1981) 'How Important is it to Defeat Inflation? – The Evidence', *The Three Banks Review*, 132, pp. 23–47.

BIBLIOGRAPHY

Brunner, K. (1981) 'The Case Against Monetary Activism' *Lloyds Bank Review*, 139, pp. 20–39.

Bruno, M. and J. Sachs (1985) *Economics of Worldwide Stagflation* (Harvard UP, Cambridge, Mass.).

Buiter, W.H. (1980) 'The Macroeconomics of Dr Pangloss: A Critical Survey of the New Classical Macroeconomics' *Economic Journal*, 90, pp. 34–50.

Chater, R.E.J., A. Dean and R.F. Elliott (1981) *Incomes Policy* (Oxford UP, Oxford).

Doeringer, P. and M. Piore (1971) *Internal Labor Markets and Manpower Analysis* (D.C. Heath & Co., Lexington).

Dornbusch, R. (1976) 'Expectations and Exchange Rate Dynamics' *Journal of Political Economy*, 84, pp. 1161–76.

Fellner, W. (1979) *et al.* 'The Credibility Effect and Rational Expectations' *Brookings Papers on Economic Activity*, 1, pp. 167–78.

Fellner, W. (1982) and others in 'Anti-inflation Policies and the Problem of Credibility' *American Economic Review*, 72, pp. 77–91

Fischer, S. (1977) 'Long-term Contracts, Rational Expectations and the Optimal Money Supply Rule' *Journal of Political Economy*, 85, pp. 191–205.

Fleming, J.M. (1962) 'Domestic Financial Policies under Fixed and and under Floating Exchange Rates' *IMF Staff Papers*, 9, pp. 369–79.

Frankel, J.A. and R. Meese (1987) 'Are Exchange Rates Excessively Variable?' in *NBER Macroeconomics Annual 1987* (MIT Press, Cambridge, Mass.).

Frenkel, J. (1981) 'The Collapse of Purchasing Power Parity during the 1970s' *European Economic Review*, 16, pp. 145–65.

Frenkel, J.A. and H.G. Johnson (1976) *The Monetary Approach to the Balance of Payments* (Allen & Unwin, London).

Friedman, M. (1948) 'A Monetary and Fiscal Framework for Economic Stability' *American Economic Review*, 38, pp. 245–64. Reprinted in Friedman (1953).

Friedman, M. (1953) *Essays in Positive Economics* (Univ. of Chicago Press, Chicago).

Friedman, M. (1956) 'The Quantity Theory of Money – A Restatement' in M. Friedman (ed.) *Studies in the Quantity Theory of Money* (Univ. of Chicago Press, Chicago).

Friedman, M. (1957) *A Theory of the Consumption Function* (Princeton UP, Princeton.)

Friedman, M. (1959) 'The Demand for Money – Some Theoretical and Empirical Results' *Journal of Political Economy*, 67, pp. 327–51.

Friedman, M. (1968) 'The Role of Monetary Policy' *American Economic Review*, 58, pp. 1–17.

Friedman, M. (1972) 'Comments on the Critics' *Journal of Political Economy*, 80, pp. 912–33.

Friedman, M. (1976) *Price Theory*, 2nd ed. (Aldine, Chicago). Chapter 12 is based on his 1975 *Unemployment versus Inflation* (Institute of Economic Affairs Occasional Paper No. 44).

Friedman, M. and R.V. Roosa (1967) *The Balance of Payments: Free versus Fixed Exchange Rates* (American Enterprise Institute, Washington DC).

Giersch, H. (1985) 'Eurosclerosis' *Discussion Paper 112* (Kiel Institute for World Economics, Kiel).

Gordon, R.J. (1987) *Macroeconomics* 4th ed. (Little, Brown, Boston).

Gordon, R.J. (1988) 'Back to the Future: European Unemployment Today Viewed from America in 1939' *Brookings Papers on Economic Activity*, 1, pp. 271–312.

Hibbs, D.A. (1987) *The American Political Economy* (Harvard UP, Cambridge, Mass.).

Hicks, J.R. (1950) *A Contribution to the Theory of the Trade Cycle* (Oxford UP, Oxford).

BIBLIOGRAPHY

Holden, K., D.A. Peel and J.L. Thompson (1987) *The Economics of Wage Controls* (Macmillan, London).
House of Commons (1980) Treasury and Civil Service Committee, Session 1979–80, *Memoranda on Monetary Policy* (HMSO, London).
Kalecki, M. (1943) 'Political Aspects of Full Employment' *Political Quarterly*, reprinted in E.K. Hunt and J.G. Schwartz (eds) *A Critique of Economic Theory* (Penguin, Harmondsworth, 1972).
Kenen, P.B. and P.R. Allen (1980) *Asset Markets, Exchange Rates and Economic Integration* (Cambridge UP, Cambridge).
Keynes, J.M. (1936) *The General Theory of Employment, Interest and Money* (Macmillan, London).
Krugman, P. (1989) *Exchange Rate Instability* (MIT Press, Cambridge, Mass.).
Kydland, F.E. and E.C. Prescott (1977) 'Rules Rather than Discretion: The Inconsistency of Optimal Plans' *Journal of Political Economy*, 85, pp. 473–91.
Layard, R. (1986) *How to Beat Unemployment* (Oxford UP, Oxford).
Layard, R. and S.J. Nickell (1987a) 'The Labour Market' in R. Dornbusch and R. Layard (eds) *The Performance of the British Economy* (Oxford UP, Oxford).
Layard, P.R.G. and S.J. Nickell (1987b) 'Unemployment in Britain' in C.R. Bean, P.R.G. Layard and S.J. Nickell (eds) *The Rise in Unemployment* (Blackwell, Oxford).
Leech, D. and H. Wagstaff (1986) *Future Employment and Technical Change* (Kogan Page, London).
Lipsey, R.G. (1960) 'The Relation Between Unemployment and the Rate of Money Wage Changes in the United Kingdom, 1867–1957: A Further Analysis' *Economica*, 27, pp. 1–31.
Long, J.B. and C.L. Plosser (1983) 'Real Business Cycles' *Journal of Political Economy*, 91, pp. 39–69.
Lucas, R.E. (1972) 'Expectations and the Neutrality of Money' *Journal of Economic Theory*, 4, pp. 103–24.
Lucas, R.E. (1976) 'Econometric Policy Evaluation: A Critique' in K. Brunner and A.H. Meltzer (eds) *The Phillips Curve and Labour Markets* (*Journal of Monetary Economics* supplement).
Lucas, R.E. (1978) 'Unemployment Policy' *American Economic Review: Papers & Proceedings*, 68, pp. 353–57.
Lucas, R.E. and L. Rapping (1969) 'Real Wages, Employment and Inflation' *Journal of Political Economy*, 77, pp. 721–54.
McClosky, D.N. (1983) 'The Rhetoric of Economics' *Journal of Economic Literature*, 21, pp. 481–517.
McClosky, D.N. (ed.) (1988) *The Consequences of Economic Rhetoric* (Cambridge UP, Cambridge).
McDonald, I.M. and R.A. Solow (1985) 'Wages and Employment in a Segmented Labor Market' *Quarterly Journal of Economics*, 100, pp. 1115–41.
Macdonald, R. (1988) *Floating Exchange Rates: Theories and Evidence* (Unwin Hyman, London).
Mankiw, N.G. and D. Romer (eds) (1991) *New Keynesian Economics* (MIT Press, Cambridge, Mass.).
Marin, A. (1972) 'The Phillips Curve (Born 1958 – Died ?)', *The Three Banks Review*, 96, pp. 28–42.
Mastropasqua, C., S. Micossi and R. Rinaldi (1988) 'Interventions, Sterilisation and Monetary Policy in EMS Countries, 1979–87' in F. Giavazzi, S. Micossi and M. Miller (eds) *The European Monetary System* (Cambridge UP, Cambridge).

BIBLIOGRAPHY

Meade, J.E. (1951, 1955) *The Theory of International Economic Policy* (Oxford UP, Oxford).

Meade, J.E. (1964) *Efficiency, Equality and the Ownership of Property* (Allen & Unwin, London).

Michie, J. (1987) *Wages in the Business Cycle* (Frances Pinter Publishers, London).

Minford, P. with P. Ashton, M. Peel, D. Davies and A. Sprague (1985) *Unemployment, Cause and Cure* 2nd ed. (Blackwell, Oxford).

Modigliani, F. (1977) 'The Monetarist Controversy' *American Economic Review*, 67, pp. 1–17.

Modigliani, F. and R. Brumberg, (1954) 'Utility Analysis and the Consumption Function' in K. Kurrihara (ed.) *Post Keynesian Economics* (Rutgers UP, New Brunswick).

Mundell, R.A. (1963) 'Capital Mobility and Stabilisation Under Fixed and Floating Exchange Rates' *Canadian Journal of Economics & Political Science*, pp. 487–99.

Muth, J.F. (1961) 'Rational Expectations and the Theory of Price Movements' *Econometrica*, 29, pp. 315–35.

Nickell, S.J. (1984) 'A Review of *Unemployment*: Cause and Cure by Patrick Minford et al.' *Economic Journal*, 94, pp. 946–53.

O'Driscoll, G.P. (1977) 'The Ricardian Non-equivalence Theorem' *Journal of Political Economy*, 85, pp. 207–10.

OECD (1988) *The Newly Industrialising Countries: Challenge and Opportunity for OECD Industries* (OECD, Paris).

Okun, A.M. (1981) *Price and Quantities: A Macroeconomic Analysis* (Blackwell, Oxford).

Parkin, M. (1975) 'Where is Britain's Inflation Going?' *Lloyds Bank Review*, 117, pp. 1–13.

Patinkin, D. (1965) *Money, Interest and Prices* 2nd ed. (Harper & Row, London).

Phelps, E.S. (1968) 'Money Wage Dynamics and Labour Market Equilibrium' *Journal of Political Economy*, 76, pp. 687–711.

Phelps, E.S., A.A. Alchian, C.C. Holt, D.T. Mortensen, G.C. Archibald, R.E. Lucas, L.A. Rapping, S.G. Winter, J.P. Gould, D.F. Gordon, A. Hynes, D.A. Nichols, P.J. Taubman and M. Wilkinson (1970) *Microeconomic Foundations of Employment and Inflation Theory* (Norton, New York).

Phelps, E.S. and J.B. Taylor (1977) 'Stabilising Power of Monetary Policy under Rational Expectations' *Journal of Political Economy*, 85, pp. 163–90.

Phillips, A.W. (1958) 'The Relation Between Unemployment and the Rate of Change of Money Wages in the UK 1861–1957' *Economica*, 25, pp. 283–99.

Phillips. A.W. (1962) 'Employment, Inflation and Growth' *Economica*, 29, pp. 1–16.

Pigou, A.C. (1917) 'The Value of Money' *Quarterly Journal of Economics*, 37, pp. 38–65.

Poole, W. (1970) 'Optimal Choice of Monetary Policy Instruments in a Simple Stochastic Macro Model' *Quarterly Journal of Economics*, 84, pp. 197–216.

Samuelson, P.A. (1939) 'Interactions Between the Multiplier Analysis and the Principle of Accelerations' *Review of Economics & Statistics*, 21, pp. 75–8.

Sargan, J.D. (1964) 'Wages and Prices in the UK' reprinted in J.D. Sargan *Contributions to Econometrics Vol. I* (Cambridge UP, Cambridge, 1988).

Sargent, T.J. (1976) 'The Observational Equivalence of Natural and Unnatural Rate Theories of Macroeconomics' *Journal of Political Economy*, 84, pp. 631–40.

Sargent, T.J. and N. Wallace (1976) 'Rational Expectations and the Theory of Economic Policy' *Journal of Monetary Economics*, 2, pp. 169–84.

Sargent, T.J. and N. Wallace (1981) 'Some Unpleasant Monetarist Arithmetic' *Federal Reserve Bank of Minneapolis Quarterly Review*, Autumn.

BIBLIOGRAPHY

Schultz, G.P. and R.Z. Aliber (eds) (1966) *Guidelines, Informal Controls and the Market Place* (Univ. of Chicago Press, Chicago).

Schultze, C.L. (1984) 'Cross-Country and Cross-Temporal Differences in Inflation Responsiveness' *American Economic Review*, 74, pp. 160–65.

Schultze, C.L. (1987) 'Real Wages' in R.Z. Lawrence and C.L. Schultze (eds) *Barriers to European Growth* (Brookings, Washington DC)

Sheffrin, S.M. (1983) *Rational Expectations* (Cambridge UP, Cambridge).

Solow, R.M. (1980) 'On Theories of Unemployment' *American Economic Review*, 70, pp. 1–11.

Solow, R.M. (1990) *The Labour Market as a Social Institution* (Blackwell, Oxford).

Tatom, J.A. (1988) 'Are the Macroeconomic Effects of Oil-Price Changes Symmetric?' in K. Brunner and A. Meltzer (eds) *Stabilisation Policies and Labor Markets* (North-Holland, Amsterdam).

Taylor, J.B. (1979) 'Staggered Wage Setting in a Macro Model' *American Economic Review*, 69(2), pp. 108–13.

Tobin, J. (1975) 'Keynesian Models of Recession and Depression' *American Economic Review*, 55(2), pp. 195–202.

INDEX

For Product Safety Concerns and Information please contact our EU
representative GPSR@taylorandfrancis.com
Taylor & Francis Verlag GmbH, Kaufingerstraße 24, 80331 München, Germany

www.ingramcontent.com/pod-product-compliance
Ingram Content Group UK Ltd.
Pitfield, Milton Keynes, MK11 3LW, UK
UKHW020953180425
457613UK00019B/661